BRITISH MUSLIM CONVERTS

BRITISH MUSLIM CONVERTS

Choosing Alternative Lives

KATE ZEBIRI

ONEWORLD
OXFORD

A Oneworld Book

Published by Oneworld Publications 2008
Copyright © Kate Zebiri, 2008

ISBN: 978–1–85168–546–2

Typeset by Jayvee, Trivandrum, India
Cover design by Design Deluxe
Printed and bound in Great Britain
by Biddles Ltd, King's Lynn

Oneworld Publications
185 Banbury Road
Oxford OX2 7AR
England
www.oneworld-publications.com

Learn more about Oneworld. Join our mailing list to
find out about our latest titles and special offers at:

www.oneworld-publications.com

This book is printed on paper made
from fully managed and sustained
forest sources.

FSC

TT-COC-002303

© 1996 Forest Stewardship Council A.C.

Contents

Acknowledgements

F irstly, a special thank you to all the interviewees, who gave up their time and often welcomed me into their homes, and without whom, of course, this book would not exist; also to all the friends, family, students and colleagues who kindly asked after the progress of my research. I am very grateful to the British Academy for their generous financial assistance which greatly facilitated this project, and to the School of Oriental and African Studies for giving me sabbatical leave in 2005–6.

I would like to thank Aisha Masterton for her help with interviewing, for her active interest and moral support, and for the many tasks with which she helped me as research assistant; Yasmin Moll, who also provided very able research assistance; Philip Herlihy, for creating an extremely useful and user-friendly database for my interview material; and my brother Robert, whose intricate knowledge of word-processing software was invaluable in the final stages of preparing the typescript. I am also indebted to those converts who were not part of my sample but who kindly helped, in one case by reading and commenting on sections of the typescript, in another by lending research materials, but mostly in conversations and email correspondence which increased my knowledge and understanding; Batool al-Toma and Yahya Birt deserve particular mention. I would, however, emphasize that any shortcomings in the present work are entirely my own responsibility.

And finally, my deepest gratitude to my 'other half', David Stretch-Dowse, for his unfailing support – emotional, intellectual and practical – and for many enlightening conversations which were of enormous help to me in conceiving and shaping this work.

Introduction

Western converts to Islam transcend the often invoked Islam-and-the-West dichotomy simply by virtue of who they are. It is becoming increasingly difficult for non-Muslims living in Western Europe and North America to maintain the image of Islam as 'foreign' and 'other' in the face of the growing numbers of indigenous people who choose to embrace this religion. Among Muslims, there is evidence to suggest that converts are making a disproportionate contribution to the indigenization of Islamic practice, thought and discourse in the West. In relation to Western society, it is tempting to see Muslim converts as part of a new counter-culture, in which a minority of born Muslims also participate, comparable to the so-called 'conservative counter-culture' in the US, a growing movement of young people in both evangelical and Catholic churches who reject premarital sex, alcohol and drugs.

There are two themes which are central to this study: identity change, and converts as critics of Western society.[1] These themes are closely related, in that the aspects of identity which converts seek to change reflect aspects of mainstream society with which they are dissatisfied. For example, a woman who feels that she has been treated as a 'sex-object' in a society which commodifies women's bodies converts to Islam and modifies her dress in such a way that she can no longer be seen in that light. For those who come to Islam, conversion affects not just their beliefs and values but often their whole lifestyle; far from being confined to their inner, spiritual world, their

---

[1] Although these themes are dealt with specifically in chapters 3 and 4, they are not confined to those chapters.

faith is nothing less than revolutionary in terms of the impact it has on their whole lives, often affecting not just their general social and political attitudes but also their choice of marriage partner, their social world, leisure activities, and sometimes their occupation. In view of the fact that some of the most radical changes occur in gender attitudes and behaviour, an entire chapter (chapter 5) has been devoted to that subject.

Dissatisfaction with Western society is widely cited as a motivating factor in conversion to Islam, and prominent converts such as the Frenchman Roger Garaudy (b. 1913) and the Austrian-born Muhammad Asad (1900–92) have offered powerful critiques of Western civilization.[2] Merely to follow the basic tenets of Islam (e.g. to abstain from alcohol and extramarital sex, and, for women, to wear the *ḥijāb*), is to take a strong stand against norms and values that are prevalent in Western societies. Converts (and some practising born Muslims) often go much further than this; they may, for example, give up listening to music, avoid taking out a mortgage (even an 'Islamic' mortgage, in some cases), and refrain from informal social interaction with members of the opposite sex.[3] Actively resisting what appears to be an irresistible sweep in the direction of greater individualism, permissiveness and decreased familial and social stability, Muslim converts espouse choices and values which seem to hark back to an earlier age. This study will explore the extent to which these converts are contesting some of the basic values of modern Western societies such as individualism, secularism, and gender equality.

The present work is also interested in the ways in which Muslim converts are integrating certain Western values with an Islamic identity and thus contributing to a new European or British Islam. Some new converts may subscribe to anti-Western rhetoric as they seek to distance themselves from their culture of origin, but with the passing of time many seem to reach a stage of maturity and reflexivity where they are able to integrate

---

[2] Roger Garaudy was a leading member of the French Communist Party, a member of the French parliament for almost two decades and a candidate for the presidency prior to his conversion to Islam in 1982. Muhammad Asad, an Austrian-born Jew, converted in 1926. He subsequently moved to India (Pakistan after partition) and became the first Pakistani ambassador to the UN. For more information on these two thinkers, see Gerholm, 'Three European Intellectuals'.

[3] These are matters on which there are different scholarly opinions, allowing for a diversity of practice among Muslims.

and reclaim aspects of their identity which may have been temporarily suppressed. Contemporary Islamic (including convert) discourse in Britain can be seen as part of a continuing trend of popularization and laicization of Islamic discourse, which is no longer the prerogative of those with a formal religious training (although some British Muslims and a small minority of converts have in fact received such training). There is a globalization of Islamic discourse currently taking place, but this does not preclude the simultaneous emergence of particular expressions of Islam which might be termed 'British Islam', 'European Islam', 'American Islam', etc. Muslims living in Western countries are inevitably influenced by ideas prevalent in those societies; the contribution of converts represents a further development in that Islam is being interpreted and reinterpreted by individuals who have received their primary socialization not just in a Western country but in a non-Muslim family environment. This study will observe the ways in which converts' original socialization may be influencing their interpretations of Islamic teachings.

In addition to challenging the norms of mainstream society, converts may also find themselves challenging the norms of lifelong Muslims. Sometimes marginalized within the majority Muslim community,[4] converts often inhabit a transitional or liminal sphere. It is by virtue of this sometimes uncomfortable marginality with respect to both mainstream British society and born Muslims that converts find themselves well situated to offer a critique of both. They raise new and challenging questions about the relationship between religion and culture in Islam. Not having been socialized in a Muslim culture themselves, they often face difficult choices about how far to adopt or borrow cultural elements from those who were born Muslim. Like second- and third-generation Muslims in Europe and America, converts are increasingly critical of attempts on the part of the older generation of immigrants to present aspects of their own culture as normatively Islamic. Where appropriate this study makes comparisons between converts and lifelong Muslims. However, the scope for this is limited due to the relative lack of detailed research on British Muslim thought, discourse and religious practice. Where possible I will refer to what research there is, and occasionally also to born Muslim primary sources.

---

[4] I use the term 'community' here as a sociological construct, without in any way meaning to deny the diverse and heterogeneous nature of the Muslim presence in Britain.

Converts have a unique potential to act not just as critics but also as cultural mediators, and are seemingly well placed to straddle many divides: Muslim–non-Muslim; indigenous–immigrant; Islam–the West. As Franks comments, converts 'know what it is like to be on both sides of the fence'.[5] They do generally aspire to be 'bridge-builders', especially in the sense of contributing to a more positive and accurate understanding of Islam in the wider society. Some also feel that they can help born Muslims to have a more nuanced understanding of non-Muslims and non-Muslim society in general.

This study is based on fieldwork conducted among British converts, and in addition refers to British convert-authored published and internet material. In many ways Muslims in Britain are more established, organized and developed than those in other parts of Western Europe, so there is a maturity of thought that is not matched anywhere else in the West apart from North America. Converts tend to be highly mobilized, playing a disproportionately large role in Islamic institutions and activities. English is increasingly being recognized as the lingua franca of international Islamism, and Muslims in Britain now have access via translations to the work of prominent contemporary Islamic scholars such as Yusuf al-Qaradawi, and also to the works of many classical scholars. Increasingly, internet resources such as the islamonline and sunnipath websites initiate English-speaking Muslims into the finer points of Islamic law and jurisprudence (*fiqh*), these being of direct practical importance in the lives of practising Muslims.[6] British Muslims are therefore in a better position than ever before to educate themselves in Islam; some study Arabic to a high standard, and a number of these obtain university posts in Islamic studies (again, converts are disproportionately represented here). Sometimes converts complain that born Muslims do not take them seriously, believing they lack Islamic knowledge, whereas in fact many of them go to great lengths to educate themselves in Islam, and for this reason they are often more knowledgeable than many ordinary Muslims.

Relatively little work has been done on conversion to Islam in the contemporary period, and specialists in conversion studies have only recently

---

[5] Franks, *Women and Revivalism in the West*, p. 143.
[6] See www.islamonline.net and www.sunnipath.com. The islamonline site has both Arabic and English language sections.

taken an interest in this phenomenon.[7] The only monograph on Muslim converts in Britain that has so far been published is Köse's *Conversion to Islam* (1996); this study focuses on conversion theory and factors leading to conversion, though the author does include a chapter on converts' experiences after conversion. The two other main studies in the European context – Allievi's study of European converts (*Les Convertis à l'Islam*, 1998) and Roald's study of Scandinavian converts (*New Muslims in the European Context*, 2004) – incorporate more material on the post-conversion phase, but do not focus on the British context. In addition to the above sources, I have also referred to Maha al-Qwidi's unpublished Ph.D. thesis based on fieldwork conducted mainly in the north of England ('Understanding the Stages of Conversion to Islam', 2002), which provided a useful complement to Köse's work, being the only other full-length study of British converts;[8] and on occasion I have drawn on Rocher and Cherqaoui's broad-based, semi-academic study of European converts (*D'Une Foi L'Autre: Les Conversions à l'Islam en Occident*, 1986). Roald is herself a Muslim convert, highlighting the fact that converts themselves are active contributors to academic research on conversion to Islam, with several besides Roald having published articles on the subject.[9] The relative neglect of Islam in conversion studies contrasts with the considerable attention which has been devoted to New Religious Movements (NRMs). This neglect is particularly surprising in view of the potential bearing that the study of conversion to Islam has on our understanding of changing patterns (and the continuing vitality) of religiosity in the contemporary world.

THEORY, METHODOLOGY AND FIELDWORK

There are many definitions and understandings of religious conversion, which vary according to the standpoint of the scholar or person formulating the definition. 'Insiders' tend to describe their own conversion in very

---

[7] See, e.g., the September 1999 issue of *Social Compass*, dedicated to conversion to Islam. Contributors include Lewis Rambo and Thomas Luckmann.
[8] Franks's study *Women and Revivalism in the West* takes a comparative look at Christian and Muslim religious revivalist women; five of her nine Muslim interviewees are converts.
[9] E.g. Marcia Hermansen, Tim Winter/Abdal-Hakim Murad, Gwendolyn Zohara Simmons, Harfiyya Abdel Haleem (formerly known as Harfiyya Ball-Haleem) and Yasin Dutton (see bibliography for further details).

positive terms, with reference to the transcendent, as a process of spiritual awakening in which they felt they were being guided by God. 'Outsiders', on the other hand, tend to be more interested in the psychological, social, cultural and other forces which may have influenced the process, given that the inner experience of the individual cannot be directly observed or analyzed. In particular, researchers who are not themselves religiously inclined may well be drawn to seek secular explanations. Social scientific approaches to religion tend to be theory-based and analytical, and, as Rambo points out, they carry the danger of not taking the religious or spiritual aspects of conversion seriously. The desire for transcendence is rarely acknowledged as a motivating factor,[10] whereas it is often heavily stressed in converts' own accounts of their experience. The psychological and psychoanalytic literature on conversion has often seen it as a pathological phenomenon, with the convert as a passive agent.[11] While conversion has been less fully treated within the discipline of sociology, it can be argued that a sociological approach is particularly appropriate in the case of conversion to Islam, which usually entails considerable social consequences.

Almost all conversion theory has been formulated without reference to Islam; while most studies have been based on Christian subjects, as mentioned above, NRMs have more recently attracted some attention (particularly in America). Not surprisingly, researchers on conversion to Islam have often found this literature to be of limited relevance.[12] However, several have found Rambo's approach more appropriate than others in the Islamic context due to its open-ended, heuristic and inclusive nature.[13] The seven 'stages' of religious conversion suggested by Rambo are: context; crisis; quest; encounter; interaction; commitment; and consequences.[14] Similarly

---

[10] Rambo, *Understanding Religious Conversion*, pp. 10–11 and 50.

[11] However, humanistic and transpersonal approaches, which have a more optimistic view of human nature, are more willing to see conversion and religious belonging in terms of human growth and development, and to emphasize the active role of the convert in seeking out solutions to the problems in his or her life.

[12] For example, Poston finds that of Lofland and Stark's predisposing factors to conversion ('Becoming a World-Saver'), most are absent or only minimally present in the case of converts to Islam. He further finds that only two of Starbuck's eight motivational factors (*The Psychology of Religion*) really apply to Muslim converts (Poston, *Islamic Da'wah in the West*, pp. 171 and 175).

[13] E.g. Roald, *New Muslims in the European Context*; al-Qwidi, 'Understanding the Stages of Conversion to Islam'.

[14] Rambo, *Understanding Religious Conversion*.

Lofland and Skonovd's six conversion motifs (intellectual, mystical, experimental, affectional, revivalist and coercive) are sufficiently broad to have been useful to some researchers on conversion to Islam.[15] Some scholars working in the Islamic context have drawn out the implications of their study for conversion theory as a whole. Allievi, for example, looks at the specific nature of Islam and what it has to *offer*. He feels that this 'offer' is often neglected in conversion studies, which can be too deterministic in focusing on environmental factors and alleged 'causes' of conversion.[16] Some may feel there is a danger of essentialism in this approach (though Allievi is careful to stress the multifaceted nature of Islam and the corresponding multiplicity of the offers it contains), but it does perhaps have the advantage of drawing the researcher closer to the subject, since particular qualities of Islam are often stressed by the converts themselves as factors in their conversion. Roald suggests that Rambo's stage model could be adapted to take into account the majority–minority dynamic that applies in the case of conversion to Islam (and other minority religions) in the West.[17] Wohlrab-Sahr highlights the potential usefulness of a functional and biographical approach in her attempt to ascertain what problem a person may be seeking to solve by converting to Islam; she finds that converts may be seeking to solve a range of problems, e.g. of belonging, race/ethnicity and gender identity.[18]

Van Nieuwkerk outlines two main approaches to conversion studies, the functional approach and the discourse analysis approach.[19] The former looks at what conversion means in the context of a person's life, while the latter looks at how discourses are created and how they achieve their effect. Combining these two approaches enables the researcher to arrive at a more subtle and complete understanding of the phenomenon of conversion. Consequently, I have endeavoured to employ an approach which incorporates biography as well as discourse, so that the latter could be contextualized, resulting in a richer analysis. I have drawn on both interview and non-interview material, always distinguishing between the two. Conversion to

---

[15] E.g. Köse, *Conversion to Islam*; al-Qwidi, 'Understanding the Stages of Conversion to Islam'. See Lofland and Skonovd, 'Conversion Motifs'.
[16] Allievi, *Les Convertis à l'Islam*, pp. 315 ff. and 94.
[17] Roald, *New Muslims in the European Context*, p. 79.
[18] See her articles 'Conversion to Islam' and 'Symbolizing Distance'.
[19] Van Nieuwkerk, 'Gender and Conversion', p. 10.

Islam tends to be an ongoing process which continues long after the actual commitment is made (some would say it continues over a whole lifetime). The present work is primarily concerned with what happens *after* a person has formally become a Muslim rather than with the *causes* of conversion. Models of conversion theory which pay attention to the identity changes that occur *after* conversion, notably that of Rambo, are therefore of most relevance to this study.

As Rambo points out, a multidisciplinary approach to religious conversion helps to avoid reductionism;[20] I would add that a 'top-heavy', overly theoretical approach can be equally distorting, and may drown out the voices of those about whom one is writing. I have therefore adopted a broadly phenomenological approach,[21] which prioritizes converts' own understanding of their conversion in the first instance and only then, if at all, refers to social scientific theories. I have made extensive use of verbatim material in order to allow the voices of my subjects to emerge as clearly as possible.

When I began this study in early 2005 I was intending to distribute a fairly large number of questionnaires, and then follow up some of the more interesting responses with interviews. However, I soon realized that other researchers in the field (both Muslim and non-Muslim) had experienced considerable difficulty in persuading Muslim converts to fill in questionnaires, citing low response rates.[22] Several people I spoke to, including Batool al-Toma of the New Muslims Project in Leicester, mentioned that converts were becoming less receptive to approaches from researchers in view of negative media coverage following 9/11, and a very high level of press interest, some of it quite intrusive, in the wake of the July 2005 bombings (one of the bombers having been a convert). Therefore, although I was able to obtain twelve questionnaire responses in an initial pilot study, I decided to base the study mainly on interviews, and found that on the whole people seemed more willing to engage with a researcher on a personal level, i.e. through an interview, than fill in an impersonal questionnaire. Potential

---

[20] Rambo, *Understanding Religious Conversion*, p. 7.
[21] The insights that have evolved under the rubric of 'phenomenology of religion' are the most relevant to my study, in particular the need to understand conversion from the perspective of those who experience it, and the acceptance of the believer's interpretation of their experience as an intrinsic part of the experience itself.
[22] E.g. Adnan, *New Muslims in Britain* and Poston, *Islamic Da'wah in the West*.

interviewees were contacted mainly through snowballing and convenience sampling,[23] and some effort was made to ensure a spread which reflected the make-up of British converts as a whole (insofar as this is known) in terms of gender, age, ethnic background and Islamic orientation. Just under half the sample were reached through snowballing or through a variety of Muslim contacts and acquaintances, a third through advertising on e-groups and internet sites, and a fifth through Islamic events or meetings at mosques. In all, thirty in-depth semi-structured interviews were conducted between August 2005 and July 2006, lasting between forty minutes and four hours (there were also some brief follow-up interviews to clarify particular points on which interviewees had spoken). Six of the interviews were conducted by telephone, four at the request of the interviewee (for reasons of convenience) and two for reasons of geographical distance. I also had informal contacts (meetings, email exchanges and telephone conversations) with converts who were either prominent or well connected (with other converts), and who were not part of the sample. All the interviews were recorded and transcribed. The interviewees were assured of confidentiality; I have changed their names (substituting a Muslim name for a Muslim one, and a non-Muslim name for a non-Muslim one), and have also avoided giving details that might identify them as individuals.

The interviewees comprised twenty women and ten men (possibly corresponding to the male–female ratio among British converts generally, though this is not known for sure), between the ages of nineteen and fifty-nine, with an average age of thirty-four. The length of time that they had been Muslim varied from four months to twenty-eight years, with an average of ten-and-a-half years. With one exception, the interviewees were brought up in the UK and (in one case) Southern Ireland.[24] Twenty-four of them were living within the greater London area, while six lived in small towns or rural areas in the Midlands and Home Counties. The preponderance of

---

[23] Snowballing is a sampling technique whereby the researcher uses his or her initial contacts to establish contact with others, while convenience sampling is based on availability or accessibility of subjects.

[24] The exception was a woman who had been brought up in an English-speaking country and who had spent nearly all her adult life in Britain. Due to a misunderstanding this only came to light after the interview had started, and I decided on balance to include her in the sample as her strongly ideological approach suggested that her answers would probably not have been all that different had she been brought up in Britain.

Londoners will have had some impact on the research findings: converts in London have access to a wide diversity of Islamic mosques, organizations and groups, and they are likely to come into contact with born Muslims of many different origins (whereas in some areas outside London there is a high concentration of Muslims of South Asian origin, especially in the North and Midlands). Twenty of the interviewees were white (including four Irish, two Scottish, one Welsh and two mixed European), six were black African or Afro-Caribbean, one was mixed race (Afro-Caribbean and white English), and three were Asian. This tallies reasonably well with the probable national profile of converts (approximately one-third black, a tenth Asian and the rest white). The educational level of the sample was above average, with just over half being educated to first degree level or higher (including one Ph.D.). As far as professional qualifications are concerned, the sample included three teachers, a doctor, a chartered accountant, a psychologist, an engineer and a social worker, although not all of these were currently employed. As regards employment status, seventeen people were in salaried employment (including five who worked in an Islamic context), two were self-employed and three were students; in addition, five women were at home with young children, and three people were unemployed.

Needless to say, a sample of this size cannot claim to be representative; it would in any case be impossible to find a random sample due to the lack of a sampling frame (there being no way of identifying all British converts). The snowballing method on which I and other researchers in this field have largely relied does bring the risk of bias. However, this can be minimized by making sure that the relations between the people contacted in this way are not too close – ideally that they are acquaintances rather than friends – and that only a limited number of people (a maximum of two, in my study) are followed up through a single contact. A further precaution is to cross-check for any significant differences between those who were contacted via snowballing and others; this I did, and was unable to find any. I followed the above guidelines with two exceptions: a married couple, and two people who knew each other through having married into the same family. In both cases, some advantage was gained in the sense that the relationship provided a fuller picture of the lives of the interviewees concerned than would otherwise have been possible. Since there was no overriding or undue similarity in the responses of either pair (for example, they gave different responses to the question of which Islamic tendencies or schools of law they identified with), it seemed appropriate to include them all. Contacting interviewees through Muslim acquaintances proved useful in gaining access to people who might not otherwise have come forward to be interviewed, thus mitigating a possible bias in favour of those who are more open to such things. Despite the reservations with regard to representativeness, it is hoped that at the very least this research will be able to identify important trends among converts, and to indicate some possible future lines of research.

As far as possible I conducted the interviews in such a way as to minimize the power imbalance between researcher and subject. The generally high educational level of the subjects and the fact that many of them were highly articulate and reflective meant that this imbalance was already less than it might otherwise have been. It also means that they will have access to the results of the research (in fact, many wished to be notified of the publication date). I left the choice of venue to the interviewees, often interviewing them in their own homes, and I encouraged them to ask questions about the research, and about myself, both at the beginning and the end of the interview, endeavouring to be as open as possible in my responses. In accordance with the requirements and aims of qualitative research, the interviews were semi-structured and in-depth, as mentioned above. Qualitative research allows scope for exploring the complexities and subtle nuances of the issues under investigation, whilst doing more justice, by comparison with quantitative research, to the individuality of the subjects. I incorporated many open-ended questions and adopted a flexible approach, allowing space for interviewees to talk about topics in which they had a particular interest. The same protocol was followed by my research assistant, Aisha Masterton, who conducted seven of the interviews. As the interviews progressed I sometimes incorporated new questions or modified existing ones based on the responses I received, so that aspects of the research developed organically, as in grounded theory.[25]

Several interviewees asked whether I was a Muslim myself. To these I explained that in the past I had been married to a Muslim for over twenty years, for part of which time I had worn a headscarf and followed some Islamic practices, but that I had never formally converted by pronouncing the *shahādah* (declaration of faith). Most did not ask directly about my religious affiliation, and I imagine that they would have viewed me as a

---

[25] Glasser and Strauss, *The Discovery of Grounded Theory*.

non-Muslim as I was not wearing a headscarf (except in one interview which took place on the premises of an Islamic organization), and my ethnicity is white/English. However, there may have been an element of ambiguity or uncertainty arising from the fact that I invariably wear long skirts out of personal preference, and from the fact that I have retained my married name. Roald observes that the knowledge obtained by an 'outsider' in fieldwork is different to the knowledge obtained by an 'insider'; she found in fieldwork among Muslims that being a Muslim was an advantage in terms of access to certain kinds of knowledge.[26] However, Jacobson suggests that in some cases Muslim interviewees feel freer with a non-Muslim interviewer, believing that a non-Muslim is less likely to be judgemental about their Islamic thought and practice.[27] I would add that this is especially likely to be the case with Muslim interviewees who are affiliated to a minority group (e.g. Shi'is), or who have relatively liberal views. For example, the Shi'i interviewees who told me about hostility or discrimination which they had encountered on the part of Sunnis, or about practising *taqiyyah* (dissimulation), i.e. hiding their Shi'i affiliation when among Sunni Muslims, would presumably not have spoken so openly to a Sunni interviewer. Jacobson did however encounter a degree of suspicion on the part of some interviewees and their families in her study of young British Pakistani Muslims.[28] I myself did not encounter any overt suspicion, which may be at least partly due to the fact that my subjects were converts.

In the light of the foregoing, I was interested to see whether there would be a noticeable difference in interviewee responses when the interviewer was a *ḥijāb*-wearing Muslim woman. When I listened to my research assistant's interview recordings, I noticed she had a certain rapport with the women interviewees (and often a shared amusement) based on common experiences, for example in a discussion of strategies to avoid shaking hands with a man without giving offence. Having said this, the male interviewees seemed less forthcoming in certain respects when being interviewed by a Muslim woman, due to the strong boundary that is often maintained between practising Muslim men and women; because of this boundary, my research assistant did not feel it appropriate to ask the men certain

---

[26] Roald, *Women in Islam*, p. 70.
[27] Jacobson, *Islam in Transition*, p. 55.
[28] Ibid.

questions.[29] By contrast, three of the men who were interviewed by me spoke quite freely (and explicitly at times) on matters related to sexuality.[30] Two men who spoke of the pleasure they derived from seeing attractive women in the street (as described in chapter 4) would almost certainly not have been so forthcoming with a Muslim researcher, especially a woman in *ḥijāb*. I further noticed that my research assistant's interviewees used Arabic/Islamic terms and expressions (e.g. *inshallah, mashallah, alḥamdullillah*)[31] more frequently than mine, with three of them using the term *kāfir/kuffār* (unbeliever/s) to refer to non-Muslims.[32] Although most of my interviewees did use some Islamic terminology, none of them used this particular term.[33] I would suggest that while the interviewer being a Muslim probably does help in establishing rapport, at least with members of the same sex, other factors such as general appearance, manner and degree of empathy could be equally important.

I found that male and female converts came forward (e.g. in response to notices on websites) in roughly equal numbers, and none of those who came forward or who were contacted in other ways expressed an objection to being interviewed by a female researcher. However, gender issues cannot be ignored when doing research in a Muslim context. Four of the six men who were interviewed in a domestic setting had their wives present on the grounds that, Islamically speaking, an unrelated man and woman should not be alone together.[34] Köse, a male Muslim researcher, was only able to

[29] These were the questions relating to sexual morality. After one of the interviews where the interviewee was male, my research assistant mentioned that their eyes had met only once during the interview.

[30] One man went into very elaborate details concerning the health hazards of anal intercourse; another spoke of his belief that circumcision might affect his sexual function.

[31] Respectively 'if God wills', 'whatever God wills', and 'praise be to God'.

[32] Although the term *kāfir* can be used in a neutral way to denote 'unbelievers', it very often has pejorative overtones, as discussed in chapter 3.

[33] I am aware of the possibility that Muslim subjects might give more conservative responses to a Muslim researcher, and in fact my assistant's interviewees were slightly more conservative than my own in their views. However, because of the small numbers, and because the way in which interviewees were contacted differed (a significantly higher proportion of her interviewees were contacted via a mosque), it is difficult if not impossible to establish causality.

[34] The mainstream Islamic position is that a person should not be alone or in 'seclusion' (*khalwah*) with a non-*mahram* person of the opposite sex, *mahram* meaning a degree of consanguinity which prohibits marriage. Although this rule applies equally to men and women, it seems that women are less willing to be interviewed by a male interviewer than men are by a

interview twenty women (as opposed to fifty men) due to the general reluctance of Muslim women to be alone with an unrelated male.[35] In my case I chose to interview fewer males than females in order to bring the sample into line with the suggested ratio of 2:1 among British converts as a whole.[36]

In addition to interviews, I have drawn on a range of primary source material which includes books, journals, magazines, newspapers, television and radio broadcasts, and internet sources. Some converts have contributed to the academic literature on Muslims in Britain and on conversion to Islam (as mentioned above), so an author may be quoted both as a primary and as a secondary source. In terms of Muslim magazines and newspapers, I identified Q-News and emel as having a much higher proportion of relevant material than other publications, both in terms of material about converts and material by converts. I therefore systematically surveyed all issues of emel (publication of which started in September 2003), and issues of Q-News dating back to 2000. This probably led to a certain imbalance, as these two publications both incline towards the liberal or progressive end of the spectrum of Islamic thought, but this was unavoidable as more conservative publications such as The Muslim News had very little material of relevance. Meeting Point, the newsletter of the New Muslims Project at the Islamic Foundation in Leicester, also contained much useful material. I have at times quoted or cited American converts, who participate in British discourse to the extent that they contribute to British publications such as Q-News (which is now also distributed in North America). Hamza Yusuf Hanson (usually known as Hamza Yusuf) in particular has close links with Britain and frequently travels to the UK to attend various events and to give talks.

Converts are generally referred to as 'converts', 'reverts' or 'new Muslims'. I asked my interviewees which term they preferred, and about half

female, which may be due to a religio-cultural expectation that the woman should be more cautious, or needs more protection, in her contacts with outsiders. My Muslim research assistant observed in this context that it is socially inappropriate for a man to be 'asking a woman probing questions'.

[35] Köse and Loewenthal, 'Conversion Motifs', p. 104.

[36] The 2:1 ratio is cited in British Muslims Monthly Survey 10, 1, January 2002, p. 8; the same source gives the female to male ratio as 4:1 in the USA. Batool al-Toma, director of the New Muslims Project at the Islamic Foundation, agreed that women converts in Britain outnumber men, but was non-committal regarding the exact ratio (interview with the author, 13 December 2006).

said they had no preference. The rest were more or less evenly divided between 'convert' and 'revert', with none expressing a preference for 'new Muslim'.[37] Some converts object to the last term as it seems inappropriate when applied to longer-term converts, and, like 'convert', can increase the sense of marginality from which converts may already suffer.[38] Those who prefer the term 'revert' feel that it conveys the sense of returning to something which is innate, and also that it reflects the belief (contained in a well-known *ḥadīth*) that all people are born in a state of natural goodness (*fiṭrah*) but it is their parents who make them into followers of religions other than Islam. This ties in with the notion, widely held among Muslims, of Islam as the 'natural' religion, the one which accords with human nature (also denoted by the term *fiṭrah*). Many converts to Islam express the sense that prior to their formal conversion they had already, perhaps always, been a Muslim without realizing it. However, five of my interviewees did not like the term 'revert' as they felt that it did not take account of their deliberate and conscious decision to be Muslim, a decision which, some pointed out, is also necessary for those who were born into a Muslim family. Two did not like the term 'convert', and both gave the same rather unexpected reason, indicating the existence of a discourse which I had not previously encountered: '"Convert" sounds like you're being conned into something.' For the purposes of academic discourse, the term 'revert' has the disadvantage of being less specific than 'convert' as it is often used to denote those who were born into a Muslim family and who discover or rediscover their faith, not having been particularly religiously inclined before. I have therefore mainly used the term 'convert'.

I am aware that converts may not wish to be marked off as 'different' from other Muslims, and so it might seem invidious to conduct this study at all. In fact, converts do generally identify with the born Muslim community; many marry born Muslims, most if not all would say 'we' when talking of

---

[37] This contrasts with the tendency of convert support networks in Britain to describe themselves as 'new Muslim projects'. 'Revert' was the preferred term among the interviewees of both al-Qwidi, 'Understanding the Stages of Conversion to Islam', p. 202 and Adnan, *New Muslims in Britain*, p. 7.

[38] Yahya Birt asks: 'Are we always to be defined as neophytes, as newcomers to the faith? According to the current stereotype, the inimitable Umar al-Faruq, may God be well pleased with him, would have been categorised a mere "new" Muslim for life . . . We cannot be forever defined by our initial conversion, for the *shahādatayn* is just the first witnessing in a lifelong journey towards God' ('Building New Medinas').

Muslims in general, and some use the term 'we' even when talking specifically of immigrant Muslims.[39] I have tried to be sensitive to this and not to
create artificial divisions or overstate the differences between converts and
non-converts. However, my interviewees seemed on the whole to be
favourably disposed to the idea of participating in a study devoted to converts and none expressed criticism of the idea. It is my belief that converts
are distinctive in some respects (as described earlier) and therefore have a
distinctive contribution to make – to Islamic thought, discourse, identity,
and potentially to British society and culture.[40]

[39] See, e.g., Murad, 'Tradition or Extradition?'.
[40] Of course the differences may decrease in future as Muslims become increasingly encul-
turated into Western societies, but the fact of having been brought up in a non-Muslim family will remain a significant variable.

Chapter 1

Converts in the British context

This chapter attempts to situate converts in the British context, initially by giving a brief history and overview of the Muslim presence in Britain, paying particular attention to factors of relevance to this study such as changing patterns of identity among young Muslims and the impact of key issues such as the Rushdie Affair, 9/11 and the Iraq war. It goes on to give a brief history of conversion to Islam with particular reference to Britain, followed by a comparative look at second- and third-generation Muslims on the one hand, and converts to Islam on the other, which will serve to clarify the ways in which the latter are distinctive. Finally, it will provide a social and demographic profile of British converts, including their Islamic affiliation, and will incorporate details of my interview sample.

MUSLIMS IN BRITAIN

Contrary to early expectations, Muslims in Western Europe appear to be resisting prevalent trends of secularization; by and large they have not assimilated, or disowned their religious identity. While some young Muslims have adopted secular identities,[1] others are evolving new ways of

---

[1] As Gilliat-Ray observes: 'The plurality of competing secular ideologies has the potential to relativize the absolutes of Islam, and draw young Muslims away from the values and traditions their parents have nurtured into them' ('Multiculturalism and Identity', p. 347).

expressing their Muslim or Islamic identity. The Muslim presence in Western Europe poses challenges for both Muslims and Europeans; while the onus of adaptation falls on the former, as a minority, many have suggested that European countries also need to adapt – to recognize and accommodate the new, permanent, indigenous Muslim populations, and to allow some place for religion in the public sphere.[2] However, in Britain as elsewhere, many people feel threatened by the idea of a politicized religious identity, some of them beating a retreat to a classical liberal distinction between the public and the private spheres (with religion belonging to the latter).[3] The events of 11 September 2001, and more recently the London tube bombings of July 2005, have had far-reaching consequences for British Muslims, who feel pressurized and under scrutiny in a way that they have not done in the past, whilst issues of loyalty, belonging and citizenship have been thrown into sharp relief.

Religious practice and affiliation in Britain as a whole appears to be decreasing. There has been a steady decline in membership of mainstream churches over the past century, although some of the smaller independent churches have grown.[4] Recent surveys have shown that less than half of British people believe in life after death,[5] and according to the 2001 census, only 8% of the UK adult population are regular church attenders.[6] New Religious Movements (NRMs) have enjoyed some popularity in recent decades but involvement is often casual and intermittent, and there are no reliable figures.[7] A diffuse spirituality in the form of aspects of New Age beliefs has entered the mainstream with the popularization of such diverse things as horoscopes, martial arts, meditation and life-coaching. Brown suggests that those who have grown up since the 1960s are more interested in general ethical issues, such as the environment, gender issues and racial equality, than in religion per se.[8]

---

[2] See, e.g., AlSayyad, 'Muslim Europe or Euro-Islam'.
[3] Modood, 'The Place of Muslims', pp. 125–6.
[4] Davies, *Religion in Britain Since 1945*, p. 49.
[5] Bruce cites a 1991 survey which found that 27% of British people believed in life after death (*Religion in Modern Britain*, p. 51), while a YouGov survey conducted in 2004 found a rather higher figure of 44%: http://www.yougov.com/archives/pdf/OMI040101073_1.pdf (accessed 21/12/2006).
[6] Giddens, *Sociology*, p. 561.
[7] Barker, *New Religious Movements*, p. 150.
[8] Brown, *The Death of Christian Britain*, p. 190.

Figures from the 2001 census (the first to include a question on religious affiliation) show that Muslims number almost 1.6 million (the true figure may be nearer to 2 million due to under-enumeration), making Islam the second largest religion in Britain, with Muslims constituting 2.7% of the population.[9] The majority of British Muslims (about two-thirds) are of South Asian origin, while most of the rest are of Arab (especially Egyptian, Iraqi, Moroccan and Yemeni), Turkish (including Turkish Cypriot) and Somali origin.[10] Muslims have the youngest age structure of all religious groups, with 52% being under twenty-five, compared to a national figure of 31%. Possibly 10% of British Muslims are Shi'i (though figures are hard to come by);[11] within Sunnism, the main sectarian groups are the Deobandis and the Barelwis, both of which originated on the Indian subcontinent. These two groups have a long history of conflict which has spilled over into the UK (for example in disputes over control of mosques), but it should be borne in mind that both groups are amorphous and inwardly diverse. The distribution of Muslims in Britain is uneven, with almost half living in or around London, while most of the rest live in the West Midlands, Yorkshire and Greater Manchester. Outside London, most Muslims are from the sub-continent, while the London Muslim population is highly diverse, including not just South Asians but also Arabs, Africans, Eastern Europeans, Iranians and other Asians.

As with any religious group, there are variations in levels of commit-ment among Muslims. However, there is evidence to suggest that Islamic belonging is important even to non-practising Muslims. The 2001 census showed that for England and Wales, less than 0.5% of people of Pakistani or Bangladeshi descent (the vast majority of whom are Muslim) claim to have no religion, compared to 15% of the population as a whole. According to the *Fourth National Survey on Ethnic Minorities* (1993–4), religion was the most prominent factor in the self-descriptions of South Asians; 90% said that religion was important to them, compared with 13% of white Britons. Two-thirds of Muslims said that they attend the mosque at least once a week, and two-thirds of young Muslims (aged sixteen to twenty-four) of Pakistani and Bangladeshi extraction said that religion was important to how they conducted their lives, as compared with only 5% of whites and 20% of

[9] For the census figures generally see www.statistics.gov.uk/census2001.
[10] Ansari, 'The Infidel Within', p. 168.
[11] Peach gives a figure of 7% for Shi'i mosque affiliation: 'Britain's Muslim Population', p. 28.

Afro-Caribbeans in the same age-group.[12] Modood, the principal researcher in this survey, found that even Muslims who were not strongly religious saw religion in terms of public policy and not just private life.[13]

Muslims are more established and integrated in Britain than in many other European countries because they were mostly given rights of citizenship and political participation as soon as they arrived, and because migration was generally earlier. There has been a significant Muslim presence in Britain for some five decades now.[14] Although the earliest Muslim communities in Britain date back to the eighteenth century, the first mass migration began in the late 1950s, and consisted mainly of single men from rural areas of the Indian subcontinent (also from Cyprus, the West Indies and Africa) who came for economic reasons, to undertake manual labour with the idea of returning to their countries of origin when they retired, if not before. Levels of religious practice among these single men were generally low, but with the arrival of their wives and children in the 1960s (prompted by the prospect of restrictive legislation), this changed. In particular there was a concern to pass on religio-cultural traditions to the children, and organizations and institutions were rapidly established to provide for worship, education and other community needs. From the 1970s onwards there have been waves of political refugees from places such as Somalia, Iran, Bosnia, Kosovo, Afghanistan and some Arab states, as a result of political upheavals in these countries.[15]

Muslims are among the most disadvantaged groups in Britain, with neglect and racism undoubtedly playing a part in this. Those of Bangladeshi or Pakistani origin in particular score badly on all the socio-economic indicators including employment and wage levels, housing, female participation in the labour force and, to a lesser extent, education.[16] Muslims are overrepresented in the prison population (almost 10%), but underrepresented in key areas including the police force, the judiciary, the civil service and the media.[17] The figures show a higher than average birth rate among

[12] See Modood, *Multicultural Politics*, p. 160 and 'The Place of Muslims', p. 121.
[13] Modood, 'The Place of Muslims', p. 122.
[14] For a brief history of Muslim settlement in Britain, see Lewis, *Islamic Britain*, chapter 1. For a more expanded account, see Ansari, *'The Infidel Within'*.
[15] Modood, 'The Place of Muslims', p. 113; Peach, 'Britain's Muslim Population', p. 19.
[16] Peach, 'Britain's Muslim Population'.
[17] Anwar, 'Issues, Policy and Practice', pp. 44–5.

Muslims and a younger than average age distribution, as mentioned above. There have however been some modest advances in recent years. There is now a handful of Muslims in both the Lower and Upper Houses of Parliament, the first Muslim MP having been elected to the Commons in 1997. In the same year the first voluntary-aided Muslim schools were given government funding after prolonged campaigning, but only seven such schools had come into being at the time of writing in late 2006. Despite being underprivileged in many areas, South Asian Muslims have a strong record of political participation and involvement in the main political parties, especially Labour, and research has shown that they are more likely to vote than other British citizens.[18] For the majority, political participation is seen as the most effective way of having some influence on British society; a minority, however, including the fringe group al-Muhajiroun, promote an isolationist strategy of non-participation, urging fellow Muslims not to vote on the grounds that the whole system is unIslamic.

There has been a proliferation of mosques and Muslim organizations in recent decades. These often have some sectarian affiliation or transnational links to Muslim states, but increasingly there are also indigenous organizations, including separate women's networks such as Al-Nisa and the Muslim Women's Helpline. Some of the more recently established organizations such as the Muslim Association of Britain and the Islamic Society of Britain have emphasized interaction with British society, and the values shared by Muslims and non-Muslims. The most successful attempt to create a national umbrella organization has been the Muslim Council of Britain (MCB), established in 1996, which has made some progress in terms of gaining access to government and influencing policy. It has over three hundred associate members but some groups have declined to join, notably Shi'i- and Barelwi-affiliated groups, and some Muslims resent what they see as the MCB's attempt to be seen as representing British Muslims in general.[19] Also of significance has been the growth of an indigenous Muslim media, with publications like *Q-News*, *The Muslim News*, *The Muslim Weekly* and *emel* creating a new space for critical discussion and treatment of Islamic

[18] Ansari, *'The Infidel Within'*, p. 238.
[19] In a poll of 1,000 Muslims conducted by Gfk NOP Social Research for the Channel 4 *Dispatches* programme *What Muslims Want* (7 August 2006), only 4% mentioned the MCB when asked about organizations that represent Muslims in Britain; however, the two other organizations mentioned scored only 1% each.

issues, and also for the exploration of a new British Muslim identity.[20] The rise of the internet has had a major impact on Muslims in Britain and worldwide. In addition to providing a platform for myriad groups, organizations and individuals, it also provides a space for free and open discussion of controversial matters, including those which would normally be considered taboo, such as homosexuality, extramarital sex and suicide. Through the internet, young people can bypass traditional authority structures and attempt to undertake their own *ijtihād* (independent juristic reasoning). The effects of the internet are varied and complex: on the one hand, it allows much space for diversity and differentiation, giving a voice even to marginal groups; on the other, the improved communication which it brings allows for the possibility of a more unified Islamist discourse, as certain elements of that discourse are more widely circulated.[21]

During the 1980s, Muslims started to become more organized and gradually began to cooperate across sectarian divides over issues such as *ḥalāl* meat and single-sex schooling, with varying degrees of success.[22] The decade culminated in the Rushdie Affair with the publication of Salman Rushdie's novel *The Satanic Verses*, which most Muslims found deeply offensive, if not blasphemous. The affair, which galvanized many previously politically inactive and even lapsed Muslims into public protest, particularly affected British Muslims due to the strong tradition of veneration of Muhammad among South Asians. It was seen by many as a kind of symbolic battle between Islam and the West which was being played out in the media; in fact, it revealed a strong polarity between the secular-minded liberal intelligentsia, some of whom were outspoken in their condemnation and criticisms of Islam, and the protesting Muslims. The latter received very little support from anyone apart from some Christians (mainly Anglicans), who had a degree of sympathy with the religious sensibilities of Muslims, and also perhaps with the idea that religion had a role to play in public life. Media coverage was sometimes disastrous from the point of view of community relations; however, lessons were learned about campaigning and

---

[20] Britain also now has its first Islamic satellite channel, *The Islam Channel.*
[21] On the impact of the internet on Islam and Muslims, see for example P. Mandaville, *Transnational Muslim Politics: Reimagining the Umma* (London: Routledge, 2001) and G. Bunt, *Islam in the Digital Age: E-Jihad, Online Fatwas and Cyber Islamic Environments* (London: Pluto Press, 2003).
[22] See Lewis, *Islamic Britain.*

organizing, and a new confidence and assertiveness emerged. Many of the disaffected younger generation, disillusioned by their experiences of racism and marginalization in British society, began to articulate a new identity based on a largely politically motivated affiliation to Islam. More than any other single event, the Rushdie Affair marked a shift from race and ethnicity to religion as the core element in British Muslim identity.[23]

By 1991, nearly half of all British Muslims had been born in the UK. The 1990s were marked by an increasing assertiveness and a growing level of politicization due to international events such as the first Gulf war and the Bosnian, Kosovan and Chechnyan crises.[24] These events contributed to an increased global consciousness and a 'reimagining of Islam as a global religion'[25] among Muslims generally, including Muslims in Britain. Bosnia in particular raised questions about the position of European Muslims; for some, the tardiness of Western governments in coming to the aid of Muslims who were being slaughtered, even when those Muslims were white fellow-Europeans, could only be explained by a pervasive hostility to Islam and Muslims. The emergence since the early 1990s of an 'assertive Muslim identity' is described by Jacobson, who observes this phenomenon among young men engaged in social or political protest, who may or may not be practising Muslims; a minority of these young men combine mosque attendance with criminal activity, and feel empowered by the media portrayal of Muslims as fanatics or terrorists.[26] Some of the disaffected youth have been attracted to radical or fringe groups such as Hizb al-Tahrir and its offshoot, al-Muhajiroun. This political radicalization has continued into the twenty-first century, which has seen the emergence of rudimentary Jihadist networks in Britain, accompanied by a growing sense of alienation and a profound distrust of authority among some British Muslim youth.[27]

There have also been significant intergenerational changes, as younger Muslims have often distanced themselves from the cultural traditions of

[23] Ansari paints a slightly different picture; he feels that for British Muslims, Islam is not generally the main form of social and political identification, except on those occasions when Islam is under attack, and that ethnic divisions are often more significant (*'The Infidel Within'*, pp. 4–5 and 12).

[24] For more details about the impact of such crises on British Muslims see McRoy, *From Rushdie to 7/7*.

[25] Bagguley and Hussain, 'Flying the Flag for England?', p. 218.

[26] Jacobson, *Islam in Transition*, pp. 33 and 125.

[27] On the latter point see Alam, 'Vision of a New Islam'.

their parents and grandparents. While some have grown away from Islam and developed more secular identities, others are attracted to universal and normative styles of Islam as distinct from the ethno-cultural traditions of their parents. Many of them are reading the Islamic sources directly and interpreting them for themselves using the kind of rational and critical thinking which is encouraged in the Western education system, of which they are products. The younger generation appear to be less interested in sectarian division and the minutiae of religious practice, and more interested in broader social and political issues such as how to relate to the wider society. Much of the religious discussion and activism takes place away from the mosques, from which many of the younger generation have become alienated, finding the traditional leadership ill-equipped to deal with the issues that are relevant to their everyday lives. As elsewhere in the Muslim world, there has been a devolution of religious authority, with the right of *ijtihād* being claimed sometimes by those who do not have a formal religious scholarly training. Fareena Alam, the editor of *Q-News*, writes as one of this new generation: 'We are more comfortable in our own skin and we are openly critical of fellow Muslims when we think their actions are out of order. We care less about hiding dirty laundry and more with engaging in vigorous debate . . . In the aftermath of the London bombings, many have realised we have to stop hiding behind a false sense of unity and call a spade a spade.' She also illustrates the fact that the younger generation have higher expectations than their parents and are therefore less willing to put up with discrimination and more likely to assert their rights, as she continues: 'Britain must also come to terms with us . . . We are among the most politicised and engaged communities in Britain. We belong here.'[28] Despite the alienation of some, Ansari detects among young Muslims a 'greater propensity to associate with the culture of the indigenous white majority and adopt many of its traits'.[29]

Certain Islamic scholars and thinkers based in the West, such as Hamza Yusuf and Tariq Ramadan, are part of a new Muslim intellectual elite who are looking to reformulate Islamic thought in order to meet the needs of Muslims living in non-Muslim societies. They reject the classical Islamic binary division of the world into Muslim countries (*dār al-islām* or 'the

[28] Alam, 'Why I Reject the Anarchists Who Claim to Speak for Islam'.
[29] Ansari, 'The Infidel Within', p. 19.

abode of Islam') and non-Muslim countries (*dār al-ḥarb* or 'the abode of war'), on the grounds that this does not reflect contemporary global realities. Ramadan has written a number of books which deal with the situation of Muslims living in a non-Muslim context. In his books *To Be a European Muslim* and *Western Muslims and the Future of Islam*, he argues that it is perfectly legitimate for Muslims to live in non-Muslim countries provided they are able to practise their religion freely. He emphasizes the need for ongoing *ijtihād*, and envisages the creation of a 'European Islam' which will draw on the indigenous cultures of European countries. He urges Muslims in Europe to participate fully in the societies in which they live and to see themselves as being rooted in those societies and as having a contribution to make to them. He sees the European context as providing Muslims with a welcome opportunity to distinguish between Islamic essentials and cultural accretions, and believes that Western Muslims have an important contribution to make to Islamic thought in general.

As already mentioned, religion is becoming a more prominent element in the identity of young British Muslims, who are increasingly drawing a distinction between religious and ethnic identity. Islamic belonging may be felt in terms of the local Muslim community, the national Muslim community or the global *ummah*,[30] and it is likely to comprise cultural, religious and political elements in varying degrees.[31] Notwithstanding the drift away from the mosques, Jacobson found a widespread attachment to Islam among young Muslims, including those who were not fully practising.[32] Islam may be seen as offering an alternative to British or Western society, on the one hand, and to the traditional community, on the other, neither of which is able to meet their needs or address issues of relevance to them.[33] Muslim women have often been able to empower themselves by appealing to normative Islamic teachings over the cultural traditions of their parents – to oppose forced marriages, for example, or to resist restrictions on their education.

---

[30] Jacobson, *Islam in Transition*, p. 17.
[31] The shift from ethnic to religious identity should not be overstated. Jacobson envisages that Asian Muslims will continue to be influenced by the cultures of their parents and grandparents for at least another generation or two (*Islam in Transition*, p. 147), while Bagguley and Hussain found that none of the young people they interviewed were completely detached from the cultural traditions of their parents ('Flying the Flag for England?', p. 217).
[32] Jacobson, *Islam in Transition*, p. 103.
[33] Fulat, 'Recognise our Role in Society'.

Feelings of national belonging are secondary to religious identity for many Muslims. The various opinion polls conducted in recent years have shown a mixed picture, with some surveys finding a large majority who feel either 'British' or 'loyal to Britain' and others finding a rather more variegated picture.[34] Muslims' feelings of ambivalence towards 'Britishness' arise at least in part from their experiences of racism and exclusion.[35] Ansari observes that 'Britishness is often described in terms of citizenship, a birthright, but not really a deeply-held emotional and cultural bond shared with the white, secular or Christian majority'.[36] As pointed out by Jacobson, the concept of 'Britishness' can be understood on different levels: citizenship; values and lifestyle; and ancestry and colour.[37] Most of her young British Muslim interviewees saw Britishness as an 'official but not really meaningful belonging'.[38] However, there was some appreciation of British values and lifestyle, and a sense among her interviewees that they would miss living here if they moved to another country; they particularly valued certain aspects of British society such as the welfare state, general prosperity and the efficient organization of society.[39] In Muslim publications such as Q-News and emel, some of the more educated young British Muslims are contributing to a discourse which combines Muslim identity with Britishness, and which envisages a high degree of civic engagement and social participation.[40]

Most Muslims, especially the younger generation, have no problem with identifying themselves as both 'Muslim' and 'British'. Hussain argues that the question of 'which are you first: Muslim or British?' is a non-issue, explaining: 'There are two distinct identities involved here: one is a religious

[34] Research carried out in early 2006 for the Channel 4 Dispatches documentary What Muslims Want (broadcast 7 August 2006) found that 82% of Muslims felt 'strongly British', and an ICM poll conducted for the Daily Telegraph (19 February 2006) found that 91% felt loyal to Britain. However, the Dispatches programme also found that 22% felt that the July 2005 bombings were justified in the light of the 'war on terror', and a YouGov poll conducted for the Daily Telegraph (23 July 2005) found that while 46% of British Muslims described their attitude to Britain as 'very loyal', most of the rest were either 'fairly loyal' (33%) or had 'little or no loyalty at all' (18%).

[35] Bagguley and Hussain, 'Flying the Flag for England?', p. 215; Jacobson, Islam in Transition, pp. 11 and 152.

[36] Ansari, 'The Infidel Within', p. 18.

[37] Jacobson, Islam in Transition, p. 17.   [38] Ibid., p. 67.

[39] Ibid., p. 70.

[40] Moll, ' "Beyond Beards, Scarves and Halal Meat" '.

and philosophical identity and the other is a national or territorial identity. Just as one can be Christian and British, or Humanist and British, so one can be Muslim and British, without the need for contradiction, tension or comparison between the two.'[41] Seddon observes that Catholics are not considered suspect because of their loyalty to the Pope, nor are Jews who have dual nationality, nor are they expected to prioritize these loyalties.[42] Knott and Khokher have argued that the conflict model which sees young Muslims as being 'between two cultures', whether torn between them or engaging in cultural synthesis between them, is outmoded, and that it is more useful to talk of multiple and changing identities.[43] Similarly Geaves talks of a 'shift from notions of a fragmented self torn between culture and religion and ethnicity and "Britishness" to that of a multi-layered self that lies outside the traditional/modern dichotomy so often presented in right-wing minority discourse when speaking of Muslims'.[44] Looking at the new Muslim media (specifically *Q-News* and *emel*), Moll discerns the construction of 'a British Muslim identity that is firmly and unproblematically rooted in the British-European-Western context, rather than in the countries of (now increasingly distant) origin of the Muslim community'.[45] She sees this type of identity as having the potential to empower British Muslims, since 'it engages both the West and Islam on their own grounds, and in their own terms. To put it more clearly, these media construct an identity that simultaneously redefines conceptions of the West and Islam, all the while embracing both.'[46]

Muslims have come under increased suspicion following the attacks of 9/11, and more recently the July 2005 bombings. Despite the widespread condemnation of these attacks by many Muslim groups and individuals, in both cases Muslims experienced an immediate backlash in the form of a significant rise in verbal and physical abuse of varying degrees of seriousness.[47] The term 'Islamophobia' is increasingly used to refer to religiously motivated

---

[41] Hussain, 'British Muslim Identity', p. 103.
[42] Seddon, 'Locating the Perpetuation of "Otherness"', p. 155.
[43] Knott and Khokher, 'Religious and Ethnic Identity', p. 595.
[44] Geaves, 'Negotiating British Citizenship and Muslim Identity', p. 76.
[45] Moll, '"Beyond Beards, Scarves and Halal Meat"'.   [46] Ibid.
[47] J. Nielsen and C. Allen, *Anti-Islamic Reactions within the European Union after the Recent Attacks of Terror against the USA* (Vienna: European Monitoring Centre on Racism and Xenophobia, October 2001); *The Scotsman*, 4 August 2005.

hostility directed at Muslims. It was popularized by the publication in 1997 of the Runnymede Trust's report entitled *Islamophobia: A Challenge for us All*, and it became more prominent in public discourse after 9/11. The report acknowledged that the term was 'not ideal', but described it as 'a useful shorthand way of referring to dread or hatred of Islam – and, therefore, to fear and dislike of all or most Muslims'.[48] It concluded that Islamophobia was a pervasive feature of British society and that media reporting on Muslims and Islam was biased and unfair.[49] In 2002, the European Monitoring Centre on Racism and Xenophobia (EUMC) reported that there was a real possibility of Islamophobia and anti-Semitism becoming acceptable in European society.[50] Allen believes that although 9/11 did not mark the beginning of Islamophobia, it has nevertheless been 'the dangerous catalyst driving its evolution, diversification and acceptance'.[51] Despite its growing popularity, a number of reservations have been expressed with regard to the term 'Islamophobia'. Some people have expressed a fear that its use will stigmatize any criticism of Islam, and a relatively small minority of Muslims have rejected it on the grounds that it is disempowering for Muslims as it casts them in the role of victims. Modood points out that it is often difficult to distinguish between religious and racial discrimination.[52] However, a recent study by the Home Office suggests that *religious*, and not just racial, discrimination against Muslims is on the increase;[53] furthermore, the far right, both in Europe generally and in Britain, have begun focusing on religion rather than just race, often singling out Islam.[54]

In the wake of 9/11 and the July bombings, more questions are being raised about Muslims' commitment to core European values such as freedom, democracy and sexual equality, and there is a new emphasis on societal cohesion,[55] with the blame for lack of integration sometimes being

---

[48]   Runnymede Trust, *Islamophobia: A Challenge for us All*, p. 1.
[49]   The follow-up report in 2004, *Islamophobia: Issues, Challenges and Action*, found that while there had been some improvements, levels of anti-Muslim prejudice had increased in certain quarters (p. 73).
[50]   Cited in Anwar, 'Issues, Policy and Practice', p. 31.
[51]   Allen, 'From Race to Religion', p. 65.
[52]   Modood, 'The Place of Muslims', p. 127.
[53]   Weller, Feldman and Purdam, *Religious Discrimination in England and Wales*.
[54]   Allen, 'From Race to Religion', p. 54.
[55]   Geaves, 'Negotiating British Citizenship and Muslim Identity', p. 71.

placed on Muslims rather than on racism and discrimination.[56] The so-called 'war on terror' is seen by many Muslims as a war on Islam, especially as even moderate Muslims such as Yusuf Islam, Yusuf al-Qaradawi and Tariq Ramadan have come under suspicion on different occasions. Anti-terrorist measures and controls on immigration and asylum have added to the sense that Muslims are being targeted. Guantanamo Bay and the torture of Iraqi prisoners have greatly increased anti-US feeling, and the growing US hegemony (aided and abetted by Britain) is seen as cause for alarm, by Muslims and others. On the other hand, there have been some positive developments for Muslims in the wake of 9/11. Hussain points out that alongside the negative media coverage there has also been an unprecedented openness in some sections of the media; new opportunities for dialogue between Muslims and government have arisen, and certain Muslim initiatives, such as the annual Islam Awareness Week, have gained a higher profile.[57] Leading public figures, including the prime minister, have made a point of upholding the distinction between terrorism and its perpetrators, on the one hand, and Islam and ordinary Muslims, on the other. A further consequence of 9/11 and the London bombings has been to open up the intra-Muslim discussion on the problem of extremism; mainstream Muslims have been more willing to speak out against extremists, and prominent figures such as Tariq Ramadan and Hamza Yusuf have done so in uncompromising terms.

The Iraq war, and to a lesser extent the invasion of Afghanistan, have given rise to a sense of anger and frustration which goes far beyond the Muslim community, and have mobilized many people who were previously politically inactive, both Muslims and non-Muslims, from a broad political spectrum. A survey carried out by *The Muslim News* in late 2001 suggested that Muslims were 'comfortable with their citizenship' but that there was 'a strong element of dissent on the Government's conduct of international affairs'.[58] There can be no doubt that this 'element of dissent' has been greatly strengthened by developments in Iraq. The anti-war movement has involved Muslims in wider campaigns and alliances, in particular the Stop the War Coalition (SWC). In March 2003, the Muslim Association of Britain

---

[56] Modood, foreword in Abbas (ed.), *Muslim Britain*, p. viii.
[57] Hussain, 'The Impact of 9/11 on British Muslim Identity', pp. 125–6.
[58] Sheriff, 'The Muslim News Survey'.

cooperated with the SWC to organize the largest ever public demonstration to take place in Britain. Birt points out that the forming of alliances with non-Muslim groups contrasted with the failure to do so at earlier junctures such as the Rushdie Affair and the first Gulf war, and that by lobbying and marching, Muslims were 'operating as critical citizens within the norms of democratic dissent'.[59] Geaves sees this as 'a sea-change in Muslim participation in citizenship', and shows how the protest was more effective than earlier events in providing a 'platform for expressing their sense of injustice without jeopardising either their sense of Britishness or the recognition of their loyalty by the wider community and the media'.[60]

A BRIEF HISTORY OF CONVERSION TO ISLAM, WITH PARTICULAR REFERENCE TO BRITAIN

Converts sometimes point out that the Companions of the Prophet, much revered by subsequent Muslims and described in a *ḥadīth* as 'the best generation', were in fact converts. There is no technical term for conversion in the Qur'an or in Islamic scholarship; the most common Qur'anic term for becoming a Muslim is *aslama*, meaning 'to submit' (i.e. to God). There is, however, evidence of a missionary impulse in the Islamic sources; the Qur'an urges the Prophet Muhammad to invite people to Islam (e.g. Q 12:108), and Muhammad is said to have written to the leaders of neighbouring countries inviting them to adopt it. In the classical provisions on *jihād* in the military sense, opponents were to be invited to embrace Islam before the commencement of hostilities, and when defeated they still had the choice of converting or paying the *jizyah* (a poll tax imposed on non-Muslim subjects). While there are stories of individuals contemporary with Muhammad converting out of personal conviction (the most famous case being that of 'Umar, who, having been active in persecuting the Muslims, is said to have been struck by awe and wonder upon reading a portion of the Qur'an), there are also reports of whole tribes converting, which presumably were cases of 'adhesion' rather than 'conversion', in Nock's terms.[61] This

---

[59] Birt, 'Lobbying and Marching', pp. 102 and 92.
[60] Geaves, 'Who Defines Moderate Islam?', pp. 68 and 72.
[61] Nock, *Conversion*, p. 7. 'Conversion' is defined as a 'reorientation of the soul . . . a turning which implies a consciousness that a great change is involved', while 'adhesion' refers to

is corroborated by the fact that some of them recanted on Muhammad's death, having considered their initial 'conversion' to have been an act of political allegiance to a specific leader.

The early non-Arab converts to Islam following the first wave of conquests were known as *mawālī*, or clients, because they had to be affiliated to an Arab tribe in order to be recognized as Muslim; many of them were of low social status (as in all times and places, those from the lower echelons of society have the least to lose and the most to gain by changing their religion). During the Umayyad period (661–750 CE), these converts were treated as second-class citizens and were not given the same rights as the ruling Arabs; there were only small numbers of upper-class converts during this period, such as those from the Iranian cavalry who received a high stipend after their conversion. The idea that Islam was 'spread by the sword' has long been discredited; in fact it was the Muslim polity rather than the religion that was spread by military expansion, with mass conversion coming at a later stage. In most cases conversion was neither encouraged nor discouraged, rulers being happy to take the *jizyah*, and there was no deliberate proselytization during the early period – on the contrary, the Muslim conquerors were often kept apart from the conquered populations in special military garrisons such as Fustat in Egypt and Basra in Iraq. It was only later, as these towns became thriving commercial centres, that there was social mixing on any large scale between Muslims and non-Muslims.

In the early centuries of Islam, conversions were closely related to the Islamization process.[62] The appearance of Islamic institutions such as mosques, *madrasahs* (Islamic religious schools), and the *sharī'ah* court system created an Islamic ambience which filtered down into the culture, making conversion to Islam more socially acceptable and appealing. Research done by Bulliet and others suggests that there was often social, political or economic advantage to be gained by converting, such as evading the *jizyah*, being able to participate in the credit system for traders, gaining a more

communal conversions, which involve 'no definite crossing of religious frontiers'. Dutton similarly draws a distinction between two types of conversion, the 'way of light' (i.e. conversion out of personal conviction) and the 'way of power' (i.e. conversion for motives other than personal conviction; this would include the 'hypocrites' often referred to in the Qur'an): 'Conversion to Islam', pp. 156–7.

[62] A fuller account of conversion in this period can be found in Bulliet, *Conversion to Islam*, and Levtzion (ed.), *Conversion to Islam*.

advantageous position in society or escaping discrimination; this last became more common later on when society was majority Muslim. However, there were also possible deterrents to conversion, including the prospect of ostracism from the community of origin, losing the right to inherit from non-Muslim relatives, and the demanding nature of Islamic religious practices.[63] There were certain factors which contributed to the rapid and widespread growth of Islam. First, conversion was a simple and straightforward process with no official registration, the pronouncement of the *shahādah* (testifying that there is no God but God and Muhammad is His messenger, normally in front of two witnesses) being the sole formal requirement. Second, where intermarriage between Muslim and non-Muslim occurred, the children would be brought up as Muslims; and third, conversion to Islam was considered a one-way process, as leaving Islam had serious civil and legal consequences.[64] There was of course a snowball effect: as people converted, contacts between (newly converted) Muslims and non-Muslims increased, giving rise to further conversions. By and large this primary phase of conversion in the central Islamic lands was completed by about the late tenth or early eleventh centuries. Later on, traders and Sufis played a prominent part in bringing about conversions in territories which had not been conquered by Muslims. Even though Muslims did not hold political power in these areas, the advanced Islamicate civilization and the success of Muslim traders enhanced the appeal of Islam for many. Sufis and mystics appealed to individuals as well as groups, and they were particularly effective in the peaceful spread of Islam because of their tolerance of syncretism, with converts not necessarily having to abandon all their previous beliefs and practices.

Conversion to Islam by Europeans dates back several centuries. It is estimated that between 1500 and 1600 there were around three hundred thousand 'renegades' (such was the term applied to European converts by other Europeans).[65] These were a mixed bag of adventurers, pirates, slaves seeking their freedom, mercenaries and traders, some of whom went on to enjoy distinguished careers in politics or military life. As before, conversion to

---

[63] Winter, 'Conversion as Nostalgia', pp. 99–100.
[64] According to most of the classical Islamic schools of law, apostasy carried the death penalty; however, this was not always exacted in practice.
[65] Allievi, *Les Convertis à l'Islam*, p. 51.

Islam sometimes represented an opportunity for social betterment.[66] In this period, to become a Muslim was known as 'becoming a Turk' and was equated with going over to the enemy. From the sixteenth to the eighteenth centuries, it was not uncommon to find Islamicized Europeans in Muslim countries,[67] many of whom gained quite prominent positions in society, especially in North Africa. Muslim societies were less hierarchical than European societies, which was conducive to social mobility, so that people from relatively low social backgrounds could rise to high positions to which they could not have aspired in their homelands. It is probable that some converts were disillusioned with European society and sought liberation from its values and mores. The so-called 'renegades' often occupied a position between Muslim and Christian society without ever being fully accepted by either, their sincerity doubted by Muslims and Christians alike (indeed, some of them converted back to Christianity when they returned home). Converts to Islam often continued to suffer the same kinds of discrimination as they had when they were *dhimmī*s (members of protected communities, mainly Christians and Jews). A reported saying of a certain Almohad caliph who imposed restrictions on converts illustrates the distrust which converts often encountered: 'If I were certain of your Islam, I would leave you to mix with the Muslims in their marriages and in their other business, and if I were certain of your infidelity, I would kill your menfolk, make captive your children and make your property as booty for the Muslims, but I have doubts about your case.'[68]

It was in the late nineteenth century that converts first appeared in Britain in significant numbers. At that time colonialists, travellers and Orientalists had become interested in Muslim societies and cultures, in some cases out of a romantic fascination with the 'other'. Converts in this period and those in the early part of the twentieth century were usually privileged European males, and they often wrote accounts of their travels in Muslim lands or their experiences of the Hajj. Many of these early British converts were grouped around Abdullah Quilliam, a well-to-do solicitor who converted to Islam in 1887 following a trip to Morocco.[69] Quilliam

---

[66] Bennassar and Bennassar, *Les Chrétiens d'Allah*, pp. 19 and 264.
[67] Garcia-Arenal, 'Les Conversions d'Européens'.
[68] Garcia-Arenal, 'Jewish Converts to Islam', p. 238.
[69] The following account of the Liverpool Mosque and Muslim Institute and the Woking Mosque and Muslim Mission is based on Köse, *Conversion to Islam*, pp. 12–19, and Ansari,

founded the Liverpool Mosque and Muslim Institute in the late nineteenth century and enjoyed considerable success in attracting converts; according to the monthly journal issued by the institute, *The Islamic World*, twenty converted in 1896 alone, and some six hundred, mainly from professional backgrounds, over the next twenty years.[70] The institute also issued a weekly magazine, *The Crescent*, and had an active programme of public lectures and meetings. A Muslim college was founded for the education of the children of the Muslim community; Quilliam also founded Medina House, a home for unwanted children who, once admitted, were brought up as Muslims. He travelled extensively in the Muslim world and was appointed by the Ottoman sultan as 'Shaykh al-Islam of the British Isles'.

Another group of converts was associated with the Woking Mosque and Muslim Mission in Surrey, after its revival in 1912 (it was the first purpose-built mosque in Britain, founded in 1889, but largely fallen into disuse). Prominent converts associated with the mission included Lord Headley (who presided over the British Muslim Society from its inception in 1914), and Khalid Sheldrake. The mission published a monthly journal, *The Islamic Review*, most of the contributors being converts. The *Review* included open discussion of Islamic issues, comparisons between Islam and Christianity, and convert testimonies and biographies. In 1924 it estimated the number of converts in Britain to be about a thousand (out of a total of 10,000 Muslims in Britain), but this was probably an overestimate.[71] Islamic modernist ideas were in the ascendant among those associated with the mission, who included prominent South Asian Muslims such as Yusuf Ali and Syed Ameer Ali. For example, it was denied that apostasy carried the death penalty, music and art were considered to be beneficial for humanity, and meat which was produced by Christians was considered *ḥalāl*, in accordance with a famous *fatwā* issued by the renowned Egyptian reformer Muhammad 'Abduh (1849–1905). The institution of *purdah* was considered inappropriate in Britain, and female converts were not expected to wear the veil; in fact, most converts seem to have continued to wear ordinary Western dress. A gradualist approach was adopted with respect to new converts, who were not

'*The Infidel Within*', pp. 82–4 and 21–34, which sources should be consulted for further details.
[70] Ansari, '*The Infidel Within*', p. 124.
[71] Köse, *Conversion to Islam*, p. 17.

necessarily expected to adopt all religious practices and prohibitions immediately; Headley himself took several years to give up alcohol following his
conversion. Acknowledging that the five prescribed prayers a day were too
demanding for the average English person, he suggested that one could offer
silent, inward prayer instead (i.e. without the movements). The mission
attracted many converts from the upper and middle classes, including
Sir Archibald Hamilton and Lady Evelyn Cobbold.[72] Ansari suggests that disillusionment following the First World War, which Christianity had not been
able to avert, may have played a part in these conversions, and notes that for
those who were already Unitarian in their beliefs, conversion to Islam may
have seemed a fairly natural progression.[73]

The rationalist and modernist approach to Islamic teachings described
above is one example of the way in which these early converts adapted Islam
to the British context. This adaptation was partly for missionary purposes,
but perhaps there was also an element of self-protection; in the face of hostility from the non-Muslim public, Quilliam sometimes resorted to presenting
Islamic teachings in indirect ways, for example by giving talks on temperance
without necessarily speaking of Islam in the first instance. Both Quilliam and
Headley were concerned to present Islam in a way that appealed to British
society, emphasizing that it was not inimical to Christianity (Headley even
said that converting to Islam had made him 'a better Christian').[74] At both the
Liverpool and Woking Mosques, religious services were held on Sundays; in
Liverpool hymns were sung (the words of Christian hymns being adapted
where necessary), and, from 1888 onwards, Christmas day was celebrated
(on the grounds that Jesus was honoured as a prophet of Islam) with meals
being provided for the poor. Headley used the terms 'Muslim Church' and
'Muslim Bible' for the mosque and the Qur'an respectively.

Although keen not to antagonize the British public, these Muslim
converts did not necessarily shy away from political involvement.
Quilliam, who had opposed the British intervention in the Sudan, left
Britain in 1908 because of the hostility he encountered, and the Liverpool
community subsequently declined. Another prominent convert of the time,
Marmaduke Pickthall (author of a well-known translation of the Qur'an),

---

[72] Their testimonies can be found in the Muslim World League compilation, *Islam: Our Choice*.
[73] Ansari, 'The Infidel Within', p. 131.
[74] Köse, *Conversion to Islam*, p. 18.

like Quilliam, had spent much time in Muslim countries and was sympathetic to the Ottoman cause. He was instrumental in founding the Anglo-Ottoman Society in 1914 and spent much time and energy lobbying on behalf of Turkey. During the First World War when war was declared on the Ottomans, Muslims found themselves in a difficult position, and their loyalty to Britain was questioned; many found themselves under surveillance. There is no definite information as to whether the descendants of these early converts continued as Muslims, but in the absence of evidence to the contrary it seems likely that many of them did not.

Without wishing to pre-empt the findings of the present study, a number of points of comparison between converts in history and contemporary converts in Britain suggest themselves. For example, the converts of the late nineteenth and early twentieth centuries were more prominent on the British Muslim scene than converts are today, no doubt because there was little in the way of an established Muslim community in Britain at that time. A possibly related point is that converts today come from a much broader social spectrum than a hundred years ago, when they tended to be confined to the upper and upper-middle classes, whilst the increased ethnic diversity among converts today reflects changes in the British population. The early converts were more assimilationist in some respects, for example in leaving aside the *ḥijāb* for women and in their adoption of terms such as 'Muslim Church'; the latter seems rather a quaint eccentricity in the light of today's multicultural ethos, and nearly all contemporary women converts wear the *ḥijāb*, or believe that they should. There are also parallels: then as now, converts (and also born Muslims) fell under suspicion (and sometimes found their loyalties divided) when there was conflict with a Muslim power. As in the past, converts do at times encounter mistrust from lifelong Muslims (see chapter 2). The tendency towards modernism evinced by the British converts of a century ago is apparent among some, but not all, of today's converts; in general converts today occupy a broader spectrum of Islamic thought, ranging from conservative or *salafī* to progressive or liberal.

CONVERTS VIS-À-VIS SECOND- AND THIRD-GENERATION
MUSLIMS: A COMPARATIVE VIEW

Notwithstanding the difficulties experienced by converts in relation to the older generation of Asian Muslims in particular (described in chapter 2), converts have much in common with second- and third-generation Muslims who have been brought up in Britain. The latter will have been exposed, like converts, to the ethos of questioning and critical thinking which is encouraged in the British education system, and may therefore think critically about their religion, and be more reflective in that respect than their parents and grandparents. Again, like converts, many practising young Muslims frame their religious orientation as a personal choice and commitment, not as something which is simply to be passed on from one generation to the next.[75] As with converts, living in a non-Muslim environment may prompt them to form a more consciously Islamic identity as they are pushed to define themselves more clearly in response to questions they are asked about Islam by curious non-Muslims.[76] It should also be remembered that most converts marry non-convert Muslims and so participate to a greater or lesser extent in particular Muslim cultures (though converts are often at pains to dissociate themselves from aspects of those cultures which they see as contravening normative Islamic teachings).

However, there are also many ways in which converts may be different from born Muslims. Obviously, a convert would not have been brought up in a Muslim family, and their ethnic and cultural background would not therefore be associated with Islam. Not being involved with parochial forms of Islam, converts bring a particular emphasis to the universality of Islam; compared to born Muslims, they are in some ways a 'blank slate', Islamically speaking, in that there is a sense in which they need to weigh everything in the balance.[77] Not having been socialized within a Muslim family also means that converts will have been more fully exposed to the impact of the dominant culture. One of my male interviewees, for example, talking on the subject of sexual morality, commented: 'It's different for us, because we were born and raised with it.' Similarly, the non-Muslim family background has an undoubted (though difficult to quantify) ongoing effect; as one woman who relates her conversion story in *emel* says: 'You can't run away from them

---

[75] Jacobson, *Islam in Transition*, p. 118; Schmidt, 'Islamic Identity Formation', p. 34. Schmidt points out that this is partly a reflection of values which are promoted by the host society, and may be a way of minimizing the risk of criticism.
[76] Schmidt, 'Islamic Identity Formation', p. 35.
[77] This is not to deny that converts have 'cultural baggage', but it seems that on the whole they are more likely to take a critical view of it and less likely to consider it 'Islamic'.

[your family] because the influences of your family are inside you and you've grown up with them.'[78]

Unlike converts, those born into a Muslim family usually participate to a greater or lesser extent in traditional cultures which may entail such things as visits to the country of origin, obligations to near or distant relatives and arranged (and sometimes transnational) marriages. This traditional culture is an additional factor for born Muslims which will need to be integrated with other elements such as the individualistic ethos of the education system, and (for those who make a conscious commitment to Islam) normative understandings of Islam. Also, born Muslims may need to define their own understanding of Islam over against that of their parents, often as part of the process of forming their own identity and achieving separation from them. Converts, on the other hand, do not have the support network of a Muslim family, which can lead to problems, particularly when seeking a marriage partner. An additional problem faced by converts is that they have to cope with the reaction of their family to their conversion, which is rarely positive; they may find themselves having to justify or defend their choice of Islam, not just to their family of origin but to non-Muslim society in general, a process which is likely to accelerate and intensify their Islamic identity formation. The process of constantly thinking and talking about Islam to both Muslims and non-Muslims is likely to mean that the 'objectification of Islam'[79] is highly developed among converts. Someone who has chosen a religion rather than having been born into it is perhaps more likely to explain his or her religious affiliation in rational terms and in terms of the virtues of the religion in question;[80] however, this is a difference of degree only, as both the rational and the apologetic approaches are widespread among born Muslims. Badran draws attention to another possible reason for converts to think deeply about Islamic issues: 'Convert[s] ... often experience contradictions between the Islamic ideal and its practice more acutely, or in a more raw way, than many born Muslims, for whom these contradictions may have become "naturalized" over time. Converts have not inherited coping mechanisms, thus compelling some to work through these inconsistencies.'[81]

---

[78] *emel*, issue 7, September/October 2004.
[79] This 'objectification' refers to a new, self-conscious way of thinking and talking about Islam; see Eickelman and Piscatori, *Muslim Politics*, pp. 37–45.
[80] Allievi, *Les Convertis à l'Islam*, p. 319.
[81] Badran, 'Feminism and Conversion', pp. 194–5.

Another important difference is that while the mainstream Muslim community covers the full spectrum of religious commitment, from nominal to fully practising, converts are more concentrated at the latter end of the scale, for the obvious reason that they have made a definite and conscious decision to be Muslim.[82] For this reason converts are more likely to have a high level of religious involvement, for example by being active in Islamic groups and organizations; they are also more likely to exert efforts to educate themselves in Islam, especially as they did not receive any Islamic instruction or education as children. They also tend to be more '*da'wah*-minded', partly as a result of having close non-Muslim relatives; many converts express the hope that members of their family might one day convert. One researcher who compared born Muslim 'reverts' (Muslims who discover or rediscover their faith) with converts to Islam found that the element of seeking was less pronounced for the former, as was the element of crisis; also, their reversion was less likely to have major social implications.[83] Born Muslims in Britain (most of whom are from South Asian ethnic groups) are more likely than converts to suffer social deprivation or to come from families of lower social status; they are also more likely to have a stable family background in terms of parents staying together, and are more likely to continue to live with their parents after marrying and starting their own family.[84]

There are also some less obvious points of comparison – for example, converts may have greater empathy with non-Muslims because of their non-Muslim past and ongoing relationships with their family of origin.[85] They often have a heightened awareness, compared to other Muslims, of how Muslims are viewed by outsiders, so there can be a strongly reflexive element to their thought and discourse. Na'ima Robert, for example, observes that 'there are so many words that we use regularly in Islamic parlance that have negative or pejorative connotations in the modern Western context, among them, "submission", "obedience", "righteousness" and "piety"'.[86] This

---

[82] However, Allievi finds that in the European context, nominal conversion for the purpose of marriage is numerically significant (*Les Convertis à l'Islam*, p. 47).

[83] Gilliat-Ray, 'Rediscovering Islam', pp. 317–18.

[84] Ansari, '*The Infidel Within*', p. 262.

[85] Of course, the reverse can also be true, given the proverbial zeal of the converted, but I have found this to be rare.

[86] Robert, *From my Sisters' Lips*, p. 230.

awareness makes converts well equipped to be cultural mediators. White converts (almost two-thirds of British converts), unlike many born Muslims, will in all probability not have been on the receiving end of racism.[87] Although it is difficult to predict or generalize as to the effects of racism on human beings, one might tentatively suggest that those who have not encountered it are likely to be less defensive and more confident in some respects than those who have. Converts might therefore feel freer to be openly critical of the host society, and more outspoken on political issues. Yaqub, one of my interviewees, commented: 'The Asian middle class now tend to bend over backwards to accommodate people and I think that's a major problem because you're not really a Muslim when you're doing that. You stand up against oppression. I think that reverts [i.e. converts] do that more and it's easier for them.'

A PROFILE OF BRITISH CONVERTS

Conversion to Islam in Europe and America is now a much more common occurrence than in the past. This is in part a function of the dramatic social changes of recent times, which have seen individuals choosing the components of their identity to an unprecedented extent, and finding themselves faced with a 'supermarket of beliefs' (many Muslim converts report having looked into a number of religions before finally settling on Islam). Freedoms of conscience and religion are protected in law, and people generally have increased wealth and leisure time to pursue interests beyond work and home. Furthermore, individuals no longer have to travel to foreign countries in order to encounter Muslims (and foreign travel is in any case easier and more accessible to ordinary people than in the past). The presence of Muslim immigrants and their descendants, and the increased availability of information about Islam through various channels such as the internet, publications and religious studies curricula, arguably make Islam less of a 'strange' and 'foreign' religion – arguably, because these are counterbalanced by continuing sensational and negative coverage of Muslims and Islam by sections of the mainstream media.

---

[87] However, women converts who wear the headscarf do experience something akin to racism; see Franks, 'Crossing the Borders of Whiteness?'.

Conversion in recent decades, in the wake of large-scale Muslim migration to Britain, is a very different phenomenon to that described above, in the historical section. Bulliet, a historian of conversion to Islam, expresses the view that conversion does not occur where it would involve a decline in social status,[88] but this does not seem to apply to all converts in the present, some of whom suffer discrimination (for example in the job market) as a result of their conversion. Furthermore, in the European context, those who convert are associating themselves with a religion which has a predominantly negative image in the media, and with communities of immigrant origin which have a low social status and suffer from relatively high levels of social deprivation. Such conversions become easier to understand, however, if one adopts a conception of perceived advantage which does not focus on social status alone, but pays heed to the search for a sense of meaning and purpose, the desire to be part of a community, and the wish to dissociate oneself from a particular culture or society. The conversions that occur in the West today are clearly individual rather than social, and are cases of conversion rather than adhesion.

It is possible to identify some broad trends in conversion to Islam in Western societies over the past few decades. The earlier converts in the 1950s and 1960s were often women who married Muslims and then converted later, partly motivated by the need to bring the children up as Muslims.[89] These converts tended to practise more 'cultural' forms of Islam, being exposed mainly to the Islam of the husband (or, occasionally, wife) and his relatives. In the late 1960s and 1970s there was a wave of conversions of those seeking a spiritual alternative, some of whom had been part of the hippy culture; of these, some had experimented with drugs and NRMs or Eastern forms of mysticism, and many were attracted to Sufism. In the 1980s and 1990s, people seem to have been motivated more by political and social issues, disillusionment with Western societies, and the reaction against liberalism. Roald, looking at Scandinavian converts, finds that many of those who converted in the 1970s and early 1980s had a leftist background, whereas those who converted in the later 1980s and 1990s were more likely to be involved in the environmental movement.[90] While converts (especially

---

[88] Bulliet, *Conversion to Islam*, p. 41.
[89] Hermansen, 'Two-Way Acculturation', p. 191; although Hermansen is writing in the American context, this also applies to Britain.
[90] Roald, *New Muslims in the European Context*, pp. 107–8.

men) in the first half of the twentieth century often converted as a result of foreign travel,[91] more recent converts are more likely to have come across Muslims at university or in the workplace.

Estimates of the number of British converts vary widely, with Nielsen suggesting an upper limit of ten thousand,[92] while Murad (writing as Tim Winter) proposes a figure of fifty thousand.[93] Birt points out that both alarmist newspaper reports and optimistic or missionary-minded Muslims tend to suggest inflated figures. With the benefit of figures from the 2001 census, he comes up with an estimate of fourteen thousand two hundred,[94] which, if correct, would mean that converts make up roughly 0.9% of the Muslim population of Britain. Based on the Scottish figures, which provide information on religion of upbringing as well as current religion, he concludes that 'Islam is the religion people are least likely to leave or convert to'.[95] As regards the average age of conversion, research in the 1990s and earlier by Köse, Poston and Adnan found it to be (based on their respective samples) around thirty.[96] However, there are indications that the average age is decreasing. Roald does not specify an average age but states that 80% of her sample of Scandinavian converts were under thirty when they converted.[97] Al-Qwidi finds an average conversion age of twenty-five,[98] which corresponds fairly closely to that of my own sample, which was twenty-three-and-a-half. If indeed the age is decreasing, the probable reasons for this are the fact that Islam has a more visible presence in society, education

---

[91] See, e.g., contributions to the MuslimWorld League publication *Islam: Our Choice*.

[92] Nielsen, *Muslims in Western Europe*, p. 44.

[93] Winter, 'Conversion as Nostalgia', p. 102.

[94] Much higher figures have been suggested for France, where intermarriage and conversion seem to be more common, and the US, which of course has a higher population than Britain. In the late 1980s Gerholm estimated the number of French converts to be between 50,000 and 200,000 ('Three European Intellectuals', p. 264), while Haddad cites a 2003 newspaper report which estimates that 30,000 Americans convert each year ('The Quest for Peace in Submission', p. 20).

[95] Birt, 'Lies, Damn Lies, Statistics and Conversion!'.

[96] Köse found it to be 29.7 (*Conversion to Islam*, p. 47), while the average age of conversion for Poston (whose sample included Americans and Europeans as well as Britons) was 31.4 (*Islamic Da'wah in the West*, p. 166). Adnan's sample, based on research carried out in 1997, suggests a slightly higher age profile, as 54% were between 31 and 60 (*New Muslims in Britain*, p. 2).

[97] Roald, *New Muslims in the European Context*, p. 109.

[98] Al-Qwidi, 'Understanding the Stages of Conversion to Islam', p. 155.

and the media, so people are able to obtain knowledge of Islam at a younger age (including in RE lessons at school). Even seemingly negative coverage of Islam can result in a higher rate of conversion, as witnessed by the waves of conversion following 9/11,[99] the most obvious explanation being that these events give rise to a curiosity resulting in higher sales of books on Islam and more enquiries at mosques and Islamic organizations.

Researchers have given widely differing accounts of the male–female ratio among converts to Islam. Poston, who looks mostly at the published testimonies of European and American converts, finds that 69% of the testimonies are written by men, and concludes that men are more attracted to Islam than women. His suggested reasons for this are the negative image of women in Islam, restrictions on women such as the veil and seclusion, and male authority and dominance.[100] However, this is not borne out by the evidence as far as the British context is concerned. Poston's sample was probably affected by the fact that many of the testimonies date back to the early or mid-twentieth century, a time when men were more socially and geographically mobile than women, and therefore more likely to be exposed to Islam. More recent studies which mention the male–female ratio tend to find a preponderance of women, with some suggesting a ratio of 2:1 in Britain, as mentioned in the introduction.[101] Possible reasons for this preponderance of women converts are the marriage factor (while it is not that unusual for a non-Muslim woman to marry a Muslim man, and subsequently take an interest in Islam which may lead to her conversion, it is rare for a non-Muslim man to marry a Muslim woman) and the fact that women are more likely to be involved in organized religion generally than are men.[102]

The religious background of converts seems to be changing in line with changes taking place in British society generally. The Scottish census of 2001

[99] *British Muslims Monthly Survey* 10, 1, January 2002, p. 11; cf. Winter, 'Conversion as Nostalgia', p. 108.

[100] Poston, *Islamic Da'wah in the West*, pp. 163–4.

[101] Roald (*New Muslims in the European Context*, p. 96), looking at Scandinavia, finds that there are more women than men converts due to the fact that more Scandinavian women marry Muslims. Anway (*Daughters of Another Path*, p. 2) and Abdel Haleem ('Experiences, Needs and Potential of New Muslim Women', p. 93, citing the *British Muslims Monthly Survey* (*BMMS*)) both agree that there are more female Western converts than male. Allievi, on the other hand, suggests that Italian converts are mostly male (*Les Convertis à l'Islam*, p. 65).

[102] Giddens, *Sociology*, p. 562.

provides the following information: 59% of converts are from Christian denominations (there is no way of knowing how many of these were nominal and how many actually practising); 27% are from a non-religious background; and the rest are from other faiths or NRMs.[103] It seems that most converts (like most British people) do not have a strong religious upbringing.[104] Köse's interviewees are mostly from nominal Christian backgrounds, with only 11% practising the religion of their upbringing prior to their conversion; some actually complained that they had been taught nothing about religion in their childhood.[105] However, 29% of his sample had been involved in NRMs (as adults) at some stage.[106] In al-Qwidi's study, most had a nominal Christian background, and only 5% were actually practising another religion at the time of conversion; those with a strong religious upbringing were mainly those of Afro-Caribbean descent.[107] In my own sample of thirty interviewees, two-thirds had either a non-religious or a nominal Christian upbringing. Of the rest, four were brought up as Catholics, three as non-Catholic Christians, and three had a Hindu background. Six (20%) had been practising Christians as adults, but only two of those were still practising shortly before their conversion to Islam. Four had experimented with or looked into NRMs prior to their conversion. From all the above findings it would seem that converts represent a normal cross-section of society as far as religious upbringing is concerned. Many converts say that they had always believed in God, which may indicate that they did absorb some kind of religious teaching as children; there are a few, though, who profess to have been atheists.[108]

The social status of converts can be inferred from factors such as class, education and professional background. In an article in *The Independent* in

---

103 Cited in Birt, 'Lies, Damn Lies, Statistics and Conversion!'.
104 This is less true in America, where converts are more likely to have a strong Christian background (see Anway, 'American Women Choosing Islam', p. 149). Poston's sample are mostly ex-Christians, but they are not contemporary; Allievi's interviewees, being European and mostly Italian, have a relatively strong Catholic socialization but are mostly lapsed (*Les Convertis à l'Islam*, p. 95); and Roald remarks that converts in Scandinavia, in accordance with Scandinavian society in general, have less of a religious background than either British or American converts (*New Muslims in the European Context*, p. 103).
105 Köse, *Conversion to Islam*, pp. 67–8 and 52.
106 Ibid., p. 53.
107 Al-Qwidi, 'Understanding the Stages of Conversion to Islam', pp. 117–21.
108 Adnan, *New Muslims in Britain*, p. 11; al-Qwidi, 'Understanding the Stages of Conversion to Islam', p. 123.

1991, Daoud Rosser-Owen, founder of the Association for British Muslims (ABM), describes the typical profile of a convert as middle class, professional and often public-school educated.[109] Sixty-six per cent of Köse's sample identified themselves as middle class, the remainder as working class;[110] however, just over half of al-Qwidi's sample, a few years later, identified themselves as working class.[111] Almost half of my sample had come from a working-class background, even if some of these aspired to middle-class status in their own adult lives. Such findings reflect the diversification of social class among converts in recent decades. Virtually all researchers (including myself) have found that converts, or at least their own sample, are educated to a higher than average level,[112] and that a relatively high proportion have professional status.[113] Such findings are even more striking when converts are compared with average Muslim figures rather than the national average. As far as the ethnic background of converts is concerned, it seems that as in America (but not nearly to the same degree) people of African or Caribbean background are disproportionately represented. According to the Scottish 2001 census figures, about a third of converts are in the Black Caribbean category, almost a tenth from an Asian background and the remaining 60% or so are White/Other.[114]

Converts have sometimes organized themselves into groups for particular purposes. Examples include the formation of a political party, the Islamic Party of Britain, in 1989 (which had very little success at the polls), and the Murabitun (originally called the Darqawiyya) founded in the 1970s by a Scottish convert, Shaykh 'Abd al-Qadir (also known as Ian Dallas).[115] A number of organizations have sprung up to cater for the needs of converts. The first of these was the Association of British Muslims (known as the Association *for* British Muslims since 1978), founded (or refounded, since it traces its origins back to Quilliam) in 1974 by Daoud Rosser-Owen.[116] In

[109] Cited in Köse, *Conversion to Islam*, p. 24.   [110] Ibid., p. 80.
[111] Al-Qwidi, 'Understanding the Stages of Conversion to Islam', p. 115.
[112] Köse, *Conversion to Islam*, p. 80; Adnan, *New Muslims in Britain*, p. 11; al-Qwidi, 'Understanding the Stages of Conversion to Islam', p. 242.
[113] Adnan, *New Muslims in Britain*, pp. 9 and 13; Köse, *Conversion to Islam*, p. 80; al-Qwidi, 'Understanding the Stages of Conversion to Islam', p. 115.
[114] Cited in Birt, 'Lies, Damn Lies, Statistics and Conversion!'.
[115] For more information on the Murabitun, see Köse, *Conversion to Islam*, pp. 175–88.
[116] For further information see the ABM website at http://members.tripod.com/~british_muslims_assn/welcome.html.

the 1970s and 1980s this organization was much criticized by those who saw it as racially divisive. It has now become more inclusive, aiming to represent not just converts but also second- and third-generation Muslims. More recently, a number of 'new Muslim' projects or networks have appeared in major cities such as Leeds, Manchester and Sheffield. The most established project is the one based at the Islamic Foundation in Leicester, which has a central role in relation to British converts. In addition to maintaining a database on Muslim converts, it publishes a monthly newsletter (*Meeting Point*) and organizes a wide range of activities including Hajj trips, seminars and workshops on Islam-related topics, Arabic classes and family holidays.

If one asks to what kind of Islam converts are attracted, the picture is rather complex. It is generally acknowledged that a disproportionate number are attracted to Sufism,[117] though it should be remembered that this covers a wide spectrum of tendencies from the perennial philosophical approach of people like René Guénon (1886–1951) and Frithjof Schuon (1907–98),[118] to the more popular approach of Shaykh Nazim's Naqshbandi group, which has attracted a high proportion of converts, both white and Afro-Caribbean.[119] True to its historical record of tolerance and flexibility, Sufism can accommodate intellectual as well as anti-intellectual tendencies, and can also attract those who are seeking emotional contact or expression, since Sufi groups often offer a close sense of community and belonging. Not all people who become involved with Islamic mysticism or Sufi groups actually convert to Islam, but those who do become Sufi-oriented Muslims tend to have a certain respect for Islamic traditional scholarship and the classical schools of law.

Not surprisingly, converts reflect the diversity of Muslim religious and political trends; Roald devotes an entire chapter to convert trends, but no research has yet attempted to quantify these tendencies among converts.[120]

---

[117] However, there seems to be a very low rate of Sufi affiliation among al-Qwidi's sample; for example, she found that none of her interviewees spoke in terms of mystical experience ('Understanding the Stages of Conversion to Islam', p. 198). This may be partly due to the fact that Sufi groups are less active in the North of England, where she mainly conducted her study.
[118] Guénon is a French convert and Schuon Swiss; Seyyed Hossein Nasr is perhaps the best-known living Muslim exponent of this philosophy.
[119] Köse, *Conversion to Islam*, p. 173.
[120] It would be difficult to do so as people are often reluctant to label themselves as belonging to a particular tendency (see below).

Roald notes the preponderance of the rational approach, which reflects the main ethos of the Islamic literature which is available in European languages, and which has affected Shi'is as well as Sunnis.[121] However, there are other significant trends such as traditionalism, Sufism and Salafism,[122] which are less rationally inclined. Most converts (apart from those who convert after marrying a Shi'i) convert to Sunni rather than Shi'i Islam, but there are some who subsequently become Shi'is. It is difficult to estimate the overall proportion of Shi'is amongst converts, but it is likely to be smaller than for British Muslims as a whole due to the fact that Shi'is are far less active in outreach than Sunnis. A small minority of converts are attracted to radical or militant Islam, although these have received a high profile in the media, creating the impression that they are more numerically significant than is in fact the case. Overall it would appear that converts reproduce the trends already extant among Muslims in their societies, with the proviso that they are less likely to be attracted to the more parochial trends such as, in the British context, the Deobandis and Barelwis. In this respect, they resemble second- and third-generation Muslims, who are increasingly moving away from the Islam of their parents and towards more universal expressions of Islam.

Of my own sample, 90% could be described as Sunni 'by default', though a few did not understand the distinction between Sunni and Shi'i, and several thought the distinction was not relevant to them since as converts they were not born into one of the two traditions. As Halima put it: 'When we as Muslims meet one another it's not something that [it] would occur to you to ask.' There were also three Shi'is, one of whom had initially been Sunni but had then moved sideways into Shi'i Islam. Another, who had come straight into Shi'ism, said that most of his friends were Shi'i converts who started as Sunnis. For these Shi'i interviewees, the Sunni–Shi'i distinction *was* relevant, and two of them said that they practised *taqiyyah*

---

[121] Roald, *New Muslims in the European Context*, pp. 116–26.

[122] The term *salafi* refers to a tendency rather than a specific movement; *salafis* hark back to the first three generations after the Prophet, known as the *salaf* (forefathers). They have much in common with the Wahhabi movement and are sometimes affiliated with it, but don't usually adhere to any of the four Sunni schools of law, preferring instead to refer directly to the Qur'an, *ḥadīth* or the earliest scholars. They tend to be socially conservative, for example the women may wear the *niqāb* (face veil) and there may be strict segregation of the sexes.

(dissimulation) at times to avoid hostility from Sunni Muslims.[123] Just over a third of the sample, including all those with Sufi tendencies and all the Shi'is, followed a particular school of law (Hanafi, which is the predominant school in the subcontinent, being the most common among Sunnis). Not surprisingly, those with *salafi* tendencies simply said that they follow 'the evidence', or 'scholars who extract their knowledge from the sources' (i.e. the Qur'an and Sunna) rather than a particular school of law, or as one put it, 'without having bigoted partisanship to any one particular scholar or school of thought'. Of the twenty who didn't follow a school of law, a few did aspire to in the future or felt it would be a good thing; two said that they took the best of each; and one had an ambition to study *fiqh* (Islamic jurisprudence, based on the schools of law) in depth with a recognized scholar.

Most of the interviewees did not wish to identify themselves as following a particular trend such as Sufism or Salafism. There was in fact a definite reluctance on the part of most to take on any label, the main reason being that such labels were felt to be divisive (in fact two people had been advised by shaykhs not to take on or accept any label). Seven interviewees clearly had Sufi tendencies, whether they followed a particular shaykh or attended *dhikr* sessions or were just attracted to Islamic mysticism. However, only one of these accepted the appellation 'Sufi'. Abdullah explained his reluctance to use the term: 'You know there's Sufis and there's Sufis. I mean we don't want to be branded as goofy Sufis, people who go about saying "I love Allah" but don't pray and don't follow the Sunna [practice of the Prophet Muhammad]', while Peter observed: 'The Prophet didn't say: "Become a Sufi." I just see it as a label for a certain style of Islam which has come along ... You can be the thing without the name, without getting caught up in the labels.' Similarly, there were four people who clearly had *salafi* tendencies – for example, following particular *salafi* scholars or their disciples[124] – but only one had no reservations when it came to applying the term to himself. Others were reluctant for a variety of reasons: a desire not to be associated

---

[123] Shi'is normally pray slightly differently than Sunnis, for example using a *turbah* (a small piece of earth or clay, preferably taken from Karbala) on which to prostrate. One Shi'i convert who was not part of the sample told me that someone had once placed a chair over his head while he was prostrating in a major Sunni mosque in Britain. Others said that when praying in a Sunni mosque they would make sure to pray in the Sunni way.

[124] The most frequently cited names in this context were Shaykh Albānī, Shaykh Ibn Bāz (d. 1999) and Shaykh Ibn al-'Uthaymin.

with others who are known as *salafīs*, in particular because of their harsh-ness and 'lack of Islamic etiquette'; one person felt that to call himself '*salafī*' would be to imply that he had a certain amount of religious knowledge, whereas in fact he didn't know Arabic. Overall, it seemed that these converts did not take these sectarian divisions too seriously. One interviewee said: 'You find the path that suits you, it partly depends on what your personality is I reckon', while another commented: 'You have to be a bit more chameleon-like at stages, you have to kind of blow with the wind a little bit. If your environment is *salafī*, then you have to act a little bit more *salafī*.' One interviewee described herself as a supporter of Hizb al-Tahrir, while another had a high regard for Omar Bakri Mohammed (the founder of al-Muhajiroun), and respected him as a scholar. A few interviewees mentioned the well-known *ḥadīth* to the effect that on the Day of Judgement there will be seventy-three Muslim sects and only one will be on the right path, so felt it better to stay away from any particular group.

When I asked interviewees about their general reading habits (and lis-tening habits, as several used tapes and CDs) it became clear that many of them were avid readers of Islamic literature, including a wide range of didactic, devotional and Islamic scholarly sources. Names emerged of par-ticular scholars, thinkers and authors who were admired: Hamza Yusuf was foremost (mentioned by eight interviewees), while Yusuf al-Qaradawi, Abu Amina Bilal Philips and Yusuf Islam were each mentioned by three intervie-wees. Almost half of the authors or figures cited in this context were converts; in addition to Hamza Yusuf, Yusuf Islam and Bilal Philips, inter-viewees cited Yusuf Estes, Malcolm X, Muhammad Ali, Abdal-Hakim Murad, Yahiya Emerick, Ahmad Thomson and Zaki Nike as favourite authors or leaders. Most, like Rachel, who spoke of 'the danger of being influenced by one person's opinion', made a point of reading a diverse range of sources. Many were quite eclectic in their choices, for example one inter-viewee mentioned Shaykh Fadlallah Haeri, Hamza Yusuf, Malcolm X and Khomeini as figures that he liked or admired. When asked to whom they would go for moral or religious guidance if they needed it, almost half knew particular *imāms* or scholars that they could approach (whether in person, by phone or online), while almost as many would speak to a friend, relative or acquaintance who they (in most but not all cases) considered to be more knowledgeable than themselves. Others mentioned books and the internet as sources of knowledge and guidance. As regards attitudes to religious authority, therefore, converts were fairly evenly divided between those who would consult a scholar and those who would use other means to find the information they needed. Only four interviewees had a knowledge of Arabic that was sufficient to allow them to read original scholarly sources, but many of the others consulted sources in English translation. Rachel, who did not read Arabic, nevertheless felt able to derive guidance directly from the sources; asked to whom she would go for guidance, she replied: 'I would much rather read the sources and read the *ḥadīth* myself and make my own judgement.' Charlene was part of a 'friendship group' who had all converted around the same time: 'I'll call up one if I'm having an issue, okay let's figure this out – what do we do? – our mentalities are pretty much the same.'

In the last decade or two, European and American converts have been active contributors to a growing body of Islamic literature available in English and other European languages, although the most widely distributed convert-authored works, such as Muhammad Asad's *The Road to Mecca* (1954) and Maurice Bucaille's apologetic work *The Bible, The Qur'an and Science* (first published in French in 1976), date from an earlier era. Among the most prolific or well-known contemporary authors are the German-born Murad Hofmann and the American Hamza Yusuf. The latter is a frequent visitor to the UK, as mentioned in the introduction, and his books, tapes and videos are widely circulated here. Converts such as Aisha Bewley in the US and Abdal-Hakim Murad (also known as Tim Winter) in Britain have been active in translating classical Islamic works. In the British context, as far as published books are concerned, one could mention the academic or semi-academic work of Martin Lings and Hasan (also known as Charles) Le Gai Eaton; the textbooks and Muslim 'self-help' books by Ruqaiyyah Waris Maqsood and Huda al-Khattab; the book on women converts by Na'ima Robert, and the polemical writings of Ahmad Thomson on Christianity and Western society.[125] Some of those who have contributed to contemporary Muslim or Islamic discourse on an academic or quasi-academic level are Abdal-Hakim Murad, Mohammad Siddique Seddon, Yahya Birt, Jeremy Henzell-Thomas and Harfiyah Ball.[126] Historically there

---

[125] I am not interested here in any academic or non-academic output which cannot be considered a contribution to Muslim discourse or Islamic thought, so will not be taking into consideration all works authored by the people mentioned.

[126] Again, I am thinking here of published or internet material which is written from an explicitly Muslim or Islamic standpoint.

is a strong tradition of converts to Islam, for example 'Ali al-Tabari in the ninth century CE and 'Abdullah al-Tarjuman in the sixteenth, becoming prominent contributors to Islamic literature and scholarship (especially apologetic and polemic). Converts in the present day are clearly continuing this tradition, making a significant contribution to Islamic thought and debate.[127]

[127] However, their contribution to the Islamic religious sciences, such as jurisprudence and Qur'anic commentary, is limited by the fact that most converts do not have the requisite level of Arabic.

Chapter 2

The 'double marginality' of converts[1]

his chapter explores the position of converts in relation to both
British society and the Muslim community. It begins by asking how
far attitudes to British society are a determining factor in conversion,
looking at selected aspects of conversion theory and the findings of previous
studies on Muslim converts, as well as my interview material and published
sources. While it is clear that attitudes to society are an important factor in
conversion to Islam in the West, it is generally *after* conversion that new
Muslims develop a fuller and more wide-ranging critique of British and
Western society; this will be dealt with in chapter 4. The present chapter will
also look at some of the experiential aspects of being a Muslim convert: how
do converts relate to born Muslims, on the one hand, and their non-Muslim
family and friends, on the other? Finally, it will investigate the extent to
which converts see themselves as having, and whether they actually do have,
a special role to play, in relation to both British society and born Muslims.

CONVERSION AS SOCIAL PROTEST?

Almost all studies on conversion to Islam in Europe and America have cited
disillusionment with Western society as a contributing factor; in fact, Köse

---

[1] The phrase 'double marginality' in this context is taken from Yahya Birt, 'Building New
Medinas'.

describes it as an essential predisposing factor,[2] while al-Qwidi observes of her sample that 'they had each found, during the period prior to the conversion process, different levels of disaffection with the values and lifestyle of the society in which they lived'.[3] Wohlrab-Sahr, in a study of German and American converts, finds that the adoption of a 'foreign'[4] religion such as Islam is related to problems of integration or disintegration in one's own social context, and is a means of articulating one's distance from that context.[5] The 'rebellion' factor in conversion, in the sense of the adolescent rebellion against one's parents, has not generally been found to be prominent among converts to Islam, which is not surprising in view of the relatively late average age of conversion. However, Roald points out that because of the generally negative image of Islam, conversion can sometimes be an act of 'rebellion' against the wider society, and that this especially applies to those who join Islamic radical or extremist groups.[6] Roald senses a 'strong link between conversion and converts' relationships to society', and finds that even those of her respondents and interviewees who had not been involved in leftist or environmental movements before their conversion expressed a generally negative attitude to Scandinavian society.[7]

As discussed in chapter 1, the average age of conversion has been found to be relatively high in the case of Islam as compared to other religions. This implies that Muslim converts have sufficient life experience and maturity to have arrived at informed opinions on social and political issues. Most researchers have found that intellectual and cognitive factors figure prominently in conversion to Islam, and seem to be at least as important as emotional factors, if not more so.[8] Conversion to Islam is very often a gradual process occurring over months or years, involving much reflection and

---

[2] Köse, *Conversion to Islam*, p. 122.
[3] Al-Qwidi, 'Understanding the Stages of Conversion to Islam', p. 193.
[4] The inverted commas are my own, to indicate that it is debatable whether Islam is in fact a 'foreign' religion, now that most British Muslims were born and bred in Britain.
[5] Wohlrab-Sahr, 'Conversion to Islam', pp. 352 and 361.
[6] Roald, *New Muslims in the European Context*, pp. 281 and 339. This element is likely to have increased since 9/11 and the July 2005 London bombings; an increase in conversions to Islam following 9/11 has been widely cited, though no doubt this is due in large part to wider dissemination of information on Islam at such times.
[7] Ibid., p. 106.
[8] Köse, *Conversion to Islam*, pp. 94 and 98; cf. al-Qwidi, 'Understanding the Stages of Conversion to Islam', p. 152.

study. A common motif in Muslim conversion narratives is that of the 'seeker', who explores a range of religions before finally settling on Islam;[9] the reasons given for preferring the latter often include the fact that it incorporates a practical and social dimension which was found to be lacking in other religions.

The 'crisis' element in conversion refers to the role of life crises (such as divorce and bereavement) as a predisposing factor in conversion. In contrast to cognitive factors, the crisis element, which has more to do with personal and emotional rather than social matters, does not seem to be particularly prominent for Muslim converts, although it has been found to be significant in many conversion studies focusing on Christianity. Köse does find that nearly half of his sample experienced some kind of emotional trauma such as divorce during the two years preceding conversion, but that it was the existential and cognitive concerns *arising from* the emotional turmoil that were the immediate cause of conversion.[10] Al-Qwidi, on the other hand, finds that none of her sample went through a crisis significantly close to their conversion.[11] According to Roald, any crisis, if there is one, is more likely to occur after conversion than before, given the often negative reaction of family, friends and society at large, and suggests that in a crisis one is more likely to choose a religion which is 'within the established frame of references' rather than one which incurs hostility from mainstream society.[12]

The 'affectional' element, i.e. personal attachment to members of the religion in question, is generally prominent in religious conversion. Researchers on conversion to Islam, however, are divided as to its importance. Roald suggests that this element, or its near equivalent, the element of 'encounter' (one of Rambo's seven stages), is particularly important in conversion to Islam, since a positive experience is needed to counteract the negative image of Islam in the media; of her sample, 91% had 'a form of personal relationship with Muslims' at the time of conversion.[13] Köse states

---

[9]   Twenty-nine per cent of Köse's sample had been involved in NRMs at some stage prior to conversion (*Conversion to Islam*, p. 53). Al-Qwidi, by contrast, finds that the 'quest' aspect (one of Rambo's seven stages) is less important, and that her interviewees tended to stumble on Islam by accident, as it were ('Understanding the Stages of Conversion to Islam', pp. 247–58).

[10]   Köse, *Conversion to Islam*, pp. 81–3 and 86.

[11]   Al-Qwidi, 'Understanding the Stages of Conversion to Islam', p. 141.

[12]   Roald, *New Muslims in the European Context*, pp. 93–5.

[13]   Ibid., pp. 97–8.

that conversion is highly unlikely to occur without such affective bonds.[14] However, Allievi finds that it is not unusual for conversion to occur without contact, particularly in intellectual conversions which arise from reading the Qur'an or other Islamic literature. He divides conversions into two broad categories: 'relational' and 'rational', and feels that Islamic conversions tend to be rational rather than relational.[15] Al-Qwidi broadly agrees with Allievi, claiming that in only about 10% of her sample was the affectional element definitely paramount.[16] These somewhat contrasting findings highlight the fact that the quality and significance of the contact should be carefully assessed; in fact, all of al-Qwidi's sample had had some kind of contact with a Muslim, but in most cases it was relatively brief.[17]

The above findings taken as a whole point to the relative importance of cognitive and rational factors vis-à-vis affectional and crisis elements, and are consistent with the idea of conversion to Islam as a carefully considered choice which takes into account not just personal and spiritual issues but also social and sometimes political factors. It is also important to take into account the religious and spiritual aspects of conversion, which have sometimes been neglected in conversion studies. A commonly occurring motif in Muslim conversion accounts is the impact of reading the Qur'an; converts often speak of this in spiritual and not just cognitive terms, expressing a sense that the Qur'an was speaking to them directly, and that they were overcome by a conviction that it really was the word of God.[18] The search for meaning and purpose is often prominent in these narratives.[19] Human motivation is complex, and a religious conversion may represent the culmination of a person's whole life-experience. In the case of converts to Islam, it seems that a spiritual search and a search for a better society often go hand in hand. An inherent part of the Muslim critique of Western society is its perceived materialism and lack of spirituality, and in this case social criticism and spirituality are clearly interrelated.

---

[14] Köse, *Conversion to Islam*, p. 121. He finds that women are more likely to have been influenced by this factor than men, and Sufis more than non-Sufis (pp. 194 and 103).

[15] Allievi, *Les Convertis à l'Islam*, pp. 310 and 120.

[16] Al-Qwidi, 'Understanding the Stages of Conversion to Islam', p. 186.

[17] In fact, she found that reading the Qur'an played a crucial role in the conversion of every single one of her sample (ibid., pp. 172 and 195–6).

[18] Ibid., p. 182.

[19] Köse, *Conversion to Islam*, pp. 31 and 86–92; al-Qwidi, 'Understanding the Stages of Conversion to Islam', pp. 155 and 252.

In the following brief analysis of convert narratives I have drawn not only on my interview material but also on conversion stories on the internet and in magazines and books.[20] Most scholars agree that the testimonies of converts are useful for the purposes of academic study, but warn that they are to be treated with caution, since there is a natural dialectical process whereby people formulate and reformulate past experiences from the standpoint of who they are and what they know in the present. This process of reconstruction is likely to occur as the convert changes and develops as a person and learns more about the religion he or she has joined.[21] One convert, for example, said of her parents: '[They] threw me into the middle of a corrupt society and expected me to find my own husband which was such a pressure, especially while alcoholism was going around.'[22] Conversion testimonies may fulfil various functions, including demonstrating the commitment of the new convert, validating the community the convert has joined, helping to maintain or increase the faith of other members of the religious community, and encouraging others to convert. There is clearly less scope for these functions to be served in the private, informal and interactive context of the interview, which means that the conversion accounts are likely to be less premeditated or 'packaged'. I have therefore prioritized this material.

Among my interviewees I found that, as in other studies, the cognitive element was prominent, with thirteen people mentioning reading (including reading the Qur'an) and debating with Muslims as key factors in their conversion.[23] Amin said that in discussions with Muslims he got 'thoroughly satisfying answers' to all his questions, while Sakina said that when she was reading books on Islam, 'everything clicked into place, my brain accepted it and my heart accepted it'. Another interviewee, Samia, said that on reading

---

[20] There is a growing body on convert narratives on the internet; see, e.g., www.thetruereligion.org and www.islamfortoday.com. Most of the testimonies on these sites are by American converts.

[21] Taylor, 'Recollection and Membership'.

[22] Quoted in Köse, *Conversion to Islam*, p. 89, though Köse does not make the point about biographical reconstruction. The somewhat generic quality of testimonies is further demonstrated by the fact that they often echo Islamic revivalist literature in style and content (Haddad, 'The Quest for Peace in Submission', pp. 41–2; Roald, *New Muslims in the European Context*, p. 112).

[23] 'Debating with Muslims' would of course include a relational element, but for most interviewees there was a strong emphasis on rational processes.

the Qur'an 'I just knew from the first few verses that it was the truth'.[24] Although about a third had been in a marriage or a relationship with a Muslim prior to their conversion, suggesting that the affectional element was important, in many cases the Muslim in question was not very practising (in at least three cases, the husband became more practising as a result of his wife's conversion), or the relationship had ended prior to the conversion. Most often, the relationship served as a trigger which caused the person to be curious about Islam and to start enquiring or reading about it. In almost all cases people stressed that they had not converted 'because of' their relationship or marriage, but out of conviction resulting from their own investigation into Islam.

When interviewees were invited to speak freely about their conversion and what attracted them to Islam, the most common themes that emerged in their accounts were: *tawḥīd* (oneness of God, mentioned by ten interviewees); social and political issues (nine); the contrast between Islam and Christianity (eight); the exploration of other faiths, culminating in the discovery of Islam (six); the fact that Islam was seen as a complete way of life (four); the sense of brotherhood or sisterhood (four); and the similarities with Christianity, which helped to remove the 'obstacle' of Islam being seen as a strange or foreign religion (four).[25] Religious converts generally tend to frame their conversion in terms of the aspects of the religion which they find attractive, so it is worthy of note that social and political factors were almost as prominent as the central Islamic tenet of faith (*tawḥīd*) amongst my own sample, reflecting the 'disillusionment' factor observed by other researchers on conversion to Islam. In fact, the attraction to particular aspects or qualities of Islam (e.g. a sense of brotherhood, warmth or hospitality) sometimes corresponds to a perceived lack of these qualities in British or Western society in general.[26]

---

[24] As is clear from the last two quotes, the cognitive element may be combined with a spiritual/emotional element.

[25] As some interviewees mentioned more than one theme, the total number of occurrences of these themes comes to over thirty.

[26] The perceived contrast between Western and Muslim societies in this respect is highlighted in a statement which one interviewee had included in some personal correspondence which she showed me, dating from the time of her conversion: 'I am not comfortable in the selfish, shallow, capitalist world of the West. From Muslims I have experienced nothing but kindness, warmth, gentleness and generosity.'

Of those who mentioned social or political factors in their conversion accounts, Fatima said that she had never really felt part of British society: 'As a teenager I hadn't wanted to be part of what I saw as a big sort of machine, a capitalist machine, and I dreaded just becoming a cog in the wheel, submerged in the workaday kind of existence ... When I found Islam, it enabled me to retain my distance from a sort of capitalist society, but without having to damage myself in the process.' Yaqub had been a socialist prior to his conversion, and had felt the need for 'a worldwide revolution, because it's a global economy, a global disease'; he continued: 'Islam for me is an alternative, it's a way of life instead of just a religion.' Another interviewee, Mahmud, said that prior to his conversion he felt there was 'something wrong with the society, what was happening in the society didn't make sense for me, because basically people were living for what they could get'. The theme of materialism was echoed by other interviewees, and several mentioned that they had become disillusioned with the clubbing and drinking culture. Two of the women spoke of the Islamic teachings on women as a factor that attracted them to Islam, and one of them showed me a letter to a friend from around the time of her conversion, in which she wrote: 'I feel disgusted with the emphasis on appearance in the West. As a female I tend to feel inadequate if I am not dressed in fashionable clothes. People judge each other on the shallowest of bases. It's all so plastic and cheap. I guess my desire to convert partly comes from wanting to visibly reject the West's plastic values.'[27] One man, who had himself suffered a lot from racism, spoke of 'the clarity it [i.e. Islam] gave on matters of race'. Several interviewees, like Fatima quoted above, expressed a sense of not fitting in with British society or youth culture prior to their conversion; one such was Peter: 'Even before I was Muslim, I wasn't really at home. I mean I was fine with my friends but I was never into football, I was never into pubs, I didn't even drink tea. I was quite at odds with English culture.' According to another interviewee, Abdullah: 'There is a sense of being lost I think – or there was – within my generation, whether that goes back to society or not I don't know, but just

---

[27] It is interesting to observe that in this woman's case the sense of disillusionment with Western society as a factor in her conversion came out much more clearly in the correspondence at the time than in her interview, which took place several years after her conversion. When I put this to her in a follow-up interview, she said that her feelings had not really changed but that she had 'learned to tone down the rant as it can be counterproductive'.

elements of it I suppose in terms of the drinking culture, the non-inquisitive side of our society, just get up, do your job, get drunk and go to sleep.'

Out of twenty or so British internet conversion stories which I surveyed, that of Abdurraheem Green is the one that contains the most wide-ranging critique of British and/or Western society. His account covers many areas, including education, international politics and the media, as well as lifestyle and the general culture and ethos of society. In an interview with *The Islamic Voice*, he describes how he became disillusioned with the British education system after he began studying for a degree in history, finding that it was 'thoroughly Eurocentric and projected world history in a way that suggested that the civilisation attained its full glory and apogee in Europe'. Time spent living in Egypt for periods of his childhood and youth had had a profound effect on him, highlighting the contrast between a Muslim society and a non-Muslim one. In Egypt, he found the people poor but happy: 'They left everything in the hands of Allah'; in England, by contrast, he found people shallow and materialistic: 'They try to be happy but happiness is superficial.' He writes that '[the] West's prelaid, programmed life intensely repelled me. I began to question if a person has to live a life merely to get strait-jacketed in a rigorous schedule. I found Europeans struggling a lot to enjoy life. They had no higher purpose in life.'[28]

Another frequently recurring theme, often directly or indirectly related to the critique of Western society, is the contrast between Islam and Christianity. This is still a relatively common motif despite the decline in Christian religiosity and practice in Western societies over recent decades, and despite the fact that most converts nowadays have not themselves been practising Christians. Leaving aside the theological differences between the two faiths, and the emphasis on Islam's perceived simplicity and logical nature as compared with Christianity, a commonly adduced contrast is the way in which Islam pervades all areas of life while Christianity is confined to church on a Sunday. Islam is seen as having a this-worldly, practical ethos, while Christianity is seen as rather vague and ineffable. Islam alone is therefore believed to have the potential to bring about social justice. The issue of race is mentioned by some converts, especially those from a non-white background. In such cases there is often an implicit or explicit comparison with the historical baggage (rather than inherent ideal) of Christianity, in

---

[28] Green, 'Why I Embraced Islam'.

particular colonialism and the slave trade. Most important, perhaps, is the fact that Christianity is perceived as having 'sold out' to liberalism or secularism (as evidenced by, for example, liberal Christian attitudes to homosexuality and women priests), and as unable to combat social problems such as drugs, delinquency and family breakdown. Tim Winter (also known as Abdal-Hakim Murad) feels that the Church has undergone 'too many reforms, too much laxity . . . while Islam has never changed. It is an immutable force.'[29]

As indicated above, the Islamic teachings on women, marriage and the family are another aspect which many find attractive. Clearly defined gender roles and the emphasis on a stable family life, for example, may be seen as contrasting with the social fragmentation in Western or British society. For Emira Topham, family life and 'the value that Islam places on motherhood' were deciding factors in her conversion.[30] Melissa, a convert who relates her conversion story in *emel*, was affected by the pressures on women to conform to glossy media images, and this played a part, albeit indirect, in leading her to convert to Islam.[31] Harfiyah Ball-Haleem says that prior to her conversion she was 'terribly confused' about the values that society held in relation to women, and was relieved to find in Islam clear teachings on women's role.[32] In each case it is the contrast with Western norms that potential converts find attractive.

CONVERTS IN RELATION TO BORN MUSLIMS

Converts fulfil various functions in relation to the Muslim community as a whole, in particular that of legitimization in the eyes of the host society. Muslims draw much encouragement from the conversion of Westerners to Islam, particularly in the case of high-profile figures such as Yusuf Islam (formerly the singer Cat Stevens).[33] Converts are living proof of the dictum

[29] Cited in Rocher and Cherqaoui, *D'Une foi l'autre*, p. 26. These are all prominent themes in Muslim anti-Christian polemical literature, to which converts are often active contributors; see Zebiri, *Muslims and Christians Face to Face*, pp. 78–84.
[30] Berrington, 'Islam Sheds its Image'.
[31] Chaudhry, 'Getting Spiritual in Syria'.
[32] Petre, 'My Dad Buys me Books about Islam'.
[33] The British Muslim lifestyle magazine *emel* regularly features converts' stories, and *Q-News* also had a regular feature for a time.

that Islam is valid for all times, places and peoples, and their very existence refutes the idea that Islam is a foreign or alien religion, or a religion which is for Asians, Arabs and Africans. Allievi observes that they may also provide a kind of psychological security for immigrant Muslims and their descendants in that there can be no question of converts being expelled from the country.[34] The colonial or post-colonial dynamic helps explain why such conversions are often seized on with such alacrity: whereas in the past the more powerful and seemingly superior Westerner/outsider/white man imposed his dominance, in the present the former colonizer acknowledges the superiority of the religion/culture/way of life of the formerly colonized. Those who embrace Islam, especially when they marry into Muslim communities, are in a sense subverting the 'otherization' or stigmatization of Muslims. However, many converts feel that the acclaim with which they are greeted by their co-religionists rings hollow if they are not taken seriously as Muslims. Yahya Birt remarks that converts 'are sometimes seen as having little to contribute except a sort of Caucasian tokenism in glossy brochures for raising money in the Middle East'; as Westerners, they are treated like 'a few shiny pieces of silverware, who are paraded as hard-won trophies for the faith at a time when Western . . . influence appears ever more pervasive around the world'.[35] Gerholm says of the prominent French convert Roger Garaudy: 'It is not possible for him to intervene in internal Islamic matters. His cultural capital as a master-thinker of western civilization can only be used for legitimizing Islam *in general*. Were he to propagate his own version of Islam among Muslims who were born as such, it is likely that his origin . . . would be held against him.'[36]

Notwithstanding the warmth and hospitality mentioned above as a factor in the conversion of some, nearly all my interviewees had had difficult experiences with born Muslims at some point following their conversion.[37]

---

[34] Allievi, *Les Convertis à l'Islam*, p. 289.
[35] Birt, 'Building New Medinas'.
[36] Gerholm, 'Three European intellectuals', p. 276.
[37] In fact, virtually all studies on converts (including those by Roald, al-Qwidi, Köse and Adnan) have shown that converts frequently experience disappointment in their dealings with the Muslim community and with the lack of support they receive as new Muslims. Adnan relates that she found her study becoming 'a study of the failings of the Muslim community' (*New Muslims in Britain*, p. 24). Roald points out that the sense of disappointment may be exacerbated if the convert has formed an idealized image of Islam through reading prior to actually meeting Muslims (*New Muslims in the European Context*, p. 263).

Many had been quite warmly received initially, but encountered problems later on. One interviewee, Peter, sums up the ambivalence that converts often encounter: 'There's people who are very curious and well-meaning, they'd love to have you round for dinner, but wouldn't let you marry their sister or daughter.' Lisa felt that 'the reactions are strange because a lot of people assume that you don't know anything, this is from Muslims, and they can be quite patronizing . . . it's like you're an oddity, a bit peculiar, and that you'll never really get it'. A small minority had become extremely disheartened. One male interviewee expressed this in very strong terms: 'I know how I have suffered, and how much anguish I've gone through, and how much disappointment and disillusionment. I wouldn't wish that on my worst enemy . . . I've had so much heartache . . . I just keep myself to myself these days,' while another said: 'I no longer see Muslims as inherently good people – many will stab you in the back, cheat, lie or take advantage of you.' More typical, however, was Linda's comment: 'When I first converted I thought that everyone would be perfect. Now I know they are just like any other group of people.' Overall those who had converted more recently seemed to have suffered less disillusionment, perhaps because they received more support from fellow converts.

Converts are sometimes dismayed to discover that they have to cope with prejudice not only from British society but also from born Muslims. Adnan observes that converts may find themselves excluded from positions of influence in mosques and Islamic organizations, or, if they do gain such positions, they may be exposed to jealousy and even hatred.[38] Yahya Birt finds that 'no matter what their achievements, converts are excluded from the circle of the trusted, the responsible and those of serious piety'.[39] One of my interviewees, Abdullah, took up this theme: 'Many of the older generation of particularly Asians still see themselves as "real" Muslims. Converts are seen as second-class Muslims . . . Ask any convert and they'll tell you. We're not seen as the real deal.' He also felt that there was an issue of trust: 'If someone's picking between two people they'll usually go with the one who was born Muslim.' A more subtle form of prejudice is that of being presumed ignorant, as Rahima pointed out: 'They think you've been a Muslim for five minutes, and you don't know how to recite the

[38] Adnan, *New Muslims in Britain*, p. 42.
[39] Birt, 'Building New Medinas'.

prayer in Arabic, and as you get older it gets increasingly irritating, that people think you know absolutely nothing.' Second-generation converts who are neither Asian nor Arab in appearance may suffer many of the same problems as first-generation converts. One such is Isla Rosser-Owen, who tells how she and her sister grew up feeling rejected by both Muslims and non-Muslims, and how the family 'had to deal with accusations of being "spies"; or that we hadn't really, truly converted and we weren't "proper Muslims" '. She goes on to say that 'it seems no one really values or respects converts . . . no one really takes them seriously'; she concludes: 'I am not the only one who has tried her hardest to become a part of the Muslim community but has found herself pretty much ostracised for her efforts . . . who is constantly talked down to because I have the wrong colour [i.e. white] skin, the wrong gender, the wrong job, the wrong background, the wrong history'.[40]

A common source of unease among converts is the way they feel that some born Muslims, especially the older generation, confuse religion and culture. Converts often find their faith and practice under scrutiny, and feel they risk being labelled unbelievers if either are found wanting;[41] however, the criticism is often based on a cultural interpretation of Islam rather than on the Islamic sources. As Fatima put it: 'You're not a real Muslim because you don't wear trousers under your *jilbāb* . . . you're not a proper Muslim because – not that it's said in words but it's implied in the manner.' In Roald's study, converts complained that born Muslims expected them to throw out their cultural baggage while they (the born Muslims) held on to theirs.[42] Converts often wish to combat cultural practices which they see as unIslamic, but are often criticized or dismissed when they try to do so.[43] For example, when Sakina tried to tell some African Muslim women about the need to cover their arms, she said: 'They didn't want to listen to me because I'm just a new Muslim, I don't know anything, right?' A related problem is that converts are often more knowledgeable about Islam than born Muslims, many of whom are not familiar with the content of the Qur'an (which they may have learned to recite without understanding it) or the

[40] Rosser-Owen, 'British Muslim?'.
[41] Roald, *New Muslims in the European Context*, p. 273, citing Lena Larsen, 'Velkommen til en stor Familie: Islam og Konversjon i norsk kontekst', MA thesis, University of Oslo, 1995.
[42] Roald, *New Muslims in the European Context*, p. 272.
[43] Al-Qwidi, 'Understanding the Stages of Conversion to Islam', p. 222.

ḥadīth. This places converts in the awkward position of not knowing whether to correct them or to maintain a diplomatic silence.[44]

Even if they do not encounter actual hostility or prejudice, many converts complain of a general lack of support. Yahiya Emerick, a prominent American convert, writes that 'the convert experience is basically one of isolation which can then lead to loneliness and, in the worst cases, their leaving Islam altogether. Many are quietly ignored and beyond a few pleasantries and handshakes they may never be made to feel welcome or accepted.'[45] Halima drew a contrast between the situation in Britain and her experience in the Muslim world: 'In Arab countries you're fighting off their hospitality, everybody wants you to live with them and be their best friend but here, no. Maybe it's to do with life in London, there's a distance that people keep, they're very busy.' The situation does seem to be changing in Britain, however, in that support services for converts have improved, with many of the larger mosques now running induction courses or study circles for new Muslims. Also, converts have developed their own support networks, notably in the form of 'new Muslim' projects springing up in major UK cities. One interviewee said that things had got better with the advent of e-groups: 'We get emails saying such-and-such a sister needs help . . . and then people will respond and help that person or do whatever they can.'

Converts often feel a strong need for acceptance into the Muslim community,[46] especially as they may be experiencing difficulties with their family and friends as a result of their conversion. Halima felt that the most difficult thing for a convert was the fact that 'you're not automatically absorbed into somebody's family and taken into their heart and that's what you need'. One way in which a convert can be 'grafted in' to an established Muslim community is to marry into it, and some converts express a preference for marrying a born Muslim rather than a convert, partly for the sake of their future children, who would then have the support of an extended Muslim family.[47] However, in practice converts can find it difficult to marry into the predominantly Asian British Muslim community due to the institution of arranged marriage and preference for partners from the same ethnic background; this situation gives rise to much frustration and

---

[44] Ibid., p. 224.
[45] Emerick, 'You and your Family'.
[46] Allievi, *Les Convertis à l'Islam*, p. 28.
[47] Al-Qwidi, 'Understanding the Stages of Conversion to Islam', p. 227.

disappointment.[48] One new Muslim, recently married to a fellow convert, goes so far as to say that 'the hardest and ugliest difficulty in finding a partner, is the tribalism and sickening racism that is prevalent amongst many Muslim communities'.[49] Of the twenty-three interviewees who were married, six were married to a convert (in addition, two of the single women were in negotiations to marry a convert) and seventeen to a born Muslim.[50] Of the latter, only three were married to Asians; the rest were mostly married to Arabs and Africans.[51]

If white converts find themselves marginalized, things tend to be worse for black converts, with many complaining of racist attitudes, particularly on the part of the older generations of the Asian community. Al-Qwidi found that white converts were more accepted than black converts by the Asian community both as people and as Muslims, which is to some extent a reflection of Asian attitudes towards black people in British society generally. Some of her Afro-Caribbean interviewees had experienced 'distressing rebuttals' and found themselves unwelcome in Asian mosques. One of my interviewees, a black male convert, explained that the marriage problem is worse for black than white converts: 'If you're trying to go and marry some Asian sister good luck, good luck lad, good luck, because it's going to be very difficult for you.' As a black convert, he had found it difficult to get support for an Islamic charity which he had set up some years ago, and as a result of his experiences concluded that 'white people are actually the least racist I've met and people of colour are the ones who have amazing amounts of racism in them ... Asians definitely, Arabs definitely'. He added that the less practising Muslims were the most racist.[52] A white Shi'i convert I spoke to

[48] Ibid., p. 220; Adnan, *New Muslims in Britain*, p. 33.
[49] Dean, 'A Day in the Life'.
[50] Two of the interviewees were married to each other, thus slightly inflating the figure for marriage to a convert as opposed to a born Muslim.
[51] Some of my interviewees felt that it was becoming easier for converts to marry into Muslim families (though they generally acknowledged that it was still difficult for black converts). In fact, one was married into a family from an African background, where the father had made a point of marrying all three of his daughters to converts (although he continually had to defend his decision to people of his own community).
[52] Black Muslims in America suffer similar problems. 'Sumayya L', a black American Muslim woman, writes in *Q-News*: 'I am told that I am a Muslim of inferior quality just because I am a convert and just because I don't have beige skin and I don't speak Arabic or Urdu ... must I be treated like an outcast until I accomplish this? ... It has shaken my faith that I cannot fit into a community that boasts about being the most fair, the most anti-racist' (*Q-News*, July 2001).

had been a Sunni before making the transition to Shi'ism. He felt that because of their 'siege mentality', Shi'is were generally worse than Sunnis in their treatment of converts, and also more racist: 'The Afro-Caribbean converts ... were treated so horribly, I mean people wouldn't even shake their hands because they thought they were somehow religiously impure.'

As some converts are aware, the complexity of born Muslims' attitudes towards them is partly due to historical factors, and in particular the legacy of colonialism. Fatima believed that this legacy tends to be underestimated in assessing relations between Muslims and Westerners in general, and that it impacted on her own relationships with other Muslims: 'This whole colonial issue gets in the way, they just see you as, oh well, you've got it easy because you're white, and you don't have to suffer as much as we've had to suffer.' Aisha Masterton elaborates on this theme, saying that the convert encounters 'both outrage and irritation from some born Muslims who feel you have stolen their religion and are not practising it properly ... When one gives one's whole heart to Islam, it is difficult to hear somebody implying that you are fake, or defining you as a privileged white girl who is patronising Arab or Asian people.'[53] Yahya Birt points out that converts are still categorized as Westerners, with all the ambivalence that that entails: 'Whether as novice or trophy, the convert appears overburdened equally with low or high expectations, which mirror the simultaneous admiration, envy and distrust with which Muslims often regard the West.' He feels that many born Muslims 'have to shrug off their own racist preconceptions that Caucasians are forever entrapped in a superior mindset obsessed by the will to power.'[54] Aside from the colonial past, power relations in the present also need to be taken into account. Immigrants are generally of lower social status and the older generation in particular may feel that Islam is the one area in which they can claim some sort of authority. When even this last bastion is encroached upon by British converts, they may feel threatened.[55]

Another American suggests that the racial prejudice among American Muslims is such that if it were known about, 'it probably would add fuel to the anti-immigrant sentiment' (Q-News, July–August 2002).
[53] Aisha Masterton, 'Experiences of British Converts to Islam', talk given at Oxford University, autumn 2003.
[54] Birt, 'Building New Medinas'.
[55] Adnan, New Muslims in Britain, p. 31; Roald, New Muslims in the European Context, pp. 279–80. Al-Qwidi points out that South Asian Muslims, with their tradition of

Interestingly, some converts report that they experience the greatest hostility from non-practising Muslims, who often seem to feel guilt or defensiveness in the face of an 'outsider' who has chosen to practise the religion they themselves were born into. In such cases it seems that the colonial dynamic is still operational, but unmitigated by any sense of religious fellowship. An American convert sums up this attitude on his blog: 'You get the lapsed, non-practising Muslims, who wonder why anyone would choose to follow a faith that they themselves have rejected or are just too lazy to follow ... so they have to make it out to be that converts/reverts are sheep, they don't really know the religion, or are just people that wannabe Arabs.'[56] Fatima had a close friend who was a non-practising Muslim. When she converted, she said that her friend had felt that 'she had shown me what was sacred and I'd taken it away from her'; the friend also expected to be looked down on by her. Fatima continued: 'I think the whole colonial thing came into it. I was upset. I thought, come on, I'm your friend, I'm not a colonialist.' She had also found that non-practising Muslims who came into contact with her as a convert often felt the need to prove their Islamic credentials by 'lecturing' her about some aspect of Islam, even though she generally knew rather more than they did. Another interviewee, Janice, described a similar reaction from two Muslim friends she knew from before her conversion, one of whom said to her: 'Just because you wear the scarf you think you know everything.' Halima commented that the Westernized, non-practising Muslims 'tend to look on anything religious as being lower class, and wearing the headscarf, they think only servants do that'.

Yahya Birt, in a talk originally addressed to a gathering of converts, points out that the colonial dynamic can work both ways: 'It is never justified – no matter how disappointing one's experiences with British Muslims can sometimes be – to fall into racial stereotyping', and that converts might need to 'struggle to escape implicit notions of cultural or intellectual superiority that may persist after conversion'. Referring to the way in which converts are often complimented on being more serious about their faith than other Muslims, Birt points out the danger of converts acquiring a 'false

unquestioning respect for the elders, are somewhat bemused by converts who cite textual authority for their views on what is or is not Islamic ('Understanding the Stages of Conversion to Islam', p. 266).

[56] See http://abusinan.blogspot.com/2005/11/recently-subject-of-convertsreverts.html (accessed 14/03/06).

sense of superiority'. He reminds his audience that converts need to engage in self-criticism just like anyone else, and that 'any born Muslim who takes or who decides to take their faith seriously has made a choice that is just as self-conscious and committed as any true act of conversion'.[57] Sufyan Gent agrees: 'The devil will try to exploit human weakness and make you think you're special, and so we must pray to avoid this trap.'[58] While acknowledging that many of the complaints which converts make about born Muslims are grounded in their experience, Roald (who is herself a convert as well as an academic) feels that they should take account of the fact that many of the Muslims with whom they come into contact are immigrants with a poor educational background and low socio-economic status, and that these should be distinguished from Muslims who live as majorities, and who might be better placed to provide good role models.[59]

Among my interviewees, experiences of mosques were rather mixed. Many found Asian mosques in particular to be unwelcoming, insular, sectarian and male dominated, and many complained about the lack of facilities for women. Some people were annoyed about sermons not always being in English, or about the sometimes exclusivist, intolerant or politically radical content of the sermons. Mahmud told how he used to deliberately time his arrival at the Friday prayers so as to miss the sermon, while Peter had sometimes found his Friday prayer visits to the mosque to be a 'completely soulless experience'. On the other hand, some appreciated the activities and groups organized by the larger, more cosmopolitan mosques. Sakina had had very positive experiences; at the African mosque where she took her shahādah, she was told: 'Think of it as your second home – always come here whenever you need to.' To some extent converts' experiences depend on which area they're living in. Those living in London generally fare better because of the ethnic diversity of Muslims in London. In areas where Muslims are predominantly Asian, it can be more difficult, as one interviewee who was living outside London indicated: 'It's very racially divided ... the Asians keep to the Asians, the whites keep to the whites, nobody really mixes very well.' Some of the women living in smaller towns or rural areas had no access to a mosque at all due to the lack of women's facilities.

[57]   Birt, 'Building New Medinas'.
[58]   Gent, 'It was as if the Scales had been Lifted from my Eyes'.
[59]   Roald, New Muslims in the European Context, p. 255.

A few of my interviewees reported encouraging experiences of being welcomed into a Muslim community, and one or two remarked that they felt more at home with certain Muslim cultures than with English culture.[60] Rachel had been overwhelmed when a born Muslim woman whom she had only met twice had thrown a big party in her honour, attended by about fifty Muslim women, while Sulayman spoke of the 'wonderful sense of brother-hood' he had experienced on converting, and had found Muslims (includ-ing Asians) to be very hospitable: 'I could save an awful lot of money on food by eating out if I wanted to.' In some cases, however, the welcome could be excessive. Rahima commented that when she converted 'people would speak to you like you're some kind of VIP everywhere you go'. Hafsa had been sent off by a Muslim organization to give talks and lectures in mosques almost immediately after her conversion: 'Sometimes when you get a pink person that becomes a Muslim, it's almost like they put them up on a pedestal . . . it's a bit too much,' while Amin agreed that often 'converts are made too much fuss over'.

Converts often express a sense of relief at spending time with other con-verts, no doubt partly due to uncomfortable experiences with the majority Muslim community. Common themes here are the acceptance of difference and doubt, and an open, questioning approach to religious matters. Feedback on events and camps organized by the New Muslims Project in Leicester gives a sense of this. One woman, in a letter to *Meeting Point*, describes her experience: 'Judgement was left to Allah enabling a spiritual, physical and psychological growth of all. I was overcome by a sense of accep-tance: *a feeling I have not experienced within the Muslim community for some considerable time now*' (my italics).[61] Another person talks of the 'frank and wholesome discussion amongst all the participants leading to and provid-ing a comfortable atmosphere where doubts, hopes, fears and aspirations were heard and addressed with confidence'.[62] There is no doubt that despite the fact that most converts marry born Muslims, converts seek each other out socially, and this is at least in part due to cultural affinity. Among my interviewees, over half said that 50% or more of their friends were converts,

[60] One interviewee felt that there was much value in being exposed to born Muslim cultures, 'because it's already there in a package, there's so much you'd learn that you wouldn't learn from reading a book'.

[61] Letters, in *Meeting Point*, 27, October 2002.

[62] 'Wales . . . Where the Lambs are Rarely Silent', in *Meeting Point*, 27, October 2002.

and almost a third (nine) of the total sample said that at least 70% of their friends were. Yahya Birt tells how he used to avoid convert-only gatherings for fear of exclusivism, but goes on to say: 'A few months ago, I spent a delightful evening in the company of two "seasoned" convert brothers. I found it a liberating chance to just be British and Muslim, *just to be who I was without apology or explanation*' (my italics). He concludes that convert interactions, whether for social or practical purposes, are to be encouraged. However, converts sometimes come under suspicion when they organize events involving only converts, as Birt explains: 'No other ethnicity considering self-organisation is so easily charged with the possibility of racism, when at the same time every other ethnic Muslim grouping in the UK legitimately comes together for a number of good purposes'; he goes on to ask: 'What is the problem with this, so long as one does not develop racist or exclusive attitudes that vitiate the universal brotherhood of Islam?'[63]

There is some evidence to suggest that converts are becoming more self-sufficient (though not insular or isolationist), and less dependent on the patronage of born Muslims, an obvious example being the growth of 'new Muslim' support services and e-groups. Of the five interviewees who expressed a preference, three (who were all still single) said that they would prefer to marry a convert rather than a born Muslim; their reasons included the hope that a convert would have less 'cultural baggage', that there would be fewer family problems, and that he or she would be more committed to Islam. Several interviewees seemed able to take any problems they encountered in their stride. Halima contrasted the insularity of the Asian community with the attitude of the early Muslims: 'What brought Islam out of Arabia was that the Arabs went to different places and they traded and they intermarried. If they'd stuck to themselves then Islam would still be in Arabia. So we'll do that, we'll take Islam out, they'll stay there. Either they will follow us or they don't. If they don't, it's their loss really.' Dawud commented that 'all people who live in the world encounter problems with people in general', and that it was important not to be preoccupied with wrongs suffered: 'I guess if you're brought up with Allah *subhāna ta'āla* [praise be to Him, the Almighty] then you don't find fault and you don't demand what people owe you. Whatever happens, you accept it's Allah who's doing it.'

---

[63] Birt, 'Building New Medinas'.

CONVERTS IN RELATION TO NON-MUSLIM FAMILY AND FRIENDS

Many converts say that one of the hardest things about converting to Islam is telling their families and friends. Most of the themes treated in this book, including culture, politics, theology and gender issues, can become bones of contention in this context. Converts' ongoing relationships with their families of origin and non-Muslim friends may to some extent affect their attitudes to non-Muslims in general and also perhaps to the wider society. However, it is difficult to demonstrate this as there are so many variables, and so many other factors which might influence their views and attitudes. In practice, converts often go to some lengths to maintain their family ties, despite the difficulties around 'coming out' and the ensuing tensions; a few of the interviewees felt that their relationship with their family had actually got better since their conversion, most of them attributing the improvement to Islamic teachings on the good treatment of parents. Conversion had a rather different effect on friendships with non-Muslims, however, with many interviewees drifting away from most, if not all, of their friends from pre-conversion days.

Family reactions to conversion appear to fall into three categories. First, there are those cases where a negative reaction is followed by a period of difficulty which, over time, gives way to a gradual coming-to-terms and an eventual, if not always wholehearted, acceptance by the family of their Muslim offspring. Next there are those instances in which time does not seem to heal. Seven of my interviewees exemplify this, reporting that their conversion is continuing to cause friction up to the present day (three of these described how they had been scapegoated as a result of their conversion, in the sense of being blamed for the poor physical or mental health of other family members). Finally, and this is by far the smallest category (10% in my sample), there are those converts who say that their parents were very supportive from the outset or soon after. As might be expected, family reactions will sometimes straddle two categories, with different members responding in different ways. Eleanor's mother came to be very accepting of her daughter's Muslim identity, but matters are far from being resolved with her father and brother. Though it is now thirteen years since she converted, she still hardly talks to them. 'I don't see the point', she said, 'as they hate what I am and so therefore they must hate me.' Two-thirds of the interviewees fell into the first (coming-to-terms) category. In some of these cases, considerable effort was involved on the part of both the convert and his or her parents to maintain or restore good relations. This is illustrated by the case of Rachel, who had enjoyed a very close relationship with her mother prior to her conversion. Although she tried very hard to be gradual in introducing changes, she said that her mother 'freaked out' when she came upon her going through her wardrobe and throwing out clothes that she no longer considered suitable. She said of her mother in this early phase:

> I think she felt kind of alienated from me, very very lost and confused, she didn't understand what was going on, and she found it a bit scary ... She used to feel very uncomfortable watching me pray, she couldn't handle it, until I gave her a book which had the English translation of what I was saying and I said look, it's the same contents as a hymn, it's exactly the same, only we don't say Jesus is the son of God, that's virtu-ally the only difference, and after that she relaxed a bit.

Although it had only been two years since her conversion, Rachel said that she was now close to her mother again and their relationship was not too different from what it had been previously. Eleanor told how her mother had not been particularly happy at her conversion and 'didn't agree with the religion', but went on to say: 'Now she's wonderful, she even teaches our children what they should and shouldn't do Islamically, even though she doesn't accept it herself. She tells them not to walk in front of us when we're praying.'

Not surprisingly, in cases where the family has a strong religious back-ground, particularly where religious identity is bound up with communal identity, reactions are more extreme. Among my interviewees this was par-ticularly true for those with a Hindu background, and to a lesser extent for those with an Irish Catholic background. One woman whose family were Hindu had not told her parents that she was a Muslim for four years after her conversion, and when she had, her mother had 'wailed' and her father had cried, and all contact had stopped for a six-month period as they were too upset to speak on the phone with her (previously phone calls had been twice daily). In her case family relations were eventually restored; as she pointed out, parents of converts often have 'this ability to separate off what they don't like from the child that they love'. Another woman from a Hindu background was not so fortunate: three years after her conversion she said that her family still could not decide whether they wanted to speak to her or not, and she had gone from being the adored only daughter in a close-knit extended family to being unable to attend family events (which would generally include non-*maḥram* males such as brothers-in-law) as her parents refused to see her in *ḥijāb*. She found that her role in the family had completely changed: 'It's funny, because I guess I was such an integral part of it, it never occurred to me that I'd be pushed out.' Whereas previously she had been very close to her mother and they had often gone out to cultural events together, she could now only meet with her parents in their own home, and had to remove her *ḥijāb* in the driveway before they saw her. She described her father as a 'broken man', who pretended that he did not care about her any more but who was in reality deeply wounded. The impact of historical factors in this case is clear: this woman's grandparents had been forced to leave their homes when India was partitioned in 1947. Although her family were very liberal by Asian standards, even to the point of encouraging her to have boyfriends, she had been told from a young age that she could marry whoever she liked so long as it was not a Muslim or a black man.[64] A male convert whose parents are staunch Northern Irish Catholics took a long time to tell them of his conversion, and still had not told all of his extended family. Although his parents had accepted his conversion because they didn't want to lose him, when he had tried to talk about religion with his mother 'she broke down in tears, and couldn't hack it'; now it was something they just did not talk about. His explanation is pertinent to the Hindu context too: 'Being a Northern Ireland Catholic, you can be a lapsed Catholic but because of the wider geopolitical situation you can't become something else . . . You could be seen to be abandoning and betraying your community and going over to the enemy, given that religion and politics are so closely entwined there.'[65] Of course the same could be said of most Muslim communities.

[64] Because of the inbuilt pluralism of Hinduism, Hindu parents found it difficult to understand why their children should have to go outside Hinduism and adopt a completely different religion. When a male interviewee from a Hindu background told his mother about his conversion, she suggested that instead of becoming a Muslim he could use the insights he gained from Islam to reform Hinduism from within.
[65] I also spoke to a female convert (not one of my sample) whose family were Orthodox Christians. Brought up in Britain, she had secretly converted to Islam as a teenager and, also secretly, married her Muslim boyfriend and fallen pregnant. Fearing severe repercussions, as she knew that converting to Islam was one of the worst things that she could possibly do in the

The fact that a member of the family of origin is a practising Christian does sometimes have a positive effect. One of my interviewees, Rahima, spoke of her relationship with her practising Christian sister: 'There is a difficulty there, a tension that we don't really quite talk about, at the same time there's also a positive side to it in terms of we both have that spiritual belief and we've started talking quite a lot about what we have in common, what we share ... We're just as close, I think probably closer, than when I wasn't believing in anything.' A Christian mother profiled in *emel* with her convert daughter Anna tells how she was at first taken aback by her daughter's conversion: 'I felt inadequate in a way, that I had not done enough to teach her how important and special our faith was.' She continues: 'As time has gone by I still find it difficult to understand Anna's choice, but we have been able to find common ground between our religions. I have even found that many passages in the Qur'an are similar to passages found in the Bible.' Her daughter describes how their relationship has developed from her point of view: 'As we have progressed together we have been able to hold long discussions about God, talking for hours on end at times! We both hold the same reverence for God and this binds us together despite the religious difference.' She also relates how she stayed home from mosque in the wake of the July 2005 bombings and had a joint prayer session with her mother: 'We exchanged readings of mostly synonymous proverbs from the prophets and readings from our scriptures.'[66] In such cases, interfaith relations are actively fostered, and it seems that people in this situation sometimes modify their theology as a result. An example of this is provided by the convert who described his grandmother (who was Christian) as a spiritual woman who had never done any harm and who had suffered a lot, adding: 'I can't believe she won't be saved.'[67] Anway, an American Christian woman whose daughter converted to Islam, describes her journey towards acceptance. At first she was anxious about Jesus' saying: 'No one comes to the father but through me' (John 14:6), but she later found comfort in another Bible verse which says: 'In my father's house there are many dwelling places' (John 14:2). She eventually comes to the point where she is able to say: 'God just picked

eyes of her family, she fled the family home before the pregnancy became too visible. At the time of writing, some time after the birth, she is still living in a women's refuge and has not seen her family or told them about her conversion, her marriage or her child.

[66] 'Kith & Kin', in *emel*, 16, January 2006.

[67] Cited in Allievi, *Les Convertis à l'Islam*, p. 254 (translated from the French).

a different road for our daughter to follow, and she is following it the best she can. Which is exactly what we are all trying to do.'[68] In all these cases, the Muslim convert and Christian relative seem to have been able to acknowledge value in each other's religions.

The reactions converts encounter from their families of origin reflect the attitudes of society at large, but with the important difference that parents have a strong motivation to find a *modus vivendi* and retain the ties of affection. In some cases, a negative reaction on the part of a parent is partly the result of anxiety that their son or daughter will encounter discrimination and hostility from mainstream society. Many parents are anxious about the consequences of their daughter wearing *ḥijāb*, as Rahima explained with reference to her mother: 'I think she worries about the way that I cover, I think covering's a big issue, and in fact how much it affects all my life, and she worries that it takes me away from her. I think she feels it makes us very different in our lifestyles.' In small towns in particular, some converts' families feel a sense of embarrassment in front of friends and neighbours when their convert daughters dress Islamically and wear the *ḥijāb*, which is seen as 'not respectable'.[69] Several interviewees felt that negative media images of Muslims had adversely affected their parents' attitudes; in some cases parents insisted on bringing up political issues or even engaging in heated debates about such matters as the Taliban, Saudi Arabia and, in particular, terrorism. The conversion of a son or daughter was sometimes seen as a sort of political betrayal; a male interviewee who had been Muslim for fifteen years, and who felt that his relationship with his family had deteriorated as a result, told how his family were convinced that he was either a terrorist or a supporter of terrorism. The 'betrayal' could also be seen as cultural, as described by Fatima: 'My mother, who believes European culture is the most civilized, cannot get over the fact that I have "gone native" and adopted a "foreign culture" that seems more primitive and barbaric. She actually finds it distasteful.' The perceived 'foreignness' of Islam was also a problem for Halima; she says that her parents were not at all happy on her conversion 'because they saw it as becoming an Indian'; her mother told her: 'You need to come back down to earth and be Westernized.' The

---

[68] Anway, *Daughters of Another Path*, p. 105.
[69] See, e.g., Köse, *Conversion to Islam*, p. 139; Haddad, 'The Quest for Peace in Submission', p. 31.

parents of female converts often harbour fears about the position of women in Islam, for example Maymuna's parents were afraid that when she got married her husband would beat her, although when they subsequently got to know the husband their fears were allayed. Another common fear is that a convert daughter will go abroad to live in her husband's country of origin – here the fear is not only about separation but also about the quality of life the daughter will have.[70]

I could find no obvious correlation when I cross-checked family reaction with factors such as date of conversion, race, ethnicity, class or religion, except in cases of families with a particularly strong politico-religious or religio-ethnic background, as described above. However, I have gained the impression that compared to, say, twenty years ago, family reaction is, on average, less severe nowadays. Virtually all of the conversion stories related in *emel* (which began publication in late 2003) describe a positive parental reaction.[71] Anecdotally, and from looking at material on the internet and in published sources, it appears that things are sometimes easier for black converts; for whatever reason, their families seem to have a less negative image of Islam. In the case of male black converts some of the families express a sense of relief or a hope that Islam will keep their son away from criminal or anti-social activities, like the father quoted in *emel*: 'If this means you do not drink or steal and you don't go around sleeping with different women and bringing shame to our family, then I don't have any problem with your decision to choose Islam.'[72] Köse found that working-class parents reacted less strongly than middle-class parents to the conversion of their child;[73] this suggests that families of lower social status feel there is more to gain or less to lose from such a change, and it could partially explain the more favourable reaction of black families. It seems likely that the personality of the parent is at least as important a factor as any other in determining their reaction; as Anway in her study of American female converts and their families comments, concerning those who manage to accept their daughters' choices: 'Perhaps these families were . . . the kind to let go and let their

[70] See, e.g., Anway, *Daughters of Another Path*, p. 98.

[71] See issue 2 (November/December 2003, pp. 25 and 31), issue 4 (March/April 2004, pp. 38 and 43), issue 6 (July/August 2004, p. 29), issue 7 (September/October 2004, pp. 7 and 35) and issue 9 (January/February 2005, p. 33). Batool al-Toma agreed that this was probably the case (interview with the author, 13 December 2006).

[72] Said, 'Face to Faith'.   [73] Köse, *Conversion to Islam*, p. 137.

daughter be an individual with boundaries of her own whether or not she became Muslim.'[74]

Converts who are either married or in a relationship at the time of their conversion experience complications due to certain Islamic prohibitions. According to the main schools of law, extramarital relations are forbidden and a Muslim woman cannot lawfully be married to a non-Muslim man.[75] For four of my interviewees, a relationship or marriage came to an end as a result of their conversion. One man's wife divorced him on the grounds of 'unreasonable behaviour', citing his conversion. Another had separated from his girlfriend on his conversion, but had some regrets, speaking almost twenty years after the event:

> Did I have to? In retrospect probably not, but you know I've often thought about what I could have done, the alternatives at that stage. I'm not too sure in my mind why but I just wanted a clean break and it was probably very heartless and it was probably the one thing that I had a very guilty conscience about because all the other stuff was very positive . . . but that was the one thing where I felt I didn't handle it very well and there was some sort of guilt because she'd done nothing wrong.

Fatima had gradually grown away from her boyfriend following her conversion and eventually ended their long-term relationship; she felt that her conversion had facilitated a break-up which needed to happen anyway, as the relationship 'wasn't going anywhere'. Sakina was married at the time of her conversion, and describes the situation she found herself in:

> To give up my husband, that was quite difficult, because obviously you think you're in love with your husband. I went to a mosque, and one of the teachers gave me some really good advice . . . He said: 'There's no love except for Allah.' And I knew what he meant by that: that you cannot love something that Allah does not love, you cannot love a situation or a person, if it's not sanctioned by Allah and Islam. And that

---

[74] Anway, *Daughters of Another Path*, p. 49.
[75] A Muslim man, on the other hand, is allowed to marry a woman who follows a prescribed religion such as Christianity or Judaism. However, a *fatwā* issued by the European Council for Fatwas and Research headed by Yusuf al-Qaradawi ruled that women converts with non-Muslim husbands are allowed to remain married as long as their husband does not oppose their conversion, thus departing from the mainstream Islamic legal position – see Roald, *New Muslims in the European Context*, p. 272.

piece of advice, it took a while to work. I put it in my heart, and then
eventually one day, it took a while, a few weeks maybe, a couple of
months, I woke up one day and the love for that man wasn't there any
more... I just put my trust in Allah because I knew it was *ḥarām*, I knew
I had to get out of it, *alḥamdulillah* [praise be to God] Allah just took
that love away like it was never there.

She did also say that she tried to talk to her husband about Islam, but 'he was
so far away from God it wasn't funny'; they subsequently had a 'very amica-
ble divorce'. In Na'ima Robert's study, most of the women in relationships at
the time of their conversion separated from their partners.[76] She comments:
'As a new Muslim, you want to live an Islamic life, from the moment you
wake up to pray *fajr* [the dawn prayer] to the moment you go to bed at night.
But having a non-Muslim partner means being confronted with your old
lifestyle on a daily basis and being exposed to all its tests and trials, its *fitan*
[temptations], be it bad language, free-mixing, drink, drugs or just the smell
of a bacon sandwich.'[77] In the case of the other interviewees who were in a
relationship at the time of their conversion, their relationships survived the
conversion of one party because the other was prepared to change: in two
cases a non-practising Muslim husband or partner 'reverted' to Islam as a
result of the conversion of his wife, and in another case a non-Muslim
boyfriend converted and married his convert girlfriend, with whom he
already had children. Although none of my sample were married to a non-
Muslim, men who convert do sometimes stay with their non-Muslim wives,
particularly where there are children and where the wife is sympathetic to
the decision to convert. One convert writing in *Meeting Point* describes how
his wife has been accommodating of his faith but has not herself converted:
'My wife has accepted Islam into the household 100% ... it would not be
good manners or etiquette to reject such efforts, to turn my back and walk
away and leave or divorce my family when there is no reason ... It is now a
mixed faith marriage but that only means that you have to work a little
harder.'[78]

The situation with friends is rather different from that with families,
as there is no Islamic prescription about staying in contact with them

---

[76] Allievi also finds that in the great majority of cases, the conversion of one partner in a
marriage or relationship leads to separation or divorce (*Les Convertis à l'Islam*, p. 188).
[77] Robert, *From my Sisters' Lips*, p. 96.
[78] *Meeting Point*, 35, June 2005.

(although one woman mentioned *da'wah* as a possible religious argument in favour of socializing with non-Muslims). On the other hand, there are *hadīths* concerning the need to keep company with people of 'good character'. About a third of the interviewees had stayed in touch with at least some of their non-Muslim friends from before their conversion, while the rest had lost touch with all or nearly all of them. In many cases it was a matter of 'drifting away' due to changes of circumstance such as moving, leaving university or getting married, and the friends who were lost in this way were generally replaced by Muslim rather than non-Muslim friends. However, converts sometimes feel the need to dissociate from at least some of their friends in order to consolidate their new Islamic identity, as Halima indicated: 'I had to make a point to distance myself from some people, because if those people aren't going to understand you or be a good influence on you, you end up tearing yourself apart. You have to start to mix with people who can help you in the life that you've chosen.' Similarly, Claire, one of Na'ima Robert's interviewees, hints at the precariousness of her new-found Islamic identity, saying: 'I cut everyone off, male and female – anyone I thought could influence me in the slightest.'[79] Conversely, Lisa, the only one of my interviewees who did not describe herself as a practising Muslim (although in fact she was partially practising, for example fasting during Ramadan and abstaining from pork and alcohol), said that she had not lost touch with her former friends, but added: 'If I wore a *ḥijāb* then it might be different.' In her case, the fact that she did not have a 'strong' Islamic identity meant that she could maintain her friendships with non-Muslims relatively easily.

Generally the converts who retained some of their former friends were selective, choosing to keep those friends who were prepared to make some effort to accommodate their new faith, for example by abstaining from swearing or being prepared to socialize in an alcohol-free environment. Hafsa saw this process of selection as beneficial: 'Islam just sifted out the people that probably weren't good for me and just left the ones that were good'. Some of the difficulties of maintaining friendships with non-Muslims are illustrated by Prabha; although she described her friends as 'very supportive and accepting', she explained how she had gradually lost touch with them: 'In the beginning I would still go to a pub but wouldn't

---

[79] Robert, *From my Sisters' Lips*, p. 95.

drink, and have a coke, and then after that I stopped going to pubs, but I'd still go to dinner with them, and now I don't feel comfortable being at a table where there's alcohol or in a restaurant which serves alcohol.' This illustrates the way in which a convert's gradual enculturation into an Islamic lifestyle may be accompanied by a gradual drift away from non-Muslim friends. It is often difficult to tell whether the distancing process is initiated by the friends or by the converts; in many cases it seems to be mutual. Amin, for example, described it thus: 'It's very difficult, their lifestyles are very different, people can only take so much when... you're saying oh no I can't do this, or you remain quiet on something. It just doesn't fit really.'

As indicated by the above quotes, the most prominent factor in the loss of friendships is differing interests and lifestyles. Zaynab put it most succinctly: 'We used to go out clubbing every weekend and you can't go clubbing in a *ḥijāb*, can you?' Charlene said that she had lost all her friends 'because they weren't able to understand or accommodate to the fact that I can't go to bars any more... if we meet in someone's house the conversation is just not things I want to talk about, I don't want to talk about boys, sex and all that – that is just not my mentality any more.' Another interviewee had had to cut contact with all his friends on his conversion since they were all petty criminals, as he had been himself. Na'ima Robert describes the waning of old friendships differently, in terms of what she was gravitating *towards* rather than what she was seeking to avoid: 'My old friends thought I was changing, growing away from them. But what could I do? I wanted to immerse myself in this new faith that was unfolding before my eyes. There were so many topics to debate, so many questions to ask, so many attitudes to re-examine, and I was completely wrapped up in it all.'[80]

Interviewees who spoke in general terms about social contact with non-Muslims were cautious, with six out of seven drawing attention to the need to limit such contact. One woman, for example, felt that 'it is okay to be friends with them [non-Muslims] but not to be influenced by them or to take their advice on important issues', while another thought that in such cases there was 'always a cut-off point beyond which the friendship cannot pass'. A third woman was, like the others, concerned about compromising her Islamic faith and identity: 'If you mix with non-Muslims you end up getting asked *ḥarām* questions.' By contrast, Rachel said that she made a

[80] Ibid., p. 89.

point of socializing with non-Muslims as well as Muslims as she did not want to end up with 'tunnel vision': 'Being a Muslim . . . you should always mix and socialize with people from other backgrounds, regardless of whatever religion they choose.' She also mentioned that her parents had brought her up to socialize with people of varied backgrounds.

In some cases, there was a correlation between a convert's continuing ties with non-Muslim friends and their positive attitude to mainstream society. Rachel provided the clearest example of this. She was unusual in the sense that not only had she kept many of her non-Muslim friends, but she had also made a point of organizing women's parties and inviting both her Muslim and her non-Muslim friends. She held very strong views on the need for Muslims to integrate into mainstream society, and was herself very involved in community work, contributing her time to both Muslim and non-Muslim charities and organizations. However, there was no corresponding correlation between the degree of closeness to family or parents and the level of integration into the wider society. One female interviewee described herself as a supporter of Hizb al-Tahrir, and of all the interviewees she expressed the most radical political views and saw the culture of her upbringing as wholly incompatible with Islamic culture; she was one of the few who used the term *kāfir/kuffār* to refer to unbelievers. Although she had lost contact with most of her former friends, she had a good relationship with her parents, who were quite accepting of her Islamic faith. She was unusually empathic towards them:

> I do feel for my parents because I know how they must feel. They brought me up a certain way and they did their best for me, and they love me a lot and I've just turned round and basically kicked them in the teeth and said, oh sorry, it wasn't good enough. There's so many things that have to change, the whole free mixing thing, the way that I dress, the fact that I have to nip off five times a day to pray. It's a lot of adjustments for them and a lot of change.[81]

The lack of correlation beween family relations (as opposed to friendships) and attitudes to society could be explained by the fact that converts generally do make an effort to maintain good relations with their family (partly

---

[81] Similarly, Na'ima Robert, who adopts a very 'strong' Islamic identity, including wearing the *niqāb*, says of her father: 'Rejecting everything he held dear must have hurt him, just as it hurt me to disappoint him' (ibid., p. 83).

due to Islamic teachings on the subject) no matter what their views on other matters or their Islamic orientation.

A SPECIAL ROLE FOR CONVERTS?

In Europe as a whole, converts have played a prominent role in many sectors of society: as representatives of Islam, cultural mediators, translators, publishers, Arabists and Islamicists, personnel in Islamic organizations, etc. Their role has often been disproportionate to their numbers due to their superior communication skills and knowledge of society, as compared to immigrants. Allievi points out that their role is more significant in countries of recent immigration, but that it diminishes with the emergence of subsequent generations of born Muslims whose socialization is closer to that of converts and who are more familiar with Western society than their parents and grandparents.[82] Since Muslims have been established in Britain longer than in most other European countries, with most now having been born here, it is not surprising that converts play a less prominent role than in some other places. Nevertheless the active contribution they make to Islamic life still seems disproportionately large given that they constitute approximately 1% of the British Muslim population. There is one area where converts have until recently been less well represented, and that is the mainstream media, with almost all regular Muslim spokepersons being born Muslims. There are several possible reasons for this: historical, due to links already forged with particular spokespersons; a reluctance among some sections of the media to disrupt the familiar image of Muslims as foreign immigrants; or the fact that converts are not in leadership positions in the organizations most often called upon to comment on current affairs. It is certainly not for a lack of highly educated, articulate and knowledgeable converts upon whom the media could call.[83] However, converts such as Abdal-Hakim Murad and Yahya Birt seem to be becoming more frequent contributors to mainstream radio stations such as BBC Radio 4, perhaps

---

[82] Allievi, *Les Convertis à l'Islam*, pp. 289–90.
[83] In fact, *Newsnight* has featured interviews with converts such as Na'ima Robert (fully covered in black, including the *niqāb*) and Aisha Masterton, and Sarah Joseph has appeared on a number of radio and television programmes. Channel 4's *Sharī'ah* TV has featured a relatively high number of converts.

because converts' failure to match the popular image of what a Muslim should look like is not an obstacle for programme makers in that medium.[84]

So far the British convert community has not produced the likes of a Roger Garaudy, a Muhammad Asad or a Hamza Yusuf in terms of international Muslim recognition and political influence. In Britain, Yusuf Islam is widely admired for his educational and charitable work and his peace activism, and Hasan Le Gai Eaton and Martin Lings (1909–2005) have both authored widely read books. Among British convert contributors to Islamic discourse, Abdal-Hakim Murad is perhaps the most accomplished in terms of his knowledge of Islamic scholarship (holding an academic post at the University of Cambridge), and he moves in international Muslim intellectual and scholarly circles. As mentioned above, notwithstanding their low profile in the mainstream media, Muslim converts in Britain are strongly represented in other spheres, such as the Muslim media (especially *Q-News* and *emel*), certain Islamic organizations (e.g. the Islamic Foundation in Leicester), writing and publishing, Islamic education, *da'wah* activities, and as university lecturers in Arabic and Islamic studies.

Many converts feel that, individually or collectively, they have the potential to inject some fresh thinking into the Muslim community. Abdal-Hakim Murad refers to the vital historical contribution of Persian and Turkish converts 'with their own ethnic genius' to the classical Islamic civilization, and asks: 'Can the clarity of vision brought by novelty outweigh the absence of a Muslim upbringing? ... Might the appearance of converts in the West presage a larger revival of the fortunes of an aged and tired Islamic umma?'[85] Peter, an interviewee, expressed it this way:

> From my experience there definitely seems to be a different take on things, we can accept ideas more and perhaps think outside the box a little bit easier than most born Muslims which I've encountered anyway. Sometimes we can bring that kind of alternative argument to the table, whereas they've got a kind of cultural set up ... we don't have that set up, so we might have to look for other answers in other corners of the religion, which they might not have needed to explore.

---

[84] I was told at second hand that the editors of a documentary featuring a number of Muslim contributors, which was aired on one of the main terrestrial channels some years ago, had systematically cut out all the converts' contributions.

[85] Murad, 'British and Muslim?'.

A male Shi'i convert who I spoke to (but who was not part of my sample) felt that Shi'i converts in particular had a special role, explaining: 'The Shi'a community ... is extremely oriented around *taqlīd* (blind acceptance) ... and I think converts tend to shake that up a bit.' Roald finds that Scandinavian converts place a strong emphasis on female empowerment and women's independence,[86] and Köse suggested that converts were more liberal and dynamic in their interpretation of the role of Islam in Britain than their fellow Muslims from the immigrant communities.[87] On the other hand, there is evidence to suggest that in some matters converts are 'stricter' than born Muslims; Allievi found that converts were more likely to abstain from shaking hands with the opposite sex, and more likely to have scruples about listening to music than non-convert Muslims.[88] These seemingly inconsistent findings highlight the need for caution in drawing comparisons between converts and other Muslims; any meaningful comparison would have to distinguish between practising and non-practising Muslims, and without extensive research and fieldwork, any conclusions would have to be tentative.

Without exception, my interviewees felt that converts have a special contribution to make, both to the Muslim community and to non-Muslim society. The most frequently envisaged role was that of bridge-builder. One male interviewee whose work involves training people in cross-cultural awareness, said: 'There's a certain type of person we call a cultural deviant, where they stand between two cultures and are able to act as a bridge between them. That's what I think converts in this country can do, is really explain Islam to non-Muslims and explain Britishness to Muslims.' Many interviewees agreed that converts could play a valuable part in helping other Muslims gain a better understanding of British society. Maymuna thought that a lot of Muslims 'have the image in their head also that this is a completely immoral, corrupt and everyone-is-horrible-over-here kind of society. Because of that they probably don't want to mix with those people.' Ali picked up the same theme: 'I think we're able to make people understand what non-Muslims think and feel about the world.' He elaborated: 'We can say: look, we were non-Muslims once, we were cool, we didn't have any

---

[86] Roald, *New Muslims in the European Context*, pp. 248 and 98.
[87] Köse, *Conversion to Islam*, p. 21; it should be noted however that since Köse's book was published, the creative output of the younger generation of born Muslims has increased considerably.
[88] Allievi, *Les Convertis à l'Islam*, pp. 169 (fn. 2) and 210.

hatred or harbour any animosity towards you, we were just getting on with our lives.' At the same time, he felt that converts could help British people to stop seeing Muslims as a threat:

> Look, this is really the reality of Muslims: they're tax-payers, they're law-abiding . . . if they're observant Muslims, they're not going to steal from you, they're not going to rob you, they're perfect employees, you're laughing. You can't go wrong, really and truly, you can't go wrong employing a Muslim or having Muslim neighbours, they're the best neighbours you could wish for – no loud music, no drunkenness, watching out for you, helping you.

In relation to born Muslims, some interviewees felt that converts had an inspirational role, either because they had deliberately chosen the faith or because they tended to be more practising and more engaged in Islamic activities. One woman said that several non-practising Muslims had started to practise through meeting and talking to her, while another commented: 'I know loads of people [i.e. born Muslims] that read conversion stories to give themselves an *imān* [faith] boost.' Some felt that converts had greater credibility in the eyes of British society. As Rahima put it: 'When I talk about issues like *ḥijāb*, non-Muslims are more likely to believe me than they are to believe a born Muslim, because they think of a born Muslim, oh she's been brainwashed since she was seven . . . whereas with me they go wait a minute, she's definitely chosen this, so she might be mad, but at least we know she's not been brainwashed at age six.' Because converts generally have more contact with non-Muslims than do other Muslims, they tend to find themselves involuntarily acting as representatives for Islam; this is even more the case if they live in areas where there are few Muslims. They may see this as either a burden or an opportunity, or a mixture of the two. As Mohammad Siddique Seddon, who was at one time working as a postman in a remote area, explains: 'Being the only Muslim at work has both advantages and disadvantages: I'm constantly used as a universal spokesman for current affairs on Islam, from Usamah bin Laden to the Kosovo crisis and my non-Muslim congregation frequently asks me for *Fatwas*. The down side is that for people who have no visible Muslim community in their midst, everything I (or my wife) do or say is interpreted as "What Moslems do"!'[89] Roald

---

[89] Seddon, 'A Day in the Life'.

observes that even ordinary converts at the grassroots level feel they are acting as a bridge just by being part of society and projecting an 'image of normality'.[90]

Another area in which converts often see themselves as having a special contribution to make is that of *da'wah*. Yahya Birt feels that they should take a leading role in inviting their own people to Islam: 'This is in line with the way (Sunna) of God, who sent the Prophets to their own peoples.' He argues that converts are better placed to do this because of the fact that born Muslims tend to be more focused on global injustices: 'The West is currently the enemy ... Thus these Muslims – in their not unjustified anger – want to tell them off. They want to talk about geopolitics not God.' According to Birt, such Muslims are 'psychologically incapable of giving da'wa'.[91] Along similar lines, Prahba argued: 'It's sometimes easier for converts to give *da'wah*, because you know what that person's thinking and where they're coming from because you were like that once too.' Another interviewee painted a rather comical picture of born Muslims' attempts to proselytize: 'They go in and start reciting *āyah*s [Qur'anic verses] in Arabic, people look at them and think, what the hell's he talking about? ... It's like they're expecting people to say: "That's wonderful, how can I become a Muslim?", I mean it's ridiculous.' Sakina voiced the opinion of several interviewees when she said that converts make a contribution to *da'wah* just by virtue of being known as converts: 'People have certain images or stereotypical ideas of what born Muslims should be like, you know, either they're Arabs or Asians, and we can show them Islam is not just for Arabs or Asians or for a particular ethnic minority, Islam is for everybody'; she also felt that converts were more approachable and so would be more likely to be asked questions than would born Muslims. Some of the interviewees were quite creative in their ideas of how to give *da'wah:* one woman said she took part in sponsored events like runs or mountain climbing, both for charity and for the sake of *da'wah*, 'because you don't see *ḥijābī*s and *jilbābī*s doing that', while another said that she communicated with people via the internet and on more than one occasion had had people take their *shahādah* with her over the phone. Converts often press for a non-confrontational and culturally sensitive

[90]   Roald, *New Muslims in the European Context*, p. 297.
[91]   Birt, 'Building New Medinas'. This was written before the Iraq war, since when converts themselves are more focused on global injustices than they were before.

approach to *da'wah*. According to Zaynab: 'It's not like bible-bashing Christians, *da'wah* is very gentle. The Qur'an says "speak to them with kind words".' Nearly all my interviewees felt that *da'wah* was an important part of their role as Muslims, but most saw it as something which arises naturally, through their personal example or through people spontaneously asking them about Islam, rather than something they would deliberately set out to do.

Converts are often very active contributors to Islamic causes. Almost all my interviewees were involved in some kind of Islamic activity – as Halima said: 'I think it's essential as Muslims, if you want to achieve something you have to work with other people, you can't just stay in your house and do your own prayers, because Islam is about society.' Sulayman also emphasized the need to make a practical contribution: 'We've got lots of people who talk too much and don't do anything . . . I'd rather lay some flooring in a mosque than go to a talk.' Of my interviewees, seven were doing voluntary work in Muslim organizations or mosques, five were in paid employment working for an Islamic business or organization, and five were connected to Muslim charities (two had actually been involved in founding the charities). Five of the women were involved in running sisters' circles, and of those, three had been instrumental in setting the circle up. Three interviewees were involved in teaching Islam to Muslims, mainly but not exclusively to children. Several were involved in *da'wah* through such things as giving talks and contributing articles to the internet, and one had founded a *da'wah* organization. One was on the leadership team of a mosque, another gave a weekly Friday sermon for local Muslim workers, and two were involved in Muslim professional associations. This rather impressive list strongly suggests that the contribution converts make to the Muslim community is disproportionate to their numbers.[92]

---

[92] In no case was an interviewee approached on the basis of, or in the context of, any of these roles or positions. It could of course be argued that people who are more active are more likely to put themselves forward to be interviewed, slightly weighting the sample in that direction.

Chapter 3

A new identity?

Religious conversion often involves far-reaching changes in lifestyle and identity. This is more likely to be the case when a person converts to a 'foreign' religion which does not have strong indigenous roots; it is also more likely in the case of religions such as Islam which have detailed prescriptions pertaining to such things as dress, diet, social relations and so on. For Muslim converts, change, like conversion itself, is often effected gradually, and is usually lasting and significant. Their conversion is likely to affect their choice of friends and marital partner (for those not already married), social activities and political views; it may also affect their choice of occupation, or their choice of whether or not to pursue an outside occupation (given that some women prefer to concentrate on family duties). Rambo points out that requirements to modify specifics such as dress, diet and other daily patterns of behaviour help to reinforce the rejection of old patterns and the incorporation of new ones, and that learning and practising new rituals is a fundamental element in consolidating the conversion experience.[1] Rambo's observations are especially relevant in the case of conversion to Islam, which involves marked changes in many areas of life. Perhaps the greatest of these is the way in which ritual punctuates daily life in the form of the five prayers; as Huda al-Khattab (an English convert and author of several books on Islam) says: 'The prayer makes you conscious of God all the time. You're continually touching base.'[2]

There is a vast literature on identity, particularly within the field of sociology, but no universally recognized definition. Some emphasize the active

[1] Rambo, *Understanding Religious Conversion*, pp. 127 and 114.
[2] Quoted in Berrington, 'The Spread of a World Creed'.

agency of the human being in constructing his or her own identity, while others see people more as products of their social contexts. Identity originally denoted the subjective sense of sameness or continuity of an individual, the emphasis later shifting to the way in which a person differentiates him- or herself from others. Essentialist understandings which posit an inherent, fixed and unified identity are no longer tenable, and identity is now seen in academic discourse not as content but as process, as something which is subject to social forces, constructed rather than given. Since identity has ceased to be a function of birth, individuals now, it would seem, have the capacity to choose many aspects of their identity in a continually unfolding process of self-definition. People generally have multiple identities, whether in terms of the different roles they play (e.g. mother, sister, teacher) or in relation to overarching structures such as ethnicity, race, class, gender and sexuality. These various identities interact with each other in complex and ever-changing ways. The postmodern conception of identity emphasizes the fluidity, hybridity and plurality of identities in the contemporary period; the individual may find him- or herself strategically switching between different roles in different contexts.[3]

Identity is not just about the individual but about the relationship between the individual and society:[4] changing social structures have a huge impact on the way in which individuals construe their identity. For example, national identities are arguably being eroded by the processes of globalization, and social pluralism finds its counterpart in a growing pluralization of the self. An ever-increasing level of available options (e.g. of employment, religious affiliation, place of residence and so on) allows more and more scope for identity choices. Some see this as a positive development, affording people more opportunities for self-actualization, while others point out the dangers of fragmentation and alienation. The question of meaning sometimes arises in discussions of identity, as people seek to integrate and resolve the multiple and sometimes conflicting aspects of their identity. The search for meaning and purpose is often strongly emphasized by Muslim converts in their conversion stories.

Identity theory emphasizes concepts such as race, class, gender and ethnicity rather than faith, which Muslims and other religious people may

[3] Hall, 'The Question of Cultural Identity'.
[4] See, e.g., Berger, *Invitation to Sociology*, p. 117.

construe as a highly significant element of their own identity. As mentioned in chapter 1, Jacobson's research on young Muslims in Britain found an increasing tendency to prioritize Islamic identity over national belonging and ethnic origin. Sayyid regards the privileging by academics of other elements of identity over faith identity as a product of 'orientalism' (in a pejorative sense).[5] My sample consisted of people who were brought up in a pluralist, democratic society which allows for a relatively high degree of choice. It is worth remembering, however, that identity choices are not equally available to all people in all societies. The choices of some born Muslims, for example, may be considerably restricted by social, cultural, political, economic and other factors; and those whose lives are adversely affected by the processes of globalization may in fact choose to reassert their traditional identity if it seems to offer some refuge from the rapid pace of social and cultural change.

As observed by Haddad, converts tend to see their identity not as socially and culturally constructed, but as 'grounded in their original and natural being as a Muslim'.[6] This reflects the idea of converts as 'reverts', returning to their original nature, and helps explain why many do not necessarily see themselves as having a 'new identity' as such. A relatively rare example of an attempt to theorize Muslim or Islamic faith identity is provided by British Muslim Dilwar Hussain. He argues that a central element of Muslim identity is the conception of the individual's relationship with God, which affects all of their actions and sets the scene for their other roles in life: 'The Muslim . . . lives not for himself only but to bring goodness to humanity. The concepts of *tawḥīd*, *istikhlāf* [human stewardship], *dhikr*, *taqwā* [piety] and *rabbāniyyah* [the divine context], *inter alia*, form the core of a Muslim's being and essence.'[7] Jeremy Henzell-Thomas, an English convert with an academic background in linguistics, derives a concept of human (including Muslim) identity from English, Greek and Latin terms such as 'originality', 'individuality', 'authenticity', 'authority' and 'character', and finds that it can be 'distilled into the key concept expressed by the Arabic word *fiṭrah*. This can be translated as " primordial nature" or "original disposition" with which God . . . has invested every human being, and which is essentially good and noble'.[8]

[5] Sayyid, 'Beyond Westphalia', p. 37.
[6] Haddad, 'The Quest for Peace in Submission', p. 44.
[7] Hussain, 'British Muslim Identity,' p. 92.
[8] Henzell-Thomas, 'Passing Between the Clashing Rocks', p. 13.

Some converts reflect on the difficulty they experience in finding a strong identity of their own under the umbrella of Islam. Yahya Birt points out that since the mass Muslim migration to Britain of the 1950s, converts 'have lost their cultural self confidence and their ability to define an autochthonous Islam at ease with itself, an authentic religiosity at home with deeply-rooted British tradition and sensibilities'. A lack of role models is clearly felt to be a problem, for he asks: 'Where . . . are the Pickthalls and Quilliams of today?'[9] A male convert writing in the letters page of *Q-News* highlights the need 'to preserve the important milestones of our emerging Western history . . . North American and European Muslims are forming their identity in a historical vacuum . . . We are re-inventing the proverbial wheel of our identity over and over again in a Sisyphusian drama that leaves us frustrated and angry.' The 'great story of Islam and its civilisation', he concludes, should be embraced and written 'in our own image'. Like Birt, he sees the lives of prominent Muslim converts (including Malcolm X) as a valuable source of wisdom and inspiration in this process.[10]

It is clear that religious identity can no longer be taken for granted in the Western context, and that those who choose to assert a strong religious identity are swimming against the tide, especially in the case of a highly visible religion such as Islam. As Ziauddin Sardar puts it: 'In a world where few actually admit to believing in anything, people who overtly demonstrate their beliefs at every opportunity stand out as totally weird.'[11] Yet religion may have an increased appeal in a cultural context where tradition is rapidly being eroded, change has become the norm, identities are shifting and 'the self is no longer clearly defined and has become progressively more fragile'.[12] Furthermore, a religion such as Islam, which seems to offer clear answers and definite guidance, may have a particular appeal to those who are overwhelmed or alienated by the multiplicity of choices on offer to the average Westerner. Umm Rashid, interviewed in *The Independent on Sunday*, expresses a sense of relief at this aspect of Islam: 'With Islam, there is not this burden of weighing things up. There are obligations and you do them. It is very liberating. Especially for women. There are no longer questions such as should I wear this or that. It was a whole daily hassle in my

[9] Birt, 'Building New Medinas'.   [10] *Q-News*, July–August 2002.
[11] Sardar, 'The Excluded Minority', p. 52.
[12] Rambo, *Understanding Religious Conversion*, p. 31, citing Robert Jay Lifton, 'Protean Man', in *Partisan Review* 35, 1968, pp. 13–27.

former life.'[13] Karimah bint Dawood (also known as Deborah David) expresses the desire for structure which is commonly mentioned by converts as a motivating factor in their conversion: 'I progressed from Rasta to Islam because I needed a coherence to my faith. In Islam everything is clear, there is guidance and direction for how to live your life.'[14] In this context Islam is often contrasted with Christianity; according to Huda al-Khattab: 'Muslims don't keep shifting their goal-posts. Christianity changes, like the way some have said pre-marital sex is okay if it's with the person you're going to marry. It seems so wishy-washy. Islam was constant about sex, about praying five times a day.'[15]

Religious boundaries are generally strong and clear-cut in Islam due to its strong emphasis on correct behaviour and its prescriptions which affect all areas of life.[16] There are many opportunities in daily life for reinforcing the practising Muslim's sense of religious identity; apart from religious practices which punctuate and pervade daily life, a committed Muslim is likely to engage in private study of Islam, visits to the mosque, discussion and debates with other Muslims, and to feel some sense of solidarity with Muslims both nationally and worldwide. Foremost among Islamic prescriptions are the five daily prayers, which not only serve as a constant reminder of the believer's own religious identity but may also bring it to the attention of non-Muslims; fasting in Ramadan could have the same effect (although some Muslims choose to be discreet about this in the workplace). Dietary laws, especially the prohibition on alcohol, also promote Muslims' social distinctiveness and can inhibit social intercourse between Muslim and non-Muslim. Practising Muslims, including converts, are often reluctant to frequent pubs or clubs, and this often curtails after-hours socializing with work colleagues, and may make it difficult for the convert to maintain pre-conversion friendships, as discussed in chapter 2. Rules on social mixing between the sexes entail a distinctive pattern of socializing which is generally not compatible with the prevailing Western model of free social intercourse between men and women.

---

[13] Stanford, 'Preaching from the Converted'.
[14] Dawood, 'Face to Faith'.
[15] Quoted in Berrington, 'The Spread of a World Creed'. Sultan suggests that the rules found in Islam may 'work as a substitute for a personally adapted and revised morality', and that they may give 'a feeling of safety, being in control of one's own life' (Sultan, 'Choosing Islam', p. 331).
[16] See on this Jacobson, *Islam in Transition*, pp. 127–30.

The detailed guidance offered by Islam goes beyond the obligatory religious practices and legal requirements and extends to mundane aspects of everyday life. The Sunna, which consists of the sayings, actions and silent approval of Muhammad, provides a model of daily living and a wealth of practices and behaviours (eating with the right hand, for example) which are recommended rather than obligatory. There are collections of sayings or prayers of Muhammad to fit a wide range of daily contingencies such as leaving the house, beginning a meal, even embarking on sexual intercourse with one's spouse. Many Muslims will use some of these private prayers or sayings (known as *du'ā'*) in the appropriate situations. One interviewee described the way in which Islam permeates every aspect of her daily life:

> From the time you wake up you say *du'ā'*, you pray *fajr* [the dawn prayer], you read Qur'an, the way you talk to your children, you know you always talk to them nicely, trying not to get angry with them [laughing], you always mention the name of Allah, you know, whatever you're doing, sit up, stand up, you say *bismillah* [in the name of God]. Islam is so much a part of my life, my family's life, there's no situation, even to go to the toilet you're saying *du'ā'* to go to the toilet, Allah's name is always remembered whatever the situation.

Classical Islamic legal principles such as 'closing the avenues that lead to evil' (*ṣadd dharā'i' al-fasād*), or the *ḥadīth* that advises believers to steer clear of the doubtful or shady area between that which is *ḥalāl* (lawful) and that which is *ḥarām* (prohibited) have the effect of reinforcing religious boundaries still further. The communal aspects of certain Islamic practices, such as fasting and the breaking of the fast in Ramadan, the Friday congregational prayers and the Hajj, also reinforce group solidarity and the social distinctiveness of Muslims. These things may contribute to the powerful bonding which some converts experience; this is described by Na'ima Robert, who had a close-knit group of mainly convert friends after her conversion: 'We were living in a kind of bubble, where the *deen* [religion/way of life] was the central focus of our lives, with everything revolving around that – and only those already inside the bubble could really understand.' Safwa, one of Robert's interviewees, expresses this sense of belonging in more abstract terms: 'You feel like you're part of something, you're part of the *ummah* now and you have your place. You are united by something bigger – the worship of Allah – and you're all doing it together.'[17]

In some contexts the boundaries between Muslims and non-Muslims can be significantly weakened, for example where there is a common political purpose or where a non-Muslim has strong political sympathy with a Muslim cause.[18] This weakening is especially likely to occur where a family includes both Muslims and non-Muslims, which is almost always the case for converts.[19] Some people seem to achieve a strong social or political identification with Islam without actually converting; this often happens when a non-Muslim woman marries a Muslim man and invests time and energy in bringing their children up as Muslims. One such woman, who is now divorced from her Muslim ex-husband and who brought her children up as Muslims, is quoted in *emel*: 'I was conscious that if I did not maintain an Islamic home I would be depriving my children of their true identities ... it was by far the most important factor ... I now see Islam as something that brought us all closer.' Her daughter, a fully practising Muslim who 'dons her *ḥijāb* with confidence', says that she feels very close to her mother: 'I see perfect moral codes and values within her ... I love her for her simple and beautiful ethics, and whether Allah guides her onto a path more similar to mine is not for me to say. We all have our own paths, but I see that my mum and I will always be travelling in the same general direction ... *I feel that I've been taught the characteristics of a Muslim by a non-Muslim* ' (my italics).[20] In this case we see the boundary between Muslim and non-Muslim at its most permeable.

As regards the process of converting to Islam, the boundary between being non-Muslim and being Muslim is very fluid, and easily crossed. All that is required is the sincere pronouncement of the *shahādah*, usually in front of two adult Muslim witnesses. Crossing the boundary in the other direction, i.e. leaving Islam, has historically been rather more difficult,

---

[17] Robert, *From my Sisters' Lips*, p. 75.

[18] I know of one man, for example, who is both an Evangelical Christian and an anti-Zionist, who has been a frequent contributor to *Q-News* and who has been able to gain access to many Muslim meetings in the course of his academic research and journalistic work.

[19] For an example of this, see an account of female twins where one converts; the converted twin says her conversion has brought them 'closer together', and the unconverted twin expresses admiration of the changes in her sister and talks about 'Allah' ('Kith & Kin', in *emel*, 4, March/April 2004).

[20] 'Kith & Kin', in *emel*, 7, September/October 2004.

entailing severe civil and legal consequences (potentially including, according to most of the classical scholars, the death penalty).[21] In a context where people are free to choose and propagate a variety of different religions, and where some people with a 'seekership orientation' become 'serial converts' or 'spiritual nomads', it is inevitable that some who choose any given religion, including Islam, will fall by the wayside. This phenomenon is occasionally referred to by both converts and born Muslims, but it is generally in the context of sadness and regret that this has happened, with the onus generally being placed on the Muslim community for not having offered the necessary support which could have prevented it.[22]

Converts to Islam commonly renegotiate not just their religious identity but also many aspects of their cultural, social, political and gender identities; in fact, most of the chapters in this book deal with such changes, which are manifested in very practical and concrete ways, for example in the form of new bodily practices and new forms of behaviour. This chapter will focus on various aspects of identity formation and change, including national, racial and ethnic identity; the adoption of new styles of language and other identity markers (dress, names and circumcision); and lifestyle changes. Rambo points out the importance of converts' own perceptions of the changes that precede, accompany or follow conversion;[23] the present chapter will therefore also look at converts' perceptions of the degree of continuity or discontinuity with their former lives.

NATIONAL, RACIAL AND ETHNIC IDENTITY

Asked what 'Britishness' meant to them, many of my interviewees drew a blank or said something along the lines of: 'just a passport', although about three or four did relate in a positive way to the idea, for example saying that they were 'happy to be British'. As discussed in chapter 1, 'Britishness' is not a straightforward or self-evident concept, and it is understood differently by

---

[21] Some modern Muslim scholars argue that the death penalty is only appropriate where apostasy is accompanied by outright hostility to the Islamic polity, and thus equivalent to treason. See for an overview A. Saaed and H. Saeed, *Freedom of Religion, Apostasy and Islam* (Aldershot: Aldgate, 2003).
[22] See for example the article entitled 'Losing my Friend' in *Q-News*, November 2000 and the readers' letters in response in the following (December) issue.
[23] Rambo, *Understanding Religious Conversion*, p. 119.

different people. It is therefore not surprising that some interviewees expressed a sense of confusion over what constitutes 'Britishness' or 'British culture' – a confusion which is shared by many non-Muslims. As pointed out by Jacobson, increasing diversity, particularly among the young in multi-ethnic cities, means that ideas of Britishness and perhaps also Englishness are becoming less meaningful.[24] A number of the interviewees (including some of Asian or Afro-Caribbean background) did feel that they were English, and most of these felt positive about their 'Englishness'. On the whole, though, it was those with an Irish, Scottish or Welsh heritage who felt most positive about their ethnicity. When interviewees had these strands in their ethnic make-up, they generally felt them to be important and not infrequently took a pride in the affiliation, which was clearly not superseded by their being Muslim. One woman, for example, said: 'I love the fact that I'm Irish. I love my culture, I think it's wonderful . . . but what is the culture of Britain actually? It doesn't really exist.' Similarly, Asian, Caribbean or African strands of identity were owned without any sense of conflict. Another possible reason for reticence as regards Britishness is illustrated by another interviewee (also with an Irish background), who exclaimed: 'I could quite happily wrap myself in the flag of St George but never the Union Jack, which to my mind represents the subjugation of Ireland and Scotland by England.' This person's feelings about the Union Jack illustrate the potential common ground between people of Irish, Scottish and Welsh extraction, on the one hand, and, on the other, between these people and those born Muslims who find the concept of Britishness difficult because of colonial history. English converts' attitudes to Britishness may also be influenced by colonial history (their awareness of which is generally heightened by their conversion to Islam, as discussed in chapter 4); Britain's colonial past was specifically mentioned by one English interviewee as one of the reasons why he no longer felt any emotional attachment to being British.

Contemporary Islamic discourse tends to devalue nationalism (and to a lesser extent ethnicity) as a component of identity, seeing it as subordinate to religious identity. Some of the interviews took place during the 2006 football World Cup season, and two of the women mentioned (without

[24] Jacobson, *Islam in Transition*, p. 22, citing L. Back, *New Ethnicities and Urban Culture: Racisms and Multiculture in Young Lives* (London: UCL Press, 1996).

being asked) that they were strong supporters of England. One of these said that Englishness *was* meaningful to her, especially during the World Cup season, but added: 'Obviously we've learnt, or learnt as being a Muslim, that when someone asks what you are, you're meant to say that you're a Muslim first because your religion is most important to you, and nationality only depends on the barriers that they draw on the map.' The other told me that she would have loved to put up her England flag, but had been told by another Muslim that she should not do so as it has a cross on it. In both cases there seems to be a subtle distancing from what might be seen as the 'Islamically correct' position; in the first case this is seen in the phrase 'you're meant to say', and in the second, in the woman's seeming regret that she had not been able to put the flag up.

Many of the interviewees had a fairly minimalist concept of Britishness, perhaps seeing it in terms of attachment to a country in which they happened to have been born and brought up. Their comments included the following: 'I've travelled, and this is always home when I come back, there is always that sense of coming home, of rest and of ease, when I enter Heathrow airport'; 'I love my country, but to define what being British is, come on, even Brits who've been here more generations than me are scratching their heads';

> It means I believe God put me in a position where I've experienced a certain lifestyle, a certain culture ... What it means to me to be British is not the primary definition of who I am, it's the coincidental definition of who I am, because Allah put me in a country called Britain and I've experienced certain experiences that would make me partly British, but I've also experienced certain experiences that would make me partly Asian, but my primary reference is a Muslim.

It is of course difficult to pinpoint the effect that 'being Muslim' has on converts' ideas of Britishness, given that many non-Muslim Britons would have similarly diluted conceptions, and that Britain is not known these days for being a flag-waving, strongly patriotic nation. The last-mentioned quote does suggest that being or becoming Muslim dilutes the concept of Britishness still further (and this process seems to have been exacerbated by recent political developments, as will be seen below). Sulayman thought that Muslims have an 'inexplicable discomfort' with the idea of Britishness, even though they might have positive feelings towards the country itself; he embodied this attitude himself, saying: 'I love the country, love the tradition, love the culture, but always have this thing about saying "I love Britain".'

Several interviewees were clearly influenced in their attitudes by recent political developments, in particular the war in Iraq. Mahmud was one of these: 'Okay, it's my nationality but it doesn't have much meaning to me any more because I don't actually feel loyalty to my nationality, especially in respect of what's going on in the world . . . I'm actually ashamed of what is done in the name of Britain in the world.' Sulayman mentioned his gratitude that he was able to practise his religion freely, and his sense of pride at being part of 'this diverse British culture', but made a point of adding: 'But if it means that I then give my unconditional support to this government/ flag – never. I can't do that.' Clearly, British people are not required to give such 'unconditional support', and in reality most do not, but it is likely that many Muslims (and probably also some non-Muslims) feel an increased need to express such reservations in the light of the Iraq war and the 'war on terror', among other things. Only one interviewee gave the impression that there might be a direct conflict between being Muslim and being British: 'Being a Muslim I feel different because I feel like I'm not part of "British" any more . . . just the fact that I am Muslim, I already feel different. I would prefer not to be in this country, if I'm honest, I would like really to do *hijrah*.'[25] However, this woman's attitude seemed to arise at least in part from her personal experience of being on the receiving end of hostility because she is a Muslim; she believed that in a Muslim country she would not feel like an 'outcast'.

Converts are of varied ethnic origin, with the majority being white British. For this majority, the majority–minority dynamic, which was described in chapter 1 as affecting identity issues for born Muslims in Britain, does not apply in the same way. Similarly, the relationship between religion, ethnicity and culture does not throw up quite the same set of issues for converts as for born Muslims. As part of a religious, but not necessarily ethnic, minority, the experience of British converts varies according to factors such as how visibly Muslim or 'other' they are (*ḥijāb*-wearing women generally being the most visible, but even here there is great variation between someone who dresses in a bohemian fashion, with headscarf tied at the back, and someone who dresses from head to toe in black, including *jilbāb* and *niqāb*). British convert Mohammad Siddique Seddon observes

[25] To do *hijrah* means to 'flee' from a place where one is not free to practise one's faith to a place where one is.

that the situation for converts is complicated by the fact that the (mainly Asian) community into which he or she is entering is itself experiencing 'a shift in identity from its ethnic, cultural, geographic and traditional origins into a new environment with a religiously heightened and culturally hybrid form of Islam'.[26] Furthermore, the 'resocialization process' whereby converts are accepted into a religious community is sometimes problematic for British converts to Islam, complicated as it is by cultural differences with the receiving community.[27]

Black converts (who make up about a third of the convert population in Britain) report experiences which differ, to some extent, from those of white converts. In almost all cases they have encountered racism both from British society in general and from the Muslim community after their conversion (as described in chapter 2). For some (especially in the US, but also to some extent in Britain), a perceived history of having been enslaved by white colonizers and of having an indigenous, authentic Muslim identity which preceded slavery are factors contributing to their new Muslim identity. McCloud, who is herself an African American Muslim, sees the conversion of African Americans as in part a response to racism, and shows how Islam offers them a new identity and freedom from the yoke of Christianity which is perceived as having contributed to their oppression.[28] Al-Qwidi found that some British Afro-Caribbean converts in her sample placed particular importance on taking an Islamic name in order to get rid of their 'slave names'.[29] In some ways the transition to a Muslim identity can be easier for black converts; Hermansen, in her study of American women converts, observed that adopting Muslim dress appeared to be a natural development for some of the black women, as it seemed more continuous with their past.[30] In my own sample, one black male interviewee remarked that although he dressed in traditional-style dress, including a long robe and a tightly fitting cap, people generally took his attire to be African rather than Islamic, and he felt that this was more acceptable to most people. The sometimes complex relationship between race, religious identity and political factors is illustrated by Na'ima Robert, a British convert who grew up in a

[26] Seddon, 'Locating the Perpetuation of "Otherness" ', pp. 151–2.
[27] Al-Qwidi, 'Understanding the Stages of Conversion to Islam', p. 232.
[28] McCloud, *African American Islam*.
[29] Al-Qwidi, 'Understanding the Stages of Conversion to Islam', p. 206.
[30] Hermansen, 'Two-Way Acculturation', p. 194.

mixed-race South African family; she relates that when she visited Gambia prior to her conversion, she was struck by the fact that the Muslims were 'proud to be African', contrasting this with (mainly non-Muslim) South Africa, where people imitated the British colonialists.[31] The ability to be proud and unsubjugated is a theme that recurs in her account; she describes her own sense of pride on her conversion at being 'part of such a wonderful community'. Her sense of the historical continuity of prayer is expressed in a description which resonates with the themes of rootedness, authenticity and a reclaiming of history: 'It meant a lot to me that this ritual was the same one practised by the Prophet of Islam [peace be upon him] and his followers, and by Muslims all over the world since then.'[32]

African American Muslims are sometimes cited as an example of a strong, authentic and indigenous Muslim identity. Hassan Scott, for example, sees their self-help policies and affirmation of their own dignity as a possible model for British Muslims.[33] Yahya Birt observes that 'Afro-Caribbean converts are much further ahead in forging a self-confident sense of their Islamic self that is underpinned by well-organised collective action. They have had giants like Muhammad Ali and Malcolm X to follow. We have had no comparable recent paragon of equal stature or cultural impact';[34] this is problematic as, in his view, 'you need great transitional figures to translate something alien (like Islam) into the vernacular'.[35] Malcolm X (and to a lesser extent Muhammad Ali) is often cited as a figurehead and source of inspiration for Muslims in Britain.[36] Mohammad Siddique Seddon evokes him as a counter-example to the July 2005 London tube bombers, since he 'did not become the oppressor' in his fight against oppression, and 'his cause was not lost and the African-American community went from strength to strength inspired by the Organisation of African-American Unity that he established'. Seddon asks: 'Are British Muslims brave enough and bold enough to follow Malcolm's lead?'[37]

[31] Robert, *From my Sisters' Lips*, p. 20.   [32] Ibid., p. 22.
[33] Scott, 'Islamophobia'.
[34] Birt, 'Building New Medinas'.
[35] N. Hellen and C. Morgan, 'Islamic Britain Lures Top People', *Sunday Times*, 22 February 2004.
[36] See, e.g., *Q-News*, February 2005 and November 2005 (both on Malcolm X), and *emel*, 17, February 2006 (on Muhammad Ali).
[37] Seddon, 'The X Factor'.

IDENTITY MARKERS: LANGUAGE, DRESS, NAMES, CIRCUMCISION

Language and rhetoric play an important role in reinforcing the new religious identity; Rambo describes language as 'a powerful tool for the transformation of one's consciousness and perception of the world'.[38] In the Islamic religion and culture there are certain phrases which pervade daily life. These include *al-salāmu 'alaykum*, the Muslim greeting; *bismillah* ('in the name of God') on beginning any action; *alḥamdulillah* ('praise be to God') to express gratitude to God; and *inshallah* ('if God wills') when speaking of anything which is to take place in the future. All practising (as well as many non-practising) Muslims are likely to use these phrases on a daily basis, in my observation, not just automatically but with a degree of religious consciousness. The use of the words 'brother' and 'sister' to refer to fellow believers is very widespread among converts, as well as among born Muslims who are Islamically active, and it presumably enhances the sense of being part of a community.

Almost all converts now use the word 'Allah' in preference to the word 'God', unlike the late nineteenth-/early twentieth-century converts such as Quilliam.[39] This may be due to a growing perception that 'Allah' is the proper name of God, and also to a greater emphasis in the post-colonial era (and in the multicultural context) on cultural authenticity. It would be unthinkable, for example, for contemporary British Muslims to refer to a mosque as a 'Muslim church' as did the early converts. A convert to Islam generally needs to learn a basic Islamic vocabulary, including words referring to Islamic rituals or practices such as *ṣalāh* (ritual prayer) and *ḥijāb* (covering for a woman), or central concepts such as *tawḥīd* (unity of God), *ḥalāl* (lawful) and *ḥarām* (prohibited). This terminology is used by born Muslims (including non-Arabs), and converts are likely to pick it up from them, if not from books or the internet. Converts tend to read a lot of books and engage in much discussion about Islam, and in general I found my interviewees to have quite a wide Islamic vocabulary. Most for example were cognizant of terms such as *fiṭrah*, *dīn* (religion or way of life), *mu'min/īmān* (believer/faith) and *dunyah/ākhirah* (this world/the hereafter), and many used more unusual terms such as *rizq* (provision, i.e. from God). The use of such words

[38] Rambo, *Understanding Religious Conversion*, p. 137; cf. pp. 118–21.
[39] An exception to this is Sarah Joseph's use of the word 'God' in her *emel* editorials, perhaps with an eye to her non-Muslim readership.

is not necessarily just a formal matter, but may fulfil the function of manifesting or encouraging particular ways of thinking. An example might be the
use of the word *dīn* (roughly translated as 'religion' or 'way of life') to refer to
Islam, which sometimes connotes a particularly reified concept of religion,
as when Na'ima Robert describes the experience of herself and her friends as
new converts who became absorbed in Islamic learning and kept thinking:
'What an amazing *deen* ... what a wonderful *deen!*'[40]

Some words have a strong potential to act as boundary reinforcers.
Examples of these would be *ḥalāl* and *ḥarām*, *jāhiliyyah* (ignorance, or age of
ignorance, originally denoting the age before Islam), *munāfiq* (hypocrite)
and *kāfir* (unbeliever).[41] Na'ima Robert for example refers to the pre-conversion phase as 'the life of *jahiliyyah*',[42] which serves to strengthen the boundary between Muslim and non-Muslim life, culture and identity. The terms
kāfir and *kufr* in particular tend to denote a confrontational attitude towards
non-Muslims, and are frequently used by radical groups such as Hizb ul-
Tahrir. Ahmad Thomson, who is affiliated to the Murabitun, provides a
striking example of the use of this term in his book *Dajjal: The AntiChrist*. He
speaks throughout of the 'kafir way of life', the 'kafir state', the 'kafir university
system', the 'kafir hospital system', the 'kafir legal system', the 'kafir police', the
'kafir producer consumer system', etc.[43] He also bluntly states that 'the Fire is
for the *kafirun*. The Garden is for the *muminun*. You are either for the Fire or
the Garden.'[44] Among my interviewees, three did use the word *kāfir/kuffār* to
refer to non-Muslims (e.g. 'the *kafir*s are against us and we are against our
own selves'; 'we're not like the *kuffār*, we have no fear of death'; 'the *kuffār*
men have no shame'), while another, by contrast, said that he 'couldn't stand'
the use of the term, as he felt it denoted a dismissive and judgemental attitude
which was unhelpful to both Muslims and non-Muslims.[45] In the published
and internet sources which I reviewed, I found that, Thomson aside, the
term was more often criticized than used. A contributor to a discussion in

---

[40] Robert, *From my Sisters' Lips*, p. 242.
[41] The last two terms recur frequently in the Qur'an.
[42] Robert, *From my Sisters' Lips*, p. 105.
[43] The author actually states in the preface that in this revised edition (1997), he has tried to
reduce the frequency of the word *kāfir*.
[44] Thomson, *Dajjal*, p. 61.
[45] Similarly, Daoud Rosser-Owen deplores the 'indiscriminate' application of the term to
Jews and Christians and feels that there should be a 'moratorium on the use of the word
"kafir" and its derivatives' (*emel*, 22, July 2006).

Meeting Point (the newsletter of the New Muslims Project) laments the fact that he hears many Muslims using the term *kāfir* and argues that Muslims should be careful about labelling other people in this way; his attitude is partly informed by the fact that he is a convert: 'Should I have been regarded as such [i.e. a *kāfir*] I do not think it would have been helpful on my journey to Islam.'[46] An American convert contributing to *Meeting Point* feels that 'Islam is universal – therefore, everyone is either a Muslim, a latent Muslim, or a potential Muslim . . . today's kafir could be tomorrow's mu'min.'[47] Yahya Birt points out that according to the classical Muslim scholar al-Ghazali (d. 1111 CE/505 AH), the term cannot be applied to someone who rejects Islam out of ignorance or because of an inaccurate understanding of it.[48] The seeming discrepancy between my interview material and published sources may be partly explained by the fact that all three interviewees who used the term were among the seven who were interviewed by my Muslim research assistant; from this it would seem that the term is more likely to be used in an intra-Muslim setting.

Whilst looking at convert testimonies and writings, and whilst talking to interviewees, I often noticed phrases and concepts which were reminiscent of phrases and concepts from the Qur'an, and to a lesser extent the *ḥadīth*. One interviewee spoke of himself in the pre-conversion period in the following terms: 'I refused to really be part of the twenty to thirty-year-old drinking and womanizing, basically just following my lusts and desires.' 'Following one's own desires [*ahwā*']' is something that is frequently condemned in the Qur'an, so this person's choice of words provides an example of the reconceptualization of past experiences in the light of the new religious values and norms. Interestingly, no less than five of the interviewees referred to 'desires' in a pejorative way, using phrases such as 'the worship of vain passions and desires', and 'individuals are encouraged to follow their own desires', when talking about British society. This suggests a high level of internalization of a Qur'anic 'worldview'. Another example is provided by the conversion story of Uum [sic] Ayob, reported in *The Independent on Sunday*:

> When I graduated . . . I was turning away from rulers and governments.
> . . . Another thing my heart turned away from was opinions. In my four

---

[46] 'Point of View', in *Meeting Point*, 26, June 2002.
[47] Omar, 'Reflecting on the Ways of our Ancestors'.
[48] Birt, 'Building New Medinas'.

years at art college, I had listened to too many opinions and too many people saying what they thought life was about and what made art good. I had become really sick of opinions. I'd go into the library at college and look at books and feel physically sick because there were so many opinions.[49]

This echoes the Qur'an's negative view of 'opinions' in certain contexts, particularly when it rebukes those people who follow 'only opinions/ conjecture' (al-ẓann, e.g. 6:116; 10:66).[50]

According to Rambo, giving his or her testimony provides the convert with an opportunity to reflect on the changes that have taken place, and in the process he or she is likely to combine new uses of language with bio-graphical reconstruction.[51] Van Nieuwkerk describes the way in which iden-tities and discourses are dialectically related, with life experiences and discourse both informing identity construction in an ongoing way through-out the life of a convert.[52] Muslim convert testimonies often retrospectively express the sense that God was preparing and guiding the convert long before their actual conversion. Sometimes the dissatisfaction the person experienced in their pre-conversion life is expressed using explicitly (but not necessarily self-consciously) Islamic concepts; an example is provided by the English convert mentioned in chapter 2 who complains: 'My parents …threw me into the middle of a corrupt society and expected me to find my own husband which was such a pressure, especially while alcoholism was going around.'[53] Similarly, Kathy, an American convert, describes how she became disillusioned with Christianity because, among other things, 'women were not only no longer required to cover their heads in church but were permitted to wear pantsuits'.[54] Sophie Jenkins echoes mainstream Islamic discourse when she says that she felt that other religions she investi-gated before Islam 'all appeared so man made and contradictory',[55] while Anisa Kissoon describes Christian teachings in Islamic terms when she

---

[49] Stanford, 'Preaching from the Converted'.
[50] This convert is a member of al-Muhajiroun, and her point about rulers and governments reflects the rhetoric of that fringe group rather than Qur'anic discourse.
[51] Rambo, *Understanding Religious Conversion*, p. 137.
[52] Van Nieuwkerk, 'Gender and Conversion', pp. 10–11.
[53] Köse, *Conversion to Islam*, p. 89.
[54] Hauser, 'From a Bathing Suit to a Hijab'.
[55] Jenkins, 'The Journey of a Lifetime'.

relates how she ran away from Sunday school at the age of five because of the teacher saying that 'God was really one but was also three at the same time'.[56] Another English convert, Dawud Abdullah Mannion, provides a clear example of seeing his past through the filter of subsequently acquired Islamic concepts and values when he says in his conversion narrative that he committed 'no major *zina* [fornication]' until he was seventeen, which, he adds, was quite an advanced age 'in such a base community'.[57]

For women converts in particular, a change in dress is usually the most visible and obvious change of all, and therefore the one that elicits the strongest reaction from non-Muslims. The taking on of the *ḥijāb* is often a highly significant step, akin to a rite of passage. Jan, a convert of one year, speaking on the Channel 4 television documentary *Mum, I'm a Muslim*, remarks: 'To wear a scarf for me as an Englishwoman in Islam is a real statement, and I really feel I want to do it and it just feels the right time to do it . . . a moving on isn't it really . . . to actually go today [into work] with a scarf feels quite a journey.' Converts even surprise themselves sometimes; as Jan looks in the mirror having put on the *ḥijāb* she remarks: 'It's amazing how you sort of change isn't it?'[58] This step is sometimes preceded by much trepidation and hesitation. Amina, a convert of six weeks with an Irish Catholic background who has never met any *ḥijāb*-wearing women, writes on the *Islam For Today* website: 'I have not as yet begun to wear hijab although I am dressing modestly . . . [I] hope to find the strength to wear hijab soon.'[59] On the same website Katherine Bullock, a Canadian convert who has published an academic study on the *ḥijāb*, and who now wears it herself, describes her thought processes soon after converting: 'How will I have the courage to wear hijab? I probably won't. People will stare at me, I'll become obvious; I'd rather hide away in the crowd when I'm out. What will my friends say when they see me in that? . . . I couldn't possibly go out in public in hijab.'[60]

[56] Kissoon, 'A Different Childhood'; several conversion narratives have this theme of having objections to the Trinity from an early age.
[57] Mannion, 'Dawud's Story'.
[58] *Mum, I'm a Muslim*, Channel 4, 10 March 2002.
[59] Amina, 'Amina's Story'.
[60] Bullock, 'Twelve Hours Old'; Bullock's study is entitled *Rethinking Muslim Women and the Veil*. As Jacobson points out, born Muslims who rediscover their faith can experience similar difficulties (*Islam in Transition*, p. 119).

The majority of female converts do take on the *ḥijāb*,[61] and when this step is taken, two things generally happen (but not necessarily in the following order). One is that there is some kind of adverse reaction from family, friends or work colleagues; in many female testimonies, the family is reasonably accepting of their conversion until they take on the *ḥijāb*, at which point the attitude changes. Not infrequently a hostile reaction from family or society in general only strengthens the resolve of the *ḥijāb*-wearer, as in the case of the American convert who says: 'Now I get mad at people who stare at me or make fun of me, but that only makes me want to wear it more.'[62] The other thing that happens is that the wearer typically experiences an upsurge in religious faith, commitment and a strengthening of her Islamic identity. She has a sense of having taken a momentous step in the full knowledge that it might have awkward repercussions, that it might 'cost' something. In taking on the *ḥijāb* a strong commitment has been made, which constitutes a permanent announcement to the outside world of the religious identity of the wearer.

Some women converts comment explicitly on the way wearing *ḥijāb* strengthened their Islamic identity or heightened their sense of self-confidence. The following comment made by Kawthar, an interviewee, is typical: 'It's part of me, it's part of my identity, that's who I am. If I took it off nobody would know I'm Muslim and I'm proud to be Muslim.' Shahnaaz, speaking on the BBC television documentary *A Muslim in the Family*, says: 'I love wearing it. I know that I'm doing the right thing, and it's a progression in my faith, and it did feel wonderful being able to walk out and know that *I've got that little bit closer to being the person that I want to be*' (my italics).[63] Hilary Saunders remarks: 'I felt quite nervous putting it on at first ... I feel a lot safer now that I am wearing it; I have more self-respect. *Now I know where I belong*' (my italics).[64] Two of my interviewees spoke of how it enhanced their confidence or made them feel stronger. Some women who report a rise in self-esteem relate it to the issue of sexuality, feeling that they no longer have

---

[61] In al-Qwidi's study, fifteen out of seventeen women wore the *ḥijāb* ('Understanding the Stages of Conversion to Islam', p. 210), while in Köse's, 70% did (*Conversion to Islam*, p. 131). In my own study, seventeen out of twenty wore it. For an in-depth study of the effects of taking on *ḥijāb*, see Bullock, *Rethinking Muslim Women and the Veil*.

[62] Anway, *Daughters of Another Path*, p. 76.

[63] *A Muslim in the Family*, BBC1, 2 May 2004.

[64] Saunders, 'Why I Took the Hijab'.

to dress to please men; this aspect of *ḥijāb* is explored in chapter 5. Three interviewees said that they would feel 'naked' if they went out without their *ḥijāb*, and one of them clearly felt very strongly: 'If the government said you have to take it off, I'd say: Kill me now. I'd take my steps to do *hijrah* immediately.' Two other women said they had had dreams of finding themselves outside without their *ḥijāb*; the dreams seemed to parallel the commonly experienced dream of being naked in public.

For some women, the *ḥijāb* enhanced their identity in two specific and complementary ways: strengthening the boundary between themselves and non-Muslims; and reinforcing their sense of belonging to the wider Muslim community. Kavindra felt that 'it separates you from the non-Muslims ... It doesn't mean those non-Muslims are horrible, but the fact that you wear it separates you from them.' Janice was a relatively new convert who had previously been a Christian, and on this particular issue her way of expressing herself seemed to be influenced by Christian biblical concepts; when she took on the *ḥijāb*, despite her self-consciousness she felt a sense of comfort from Allah: 'Because I was finally separated from everybody else, I wasn't like in the world, which is what I was so not wanting to be, because I just wanted to be so close to God that I'm not associated with the things of the world.' The strengthened sense of belonging to a community is illustrated by Sarah Joseph (editor of *emel* magazine), who found that wearing *ḥijāb* 'made it easier to be accepted into the community'.[65] Prabha experienced this community acceptance in a very direct way; she said that when she started wearing the headscarf: 'There was suddenly this network of people, and suddenly there were brothers on the tube that would stand up and give me their seat, or would look out for me, and I would see that they were making sure that everything was okay and it was just completely different. I just felt like, this is making me part of something.'

Wearing the *ḥijāb* can be a deliberate attempt to play down or privatize the sexual aspect of a woman's identity, which, it is felt, is overemphasized in mainstream Western society; to that extent it is a conscious or strategic manipulation of public identity. As Na'ima Robert says of the *ḥijāb*- wearing woman: 'Whoever relates to her must relate to what she's presented – be it what she says, does or thinks', and: 'The covered Muslim woman is not

---

[65] Joseph, 'More Than Just a Scarf'. Allievi also refers to this function of *ḥijāb*: see 'The Shifting Significance of the *Halal/Haram* Frontier', p. 145.

judged by her physical appearance . . . her sense of self is not wrapped up in her looks.'[66] Emira Topham compares wearing the *ḥijāb* to when she shaved off her hair in her pre-conversion life, presumably not just because both might be construed by others as 'weird' but because both have a desexualizing effect: 'When you're bald people who would have been interested in you will be interested anyway.'[67]

Na'ima Robert highlights the close correlation for some women between wearing the *ḥijāb* and strength of religious faith or commitment, saying that when she and her friend first put on the *ḥijāb* it was as if 'Allah had put light in our faces . . . we looked beautiful.'[68] Halima, an interviewee, commented: 'Once you start wearing it then you are forced to make a change in your life anyway, so it's not like you'd put it on and go down the pub with your friends and sit there and have to face everybody's ridicule, you just wouldn't go, because you've reached that stage inside where you don't want to do those things'. This suggests a reciprocal or dialectical relationship between wearing *ḥijāb* and progressing in one's faith. Robert elaborates on the impact of wearing the *ḥijāb*, speaking of herself and her friends:

> None of us started covering ourselves without experiencing certain changes in ourselves and the way we related to those around us. The first effect that the *ḥijāb*, the headscarf, seemed to have on us was to encourage modesty – in dress and conduct. After a lifetime spent showing off our clothes and our bodies, we suddenly felt shy to flaunt ourselves in public. The *ḥijāb* reminded us of the standards of behaviour that were expected of us as Muslims and, more specifically, as Muslim women. We became more aware of upholding Islamic manners – trying not to be rude or to lie, to be kind and generous . . . We became acutely aware that we could now be identified as Muslims and, as such, were representatives of the faith wherever we went.[69]

Robert describes an ongoing cumulative process whereby she progresses from one stage to the next: from the bandana to the headscarf to the '*abāyah* (outer gown) to the *jilbāb* to the *niqāb*, each stage representing a deepening commitment accompanied by a sense of drawing closer to God: 'Wearing

---

[66] Robert, *From my Sisters' Lips*, pp. 124–5.
[67] Berrington, 'Islam Sheds its Image'.
[68] Robert, *From my Sisters' Lips*, p. 113.   [69] Ibid., pp. 114–15.

the *abayah* ... is a logical extension of a growing Islamic awareness and an increase in faith. But once you decide to cover your clothes, it is as if there is no going back – you have passed the point of no return. And in other people's eyes, you are different too – you're on a different level.' She goes on to say: 'How can I explain the impulse to cover more? There are many feelings that contribute to wanting to "step up a gear": wanting to do more to please Allah is definitely one of the main ones ... that step is also a result of higher *iman* [faith], of deeper faith and of a stronger spiritual commitment.'[70]

The minority of converts who wear the *niqāb* generally do so for religious reasons, and so are not in the same category as some women from the Gulf states, for example, who wear it as part of their cultural tradition. Therefore, for those who do wear it, it is generally an act of piety; there may also be an element of spiritual retreat, as in Fatima's description of the effect that wearing *niqāb* had on her: 'I just felt it gives you more privacy and it brings you more back to – it's an odd thing to say, but – more back to who you are as a person. So I think maybe the less of you that's visible externally, the more connected you are internally.' Halima also enjoyed the sense of privacy and space that the *niqāb* gave her: 'It did feel really wonderful because you're so free and liberated in a way and nobody can see you at all, and people sort of make space for you.' According to Na'ima Robert, the *niqāb* has a rather different impact from the *ḥijāb* on the public persona or identity of the Muslim woman:

> It is as if, once you put on the *niqab*, you cease to have a human identity. I know that the *niqab* is a shock to the system for most people in non-Muslim societies – we are used to seeing so much personal information about people around us, being able to tell their race, their age, their physique and their attractiveness. The *niqab* gives none of this information.[71]

This depersonalization may render the covered Muslim woman a blank screen on which others may project a plethora of negative images; it also has a 'shock' value. Robert shows a keen awareness of the possible impact of the fully covered woman on observers or passers-by: 'What does the non-Muslim see when he or she sees us in the street? A relic of a bygone age? A lingering symbol of oppression in a liberated world? A religious fanatic? A

---

[70] Ibid., pp. 116 and 122.   [71] Ibid., p. 127.

terrorist or terrorist's aide? An outsider, immigrant, interloper?'[72] While Robert is clearly not deterred by such reactions, some Muslims argue that it is preferable for Muslim women not to wear the *niqāb* in Western countries because of its potential to alienate non-Muslims and undermine the cause of *da'wah*.[73] Aspects of *niqāb* and *ḥijāb* which are related to reinforcing sexual or gender boundaries are discussed in chapter 5.

For men, the Islamic legal requirements for covering are compatible with normal Western dress, providing clothes are not too tight (while mainstream Islamic teachings require a woman to cover everything except her face and hands, for men it is the area between the navel and knees that must be covered). Some Muslims feel that it is religiously meritorious to dress in a manner which is distinctively Muslim, but most believe that Western dress is acceptable so long as it does not incorporate non-Muslim religious symbols, such as the crucifix, and so long as there is no intention to imitate followers of other faiths. In fact, a relatively small minority of male converts dress in a way that is identifiably Muslim;[74] while many have beards, the beard is usually not unambiguously Islamic. Of the ten men in my sample, nine wore beards, but only three of these regarded their beards as distinctively or recognizably Islamic. Only one man habitually dressed in 'Islamic' style, wearing a robe, but, as mentioned earlier, because his ethnic origin was black African, he found that people often took his attire to be African rather than Islamic. Ali, on the other hand, who was heavily involved in *da'wah*, avoided wearing anything that would identify him religiously: 'I hate the hard sell when it comes to religion ... If you want to wear a *thawb* [robe] outside, good luck to you, if you want to wear a *kufi* [skull cap] – no problem, but it doesn't make him any more a Muslim than me.' Sulayman said that he got fed up with 'petty arguments' over attire and beards: 'It's not the dress, it's actually how you act – I mean if you are blatantly following something unIslamic I would say to people you need to address that.' Three of the men

---

[72] Ibid., p. 127; interestingly, one of my male interviewees saw *niqāb* in precisely these terms.

[73] Shaikh Nuh Ha Mim Keller (an American convert who is a religious scholar and spiritual leader living in Jordan, with many followers in Europe and North America) has been widely reported as expressing this opinion. Michael Young expresses the same view in very strong terms in his internet articles 'Yes to Hijab, No to Niqaab' and 'Much Ado about Nothing'.

[74] In al-Qwidi's sample, all twenty men dressed in European style ('Understanding the Stages of Conversion to Islam', p. 210), while in Köse's, only three out of fifty men radically changed their dress (*Conversion to Islam*, p. 131).

wore Islamic dress on an occasional basis, for example at the mosque or Islamic events, or when in a Muslim country. Some male converts feel uneasy about the male–female imbalance as regards dress and visibility; Sulayman acknowledged that it was much harder for women, and expressed his admiration for what he saw as their bravery. A male contributor to a discussion on *ḥijāb* in *Meeting Point* feels that this 'burden' should be shared by men: 'If the women have to wear a scarf in this society, which let's face it can be hard, then why don't we men at least look like Muslims by wearing a hat and beard?'[75] One man who does adopt Muslim ethnic/religious clothing, John (Jamal Udeen) Standing, speaking on *A Muslim in the Family*, says to his bemused father: 'I don't feel ashamed of myself walking down the street ... I feel more than comfortable like this, I feel more than relaxed. It gives me a confidence which I don't expect you to understand.'[76] This seems to mirror the confidence that many women draw from wearing the *ḥijāb*.

The taking of a new name is a highly symbolic act, which helps to strengthen both the new identity and the sense of belonging to a group.[77] One convert interviewed by al-Qwidi expressed it thus: 'If I was in the Mosque and someone shouts you as Andrew, I do not feel like I am a Muslim. I think having a Muslim name reminds me of who I am.'[78] Most converts to Islam do take on a Muslim name, often when they take the *shahādah*, although this is not obligatory unless the original name has some undesirable meaning or connotations (as in the case of those contemporaries of Muhammad whose names referred to pagan deities).[79] Many will choose a name which is close to, or the equivalent of, their original name, or alternatively they might choose a name of a prominent religious figure such as one of the Qur'anic prophets or one of the well-known Companions of Muhammad. It is quite common for converts to use their Muslim names in Muslim contexts, and their non-Muslim names in non-Muslim contexts. The reasons for this vary, but some converts mention the possibility (or actuality, in some cases) of being disadvantaged by a Muslim name in

---

[75] 'Points of View', in *Meeting Point*, 34, March 2005.
[76] *A Muslim in the Family*, BBC1, 2 May 2004.
[77] Beit-Hallahmi, *Prolegomena*, p. 101.
[78] Al-Qwidi, 'Understanding the Stages of Conversion to Islam', p. 207.
[79] 81% of Köse's sample and 92% of al-Qwidi's sample took a Muslim name: see Köse, *Conversion to Islam*, p. 128, and al-Qwidi, 'Understanding the Stages of Conversion to Islam', p. 206.

situations such as seeking employment (this applies more to men than to most women, whose *ḥijāb* will announce their Islamic identity at the interview stage even if their name does not). One interviewee had deliberately kept his original name on his passport for many years as he noticed that when travelling with friends who had Muslim names, they were stopped more often than he was. It was rare for the new name to be used in the context of the family of origin, and most people felt it was too much to expect their parents to use their new names. Among my interviewees, five had never taken a Muslim name, and of the remaining twenty-five, eight said that they only used it among Muslims. Almost all the rest used it in all situations except with their family of origin (and pre-conversion friends, in some cases). Three said that they actually regretted taking a Muslim name (and had not known at the time that it was optional), and one of these was in the process of gradually restoring the use of her original name. A few mentioned that they had changed their names by deed poll, but the overwhelming majority had not. It seems that it is becoming increasingly common for new Muslims not to change their names; looking at the regular section in *Meeting Point* which lists those who are 'new to Islam, new to *Meeting Point* readership', the percentage of Muslim names in recent issues is noticeably lower than in issues of a decade ago (having fallen from approximately 50% to approximately 10%). This could be due to a wider awareness that it is not obligatory, but probably also reflects a new confidence among converts and less of a felt need to adapt culturally to or otherwise 'fit in' with born Muslims.

Those who choose not to take or use a Muslim name give various reasons. Michael Young, who has penned some much-read articles on the *Islam for Today* website, tells how he reluctantly took a Muslim name on conversion as he was not told that it was not obligatory, and that he has been criticized by born Muslims for not using it. He feels that 'adopting a "Muslim name" makes it easier for one's existing circle of family and friends to dismiss one's conversion to Islam as an act of eccentricity which they can brush off'. Furthermore, on his conversion he didn't want his (practising Catholic) parents to feel that he was rejecting them: 'Rejecting the name they had given me could really have been interpreted as being quite insulting to them, which in itself would be contrary to Islam.' Another argument he gives against adopting a Muslim name and clothing is that it alienates the wider society, thus 'reinforcing the preconceived notions and prejudices that non-Muslim fellow westerners tend to hold about Islam.[80]

Like changing one's name, male circumcision could be regarded as a kind of initiatory rite, though in fact it is generally acknowledged to be 'recommended' rather than 'obligatory' for converts.[81] Contributors to a *Meeting Point* discussion on this subject evince a fair degree of ambivalence.[82] While one confesses that he's too squeamish to undergo the operation, another wonders whether there's any relationship between the recommendation of circumcision and the fact that there are fewer male converts than female. Another man who is not prepared to be circumcised states: 'I fully respect and appreciate people's right to view circumcision as an act of faith. [However,] the act of faith most important to me is to stay away from the old lifestyle I used to lead and to die in a state of Islam.' His argument echoes that of some Muslim women who rationalize their choice not to wear the *ḥijāb* on the grounds that general values and behaviour are more important than external appearances. A woman contributor to the debate demonstrates an instinctive aversion to the idea of circumcision, which is probably characteristic of someone brought up in a non-Muslim context as opposed to a Muslim one. Interestingly, her objection is couched in religious terms: 'Was it not simply that the Prophet was circumcised because it was the custom in those days in that part of the world – it had nothing whatsoever to do with religion or piety at all? . . . If people aren't supposed to change their appearance in any way from the way God made us, then surely He had a reason for the minutest details in which He made us.' Of those who have been circumcized, one procrastinated for many years but says that he was glad to have done it and felt 'more complete', while the other says, 'I sought refuge in Him from cowardice and He took away my fear! I got myself circumcised for his sake, and He did not cause me to suffer for it!' The fact that these two went through with the operation despite their fears suggests that they attributed considerable importance to it, and that for

[80] Young, 'Frustrations of a Muslim Convert'. Köse and al-Qwidi both came across this motive for not taking a Muslim name (Köse, *Conversion to Islam*, p. 128; al-Qwidi, 'Understanding the Stages of Conversion to Islam', p. 207).
[81] *Meeting Point*, 29, May 2003. Most scholars see circumcision as obligatory for those who are born Muslim, including the sons of converts. Köse found that of the 80% of his sample who were uncircumcised at the time of conversion, less than half chose to be circumcised (Köse, *Conversion to Islam*, p. 131).
[82] 'Points of View', in *Meeting Point*, 29, May 2003.

them it represented an increased level of commitment. However, for the other male contributors the deterrents seem to have outweighed the incentives, and it was therefore not construed as a particularly significant or symbolic rite. It is tempting to draw a comparison between circumcision and taking on *ḥijāb* as a sort of equivalent rite of passage, as does Allievi.[83] Both may be preceded by much hesitation and apprehension, both may entail a certain 'cost', and both may indicate a strengthening of commitment. However, the differences are perhaps more substantial than the parallels: while circumcision is non-obligatory and not publicly visible, the *ḥijāb* is obligatory (according to mainstream Islamic teachings) and highly visible.

LIFESTYLE CHANGES

Elsewhere in this book there is reference to some of the important changes that converts may effect in their lives as a result of their conversion, in areas such as friendships, sexual relationships and gender relations. The focus here will be on other changes, especially those in the sphere of cultural and leisure activities. How one chooses to spend one's leisure time is an important factor in identity formation, with some converts instituting major changes before or very soon after conversion. Usually there are things that need to be given up, but aside from that which is unambiguously proscribed (such as alcohol and extramarital sex), converts vary as to what they actually do give up. It is not uncommon for new converts to dispose of their CD collections and sometimes their TVs as well.[84] Aqeel Burton, a black convert speaking on the BBC documentary *A Muslim in the Family*, thought about converting for as long as six years because he knew Islam would demand a change in his whole lifestyle, and that he would have to give up going out, drinking, smoking and chasing women – the last being 'the most difficult one'.[85] Na'ima Robert describes the difficulties involved in going to any social occasion involving non-Muslims: 'Even a seemingly innocuous place like a restaurant poses almost insurmountable challenges. Will men and women be together there? Will they be serving alcohol? Will the meat be

---

[83] Allievi, 'The Shifting Significance of the *Halal/Haram* Frontier', p. 145.
[84] E.g. Mannion, 'Dawud's Story' and Bowes, 'At This Point in my Life'.
[85] *A Muslim in the Family*, BBC1, 2 May 2004.

halal? Will the music be blasting and will they all want to dance? Will I feel strange in my *hijab*? Will I be compromising my *deen*?'[86] Sara, one of Robert's interviewees, felt she had to choose between her religion and competing in basketball tournaments (presumably because of male spectators), an activity she 'adored'. Like many other converts, she reports finding some kind of compensation for that which she gave up: '*Alhamdulillah* [praise be to God] that passion faded and, in a way, that was replaced by a passion for walking . . . and as I became more spiritually aware, I started to appreciate everything: the rain, the sky, the trees, all the different shades of green, all the things that Allah has given us.'[87]

Interviewees were asked whether there was anything that they found difficult in their transition to becoming Muslim, whether in terms of giving things up or of implementing new practices and behaviours.[88] The most frequently mentioned difficulties had to do with learning and adapting to the five daily prayers, and acclimatizing to the *ḥijāb*. Several people mentioned that they had already made certain changes, such as abstaining from alcohol or dressing more modestly, prior to their conversion. Among the things that were hard to give up, marijuana, cigarettes and alcohol were all mentioned, but only by one or two people in each case, and two people had found giving up a relationship or a marriage difficult. In fact, many said that they had found the changes relatively easy. Interestingly, more information on this topic was forthcoming when interviewees were being asked about other things. For example, when the subject of music was broached, many of those who had stopped listening to music after their conversion mentioned that they had found that very difficult (although they had not said so when asked directly about things which were hard to give up). Similarly, when the subject of celebrating Christmas came up, some of those who had given this up had found it difficult, though the difficulty was often as much to do with the reaction of the family of origin as anything else. There are several possible reasons for interviewees to be reticent on the subject of transitional difficulties. One interviewee, for example, declined to answer, citing the classical juristic principle that Muslims should not broadcast their own or others'

---

[86] Robert, *From my Sisters' Lips*, p. 88.
[87] Ibid., pp. 89–90.
[88] This seemingly 'negative' question was complemented by another one asking how interviewees felt they had changed as a person as a result of their conversion, which elicited mainly 'positive' responses.

failings and sins. Another interviewee felt that although she had experienced some difficulties, there could be 'benefit in difficultness'. It may be that when one has taken a step that one believes to be right and beneficial, one is not likely to see the accompanying changes in a negative light, especially if the religious or spiritual dimension is prioritized. Some interviewees, such as Eleanor, saw the changes as unfolding naturally and organically from their faith: 'If you can get the belief as strong as you need it to be, you know, nothing seems too hard ... If you make one step towards trying to please God, then He'll make steps to you to make it feel easier ... He makes you feel better about yourself or makes you feel happier with what you've done.'[89] Hafsa said that she had taken on the *ḥijāb* and *'abāyah* [outer garment] immediately: 'But then it just seemed normal, it just seemed like well, I've embraced Islam so this is what I've got to do now.' Other converts speak of the way they developed an aversion to things such as pork or alcohol, seemingly without any volition on their part; as one interviewee put it: 'It just happens without you noticing.' The widespread emphasis in contemporary Islamic discourse on the teachings of Islam being in accordance with human nature means that changes are seen, not as a sacrifice, but as a natural adjustment to a better way of being. This is illustrated by Sakina's answer: 'A lot of things in Islam, your initial reaction is "No! That can't be right!", but then you come round to it because Islam is geared to human nature and you have to come back to that human nature and say no, this is right, this is the right thing, and you change the way you think about things.'

I gained the impression that for converts, leisure time is often spent with family and friends, attending Islamic circles and talks, and going to the mosque. According to Sufyan Gent: 'If you are amongst a community of believers you derive your pleasure from sitting with them, discussing the wonders of our creator, or by enjoying your family and doing things together, living in a closely knit environment of mutual love and respect.'[90] Those who are still single (though converts do not often remain single for many years after their conversion) have more time for more individualistic

---

[89] This is probably an implicit reference to a *ḥadīth* in which God is reported as saying: 'If he [my servant] approaches Me by as much as one hand's length, I approach him by a cubit, and if he approaches Me by a cubit, I approach him by two hands' length. If he takes a step towards Me, I run towards him.'

[90] See http://thetruereligion.org/modules/xfsection/article.php?articleid=180 (accessed 05/10/05).

pursuits; among my sample, pastimes included kick-boxing, listening to music, and creative writing.

Most interviewees who were asked about it said that they watched less television than before their conversion, and several had actually stopped altogether. Many were selective in their viewing, for example watching news, documentaries or sport. As Amin put it: 'You are not meant to watch anything which is obviously wrong.' A few admitted to watching programmes which they knew were not particularly compatible with Islamic standards, though most said they would switch off if there was sexually explicit material or anything directly offensive to or ridiculing religion. Attitudes to fiction were generally fairly open, with the choice of reading matter being seen as a matter of common sense, though many said they were too busy to read. An unambiguously negative attitude was expressed by only two interviewees, one of whom (a female convert of nine years) thought that fiction was 'a waste of time'. The other was Janice, who had only been Muslim for a few months, and who said that she had given all her books away: 'I can't be bothered with it, I've got my Qur'an to get through, I don't need to be wasting my time with those books.' In this case reading fiction is seen as trivial rather than wrong; it seems that such activities are sometimes forsworn in the first flush of enthusiasm for all things Islamic. Prabha, who had been a Muslim for three years, had recently enjoyed the experience of rediscovering fiction, having abstained from it following her *shahādah*. Diana, who had only been Muslim for a few months, had adapted to a Muslim lifestyle in a very short period of time; like many converts she had read a lot of Islamic books leading up to and immediately after her conversion, but already felt in need of a change: 'You get a bit "Islam Islam Islam" in your head, it's a bit too much, so I read a couple of others. I've actually read other things that people don't think appropriate like Jordan's biography, because I liked the whole Jordan and Peter thing.' One woman who had been Muslim for ten years felt that 'you shouldn't read about things that might want you to have a certain lifestyle that you're not going to attain', but admitted to reading such literature herself, in the form of 'trashy fiction', romantic literature of the 'Mills & Boon' variety. She added: 'I think it would be better not to, and I think if you ask some educated scholars they'd say you shouldn't ... but I just haven't been able to stop it'; she went on to say that she wouldn't allow her young daughter to read such things when she was older, 'because my sins shouldn't be for her, she'll have her own, she doesn't need mine'.

A discussion of the merits and demerits of *Harry Potter* in *Meeting Point* reveals a variety of stances on cultural issues and illustrates the tension between religious concerns and the desire for cultural enrichment. One male contributor feels that in Islam 'there is not much place for escapism and fantasy. Having said that, fiction has a role to play, if it has a worthwhile intention . . . such as teaching higher values and morals'. Another person draws attention to the 'danger that Muslims present themselves as a bunch of miserable killjoys', and goes on to say: 'We must ensure that we ourselves are manifesting a way of life that is positive, joyful and an attractive alternative to what is on offer from the mainstream . . . I often find that Muslims have a very negative outlook and tend to look for the negative in a thing . . . before they look for a positive'. The same contributor gives a more specifically religious rationale for his position: 'It is difficult to praise and thank Allah while at the same time constantly complaining about the world that we live in, which is after all His creation, over which He has total dominion.' One convert provides a similar argument for a positive attitude to the arts in general: 'Music and film can be wonderful gifts from God when used to inspire people to see and feel the beauty of creation.' She adds that if Muslims are able to use their creative energy to better effect, a lot more people are likely to be attracted to Islam. Another cites her own conversion as an argument in favour of an inclusive attitude to fiction, saying that although she read many fantasy books as a child, she did not grow up believing that the fanstasies were literally true, nor did they prevent her from accepting Islam in later life.[91]

Music is a very prominent aspect of British culture, especially for young people, and to abjure it represents a radical lifestyle change. It is in fact a controversial issue in Islamic religious teachings, since there are a number of differing *ḥadīth*s on the subject.[92] Yusuf al-Qaradawi, an Islamic scholar of international repute who is generally regarded among Muslims as moderate (and on some issues, even progressive), has issued a *fatwā* on the subject of singing and music. He argues that singing is allowed, and considers the *ḥadīth*s prohibiting it to be weak. As for music, he considers it to be permissible and does not draw a distinction between different instruments (some scholars consider only the drum to be permissible and not other

[91] 'Points of View: Going Potty about Harry', in *Meeting Point*, 30, October 2003.
[92] This is also true of the visual arts, but this seems to be a less pressing issue for converts.

instruments). However, there are many provisos and caveats, in particular that the music should not be associated with anything *ḥarām*, such as inappropriate lyrics, the consumption of alcohol, or anything that is sexually suggestive. Another proviso is that it not be indulged in to excess, for 'spending time in permissible activities consumes time which ought to be reserved for carrying out religious obligations and doing good deeds . . . there is no excess except at the expense of a neglected duty'.[93]

Given that there are respectable and mainstream Islamic scholars such as al-Qaradawi who consider music to be permissible, I was surprised to find that just over half of the twenty-six interviewees who were asked about music confined themselves to voice and percussion, or in one case voice only.[94] The remainder did listen to other kinds of music, although many stipulated that it should meet certain conditions, for example that the lyrics should be free of sex, drugs and violence, and that it should not have an adverse effect on one's mood; or that it should be classical, religious or spiritual in nature. One of the women, who confined herself to religious or spiritual music, but not only percussion, felt that the believer should use his or her own discretion in this matter: 'I think Allah left it up to us to use our brain to decide what is right.' Of those who did listen to non-religious music, one said that she was trying not to (but without much success), and another said that she was planning to investigate the issue to ascertain whether or not music was *ḥalāl*. Only one interviewee did not express any reservations at all about music; he described himself as 'totally relaxed' about it, and continued: 'It's such a peripheral issue for me, and I wouldn't want to associate with people who take a hardline view on that. I love music and always have. You get puritans in every religion . . . you get hardliners and killjoys in all religions, but I'm not one of them.' Another said he listened to music every day and had a large collection on display, but said that he would turn it off if he felt that it was having a 'negative effect' on his state of mind.

Some converts explain the abstention from music in spiritual terms. Rahima, for example, said of her decision to stop listening to music other than *nashīd* (Islamic devotional music with only voice and percussion): 'I find it affects my kind of contemplation and my relationship with God, it

---

[93] Al-Qaradawi, 'Singing and Music'.
[94] Men who confine themselves to vocal and percussive music would generally not listen to the female singing voice as it is considered to be a potential source of temptation.

fills my head too much ... I feel that what I needed to get from music I can get from *nashīd*, and what I gained spiritually from music I can get from the Qur'an, so I don't feel like I'm missing out too much.' Timothy Bowes, author of a weblog entitled *The Neurocentric: the Journey of a Self-Centred Soul*, describes his transition to living without music in some detail:

> There was a time, back perhaps twelve years ago, when I would say 'I can't live without music.' It is interesting how times change. After eight years as a Muslim, during which I have more or less abstained from listening to song, I find there is not much I treasure more than peace ... I find this different kind of living also affects what my ears will now tolerate ... My tastes have completely altered ... What appeals to me now is the more gentle, the more raw, the more pure ... A lot of what I once considered beautiful music – that without which I believed I could not live – now seems like nothing but noise.[95]

He thus frames his abstention from music as a natural spiritual progression.

Several of the interviewees had found the transition to living without secular music difficult, and some were still struggling. One of these was Charlene: 'There was a time when I had to totally empty out my drawer because I kept on going back ... It's like "But I like Boyz II Men, that song, I really want to hear that song!"' The rule against music was not always strictly upheld in practice; Kavindra (among others) said that sometimes if music came on (for example on the television) she couldn't always bring herself to switch it off, because it was 'part of my youth'. Prabha had a more eclectic approach, having a general rule of not listening to music but making certain exceptions: 'Sometimes if I'm working out I like to listen to the Rocky soundtrack because I feel that it motivates me and *nashīd*s just don't – they don't have the tempo [laughing].'

I did not find any clear evidence among my interviewees that attitudes towards music softened over time, as longer-standing converts did not have more lenient attitudes towards music than others. However, there are examples of prominent Muslims who have undergone an evolution in attitudes, most notably Yusuf Islam (referred to below as Yusuf rather than Islam, to avoid ambiguity), formerly known as Cat Stevens. In an interview with *emel*, he speaks at some length about his musical journey:

---

[95] Bowes, 'At This Point in my Life'.

I became a Muslim and stopped singing. Contrary to popular opinion, I never gave it up irreversibly, but I suspended using my talents until I knew better . . . I was being advised that music was prohibited. At the time I didn't think for myself, but later I closely studied the sources of Islamic law and not just the fatwas . . . I discovered for myself the different views on music – there is no clear nass [religious text] against music itself but there are clearly dangers. It is not the music that is generally the problem, but all the other things that surround and accompany the entertainment industry which can lead one away from God.[96]

He comments further on his evolving stance on music in a BBC television documentary devoted to his musical career: 'When I learned something better I moved. And that's what you've got to do. I think we must not ever take the position that we know it all, God may show you something that you never knew yesteday, we've got to be ready for that.'[97] He gives a specifically religious justification for music: 'Music is around us everywhere. It is part of God's creation and harmony within the universe: the sound of rain falling on a lake; the gust of wind rushing through trees; the melody of birds singing – all this is music to be enjoyed and appreciated.' For Yusuf, music is a part of his *da'wah*: 'You have to speak to people in the language they understand and music is a universal language; it knows no racial, religious or national boundaries.'[98] The criticism directed at him following his return to instrumental music was strong enough to provoke Yusuf to post a fairly lengthy riposte on his official website, in an article entitled: 'Music: A Question of Faith or Da'wah?' In it he adduces several arguments in favour of music, including its potential beneficial effects (for example encouraging people in adverse conditions, as in Bosnia in the early 1990s), and its provision of 'an Islamic alternative' for young Muslims. He concludes that 'critics of my music and Da'wah should be aware that we are trying our best to show Muslims and non-Muslims the transcendent beauty and light of Islam, for this we must work within the media or our voices will never be heard'. Rasjid Topham, a founding member of the Yardbirds in the 1960s, underwent a similar journey, giving up music when he converted, partly through a desire to avoid the lifestyle associated with it, but returning to it later. He expresses regret over his former stance: 'For 17 years, through fear, I'd pushed aside

---

[96] Al-Rashid, 'Thinking about the Good Things to Come', p. 40.
[97] *Imagine . . . The Artist Formerly Known as Cat Stevens*, BBC1, 30 May 2006.
[98] Al-Rashid, 'Thinking about the Good Things to Come'.

and neglected a gift Allah gave to me . . . Denying that gift was wrong.' He hints at a synthesis between the spiritual and the musical when he describes how Islam has affected his musical style: 'I think it's much subtler . . . it's just being conscious of the fact that you can play in such a way that can touch people's feelings.'[99]

I asked interviewees whether they celebrated Christmas and birthdays, in the expectation that this might yield interesting insights into the ways in which converts accommodate (or do not accommodate) elements from their culture of upbringing into their Islamic identity.[100] Since the vast majority of British people do celebrate Christmas, and given the enormous hype surrounding it, a complete abstention from Christmas celebrations may to some extent signify a conscious rejection of prevailing norms in British culture and society. Converts hold a range of positions on the issue of celebrating Christmas, as do Muslims generally, but most are aware that there are several potentially problematic areas. Theologically, some find the celebration of the birthday of Jesus unacceptable (although a minority argue that there is no harm in it since he is a prophet according to Islam, and many Muslims celebrate *mawlid*, the birthday of Muhammad). Some prefer to avoid all the trappings of Christmas (e.g. cards and presents) on the basis of its pagan overtones, or on the grounds that no annual festival should be added to the two Eids which were instituted from the beginning of Islam (as specified in a *ḥadīth*); some object to the celebration of the *mawlid* on the same grounds. Socially, there may be problems with family gatherings such as the free mingling of the sexes (involving non-*maḥram* relatives or friends), or the consumption of alcohol (many converts do not feel comfortable in social gatherings where alcohol is being consumed, even though they may feel free to abstain themselves). As far as diet is concerned, those who enjoy good relations with their family of origin sometimes manage to find a compromise solution such as a *ḥalāl* turkey or a vegetarian option; others report that dietary matters cause friction or tension between themselves and other family members.

The majority of my interviewees (seventeen) said that they did not celebrate Christmas in any way. Of these, a few expressed very strong opinions to the effect that celebrating Christmas was 'completely against Islam,

---

[99] Rosser-Owen, 'A Top Brother'.
[100] Even some Asian converts with Hindu backgrounds were brought up to celebrate Christmas.

completely wrong', or that it was *shirk* (associating partners – in this case Jesus – with God, the worst sin according to the Qur'an), or that Christmas was a 'shocking pagan festival'. Apart from those seventeen, there was a certain amount of ambiguity and ambivalence among interviewees on this subject. For example, one woman who still lived at home with her family said that she did not celebrate Christmas, but went on to say: 'I'll give them cards and receive cards and everything but I don't sit down for a family meal or anything . . . I just take Christmas as another day, like they'll give me presents, I give them presents but I don't take them as Christmas presents.' Of those who said that they did celebrate in some way, all had some reservations about it and many had arrived at compromises, like the woman quoted above. Another woman had made a point of continuing to celebrate Christmas after her conversion for fear that otherwise her non-Muslim children (who in fact did convert later, in their teens) would 'hate Islam'. One man celebrated it for the sake of his elderly mother, who otherwise would not be able to celebrate: 'We make Christmas dinner for her and we'll buy her a present, but we don't do anything for it, and it's not for us, we don't feel we're celebrating it, we're doing something to make her feel happy and that's it.' Many had devised strategies to avoid giving offence to their parents or family of origin, or to try and retain the positive, family-bonding aspects of Christmas, whilst not celebrating Christmas itself. Amongst these strategies were moving the giving of presents and cards (or the family gathering) to New Year and including non-Muslim family members in Eid celebrations.

Attitudes towards birthday celebrations were slightly more relaxed, although thirteen people said that they did not celebrate birthdays at all. The main reason given for this was that Muhammad and the Companions (the first generation of Muslims) did not celebrate their birthdays. However, Rachel provided a counter-argument to this: 'The Prophet didn't celebrate birthdays not because he didn't agree with it, but because that just wasn't done at that time . . . I mean he didn't drive a car, he didn't have a computer, he didn't have a CD player, that doesn't mean those things are *ḥarām*, they just weren't around at that time.' Of those who did celebrate birthdays, some did so only for the children (often expressing concern that their children would be disenchanted with Islam if they felt deprived of something their peers were enjoying), and most did so in a low-key way, like Prabha: 'At the end of the day we don't stand around singing "Happy birthday to you", we don't copy the *jāhiliyyah* [age of ignorance] way of doing it, and we give thanks to Allah for what we've got, and I see no reason to not buy my husband a present, because I like buying him presents anyway.' Four interviewees said that their attitude to birthdays had softened over time, a pattern which did not emerge in relation to Christmas, presumably due to the fact that the theological objections to celebrating birthdays are weaker.

Some converts express impatience with what they perceive as the negative attitude of most Muslims towards festive occasions other than the two Eids. Batool al-Toma, who runs the New Muslims Project at the Islamic Foundation in Leicester, complains in a *Meeting Point* editorial that since she became Muslim

> strands in our community have, effortlessly and with great consistency, decried everything which they feel falls outside the Islamic framework from Mother's Day to Christmas, from birthdays to Valentine's Day. We are constantly introduced to the 'pagan' elements of such events and lambasted with the whole host of reasons why we should not involve ourselves under any circumstances . . . When it comes to Mother's day the Muslim line is 'every day is Mother's day', but quite honestly who of us remembers our Mother daily? . . . If Islam is all about kindness and appreciation of all things good . . . what can be wrong with a day to reflect upon the gift of a Mother and on an appropriate response for a lifetime of love and affection? Can the painful realities of a birthday and the fact that there is one year less to worship Allah or seek his forgiveness never be soothed with a slice of cake or scoop of ice cream shared with the family?[101]

It is interesting to observe that al-Toma couches her arguments in favour of Mother's Day and birthday celebrations in religious terms, lending weight to her points which are directed at a Muslim readership. The theme of *da'wah* also comes in: 'To share the story of Mary and the birth of Isa as we understand its beautiful narration in the Qur'an must surely be far more invigorating than ranting and raving about the origin of Christmas trees and such like . . . Who knows that such efforts may, by Allah's Mercy and the softening of hearts, [not] take a few more into the fold of Islam?'[102]

In addition to the lifestyle changes described above, some converts change their occupation on or relatively soon after conversion for religious

---

[101] Al-Toma, 'Enjoin Good . . .'.   [102] Ibid.

reasons. Kristiane Backer states that she gave up her job as a television presenter on MTV because it 'conflicted with my newly found values'.[103] Sakina, an interviewee, was working as a waitress when she converted and gradually came to the conclusion that she needed to leave the job: 'You take a while to realize that *rizq* [provision] comes from Allah, your provision comes from Allah, and it's not you that earns the money it's Allah that gives the provision, and Allah would never bless any provision that's *ḥarām*, so coming from serving alcohol and the whole free-mixing environment, I knew I had to leave.' Another major lifestyle change, that of settling temporarily or permanently in a Muslim country, will be discussed in chapter 4.

Although some converts have rejectionist attitudes towards elements of British culture such as music, Christmas and birthdays, I came across some interesting examples of cultural hybridity and synthesis among converts in the course of my research, from the grandmother whose daily routine includes tai-chi warm-ups, *Woman's Hour*, quilting and reading the works of Sufi scholars,[104] to the English convert who lives in Malaysia (having married a Malaysian woman), works as a freelance editor and proofreader, and is writing an Islamic science fiction novel and some English *nashīd* lyrics in his spare time.[105] Some converts convey a sense of positively relishing this cultural hybridity, drawing the best from different traditions. An American convert with a German background, 'Abu Sinan', writes on his blog: 'The Prophet (PBUH) [Peace Be Upon Him] was a great seeker of knowledge and that which is useful and he didn't care where it came from. To paraphrase . . . go even to China (a land of Kuffar) in search of knowledge . . . Because I listen to Amr Diab [a male Egyptian singer] and Asalah [a female Syrian singer] doesn't mean I have rejected or thrown out the complete works of Beethoven'; he goes on to say that his conversion to Islam hasn't changed his love of German culture at all.[106] One of my interviewees described herself as 'very English', and went on to say: 'I play a classical instrument, I go to the theatre, I love the last night of the Proms, I love traditional English art and English architecture,' adding: 'It is possible for me to like those things and be Muslim.' Hamza Yusuf's speeches incorporate a wide repertoire of cultural

---

[103] Alam and Izagaren, 'From Glamour to Glory'.
[104] 'A Day in the Life of . . .', in *Meeting Point*, 22, March 2001.
[105] 'A Day in the Life of . . .', in *Meeting Point*, 25, February 2002.
[106] See http://abusinan.blogspot.com/2005/11/recently-subject-of-convertsreverts.html (accessed 14/03/06).

references, from Confucius to Dickens to Thoreau to R.D. Laing, no doubt contributing to his broad appeal.

Isla Rosser-Owen, a second-generation convert and founder of the *Qalam* internet forum devoted to the literary arts, notes the potential importance of creative writing for Muslims: 'So many people are striving to find a voice, an outlet for their frustrations ... creative or reflective writing can be a much-needed catharsis, a therapy ... something an aggrieved individual, or indeed community, could no doubt benefit from.'[107] Converts figure prominently among the winners of literary competitions organized by the *Qalam* forum.[108] This is probably attributable to two interrelated factors: a greater desire or willingness among converts to engage in creative writing for cultural reasons (creative writing being highly valued in British culture);[109] and a greater facility with the English language and literary forms. It is not surprising, then, to find converts in the vanguard of Muslims calling for a change in attitudes towards the arts. The photographer Peter (Abd al-Adheem) Sanders expresses regret at the lack of appreciation for the arts in the British Muslim community, but senses a coming change.[110] Daniel Abdal-Hayy Moore, an American convert and poet, decries a certain narrow attitude to the arts which he senses among some Muslim communities:

One of the sad conflicts of our own psyches as Muslims is that for many years ... many people with huge talents ... have been made to feel guilty for expressing their artistic impulses, subjugated on all sides by hard rules and restrictions that go far beyond the simple halal/haram paradigms of Islam. Consequently, little cultivation of artistic talent has been developed, and it almost seems that only mediocrity is accepted as squeaking past the harsh gaze of the halal/haram police, since mediocrity at least is evidence that not much time has been taken away from worthier study and worship.[111]

In an *emel* editorial, Sarah Joseph observes the traditional bias of the British Muslim community in favour of scientific or social-scientific subjects such

---

[107] Rosser-Owen, 'In Search of a Muslim Literati'. For the *Qalam* website, see http://www.qalamonline.com.
[108] See *Q-News*, February 2006.
[109] Rosser-Owen comments on the large number of converts who entered the (2005) competition ('In Search of a Muslim Literati').
[110] Rahman, 'Framing Life'.
[111] Moore, 'Against Mediocrity'.

as law, medicine and engineering, and stresses the importance of encouraging young Muslims to go into areas such as 'art, music, film, photography, poetry, fashion design, media, graphic design' which are all 'of vital importance in the establishment of a more sophisticated and cultured faith expression'.[112]

CONTINUITY AND DISCONTINUITY

Converts' own perceptions of the changes that have occurred in their lives are in a sense inextricable from the changes themselves (and are therefore of interest in their own right);[113] this parallels the way in which the conversion process can only be discovered or accessed by the researcher through the medium of the convert's own narrative. As mentioned in chapter 1, conversion to Islam is typically more gradual and less dramatic than conversion to Christianity; Muslim converts commonly report that they studied and reflected for an extended period before taking the decision to convert. For many, the transitional process seems to span a long time, both before and after conversion. Some prospective converts 'try out' Islamic religious practices such as fasting before taking the decision to convert, sometimes in order to reassure themselves that they are capable of fulfilling the Islamic religious requirements. In fact, many converts do not identify a specific moment of conversion, but see their conversion as an ongoing process; while the *shahādah* marks a formal affiliation to Islam, the convert may have thought of him- or herself as a Muslim for months or even years previously.[114] On the other hand, there is often a period of transition and integration *after* conversion during which the convert learns how to do the prayers, gradually adopts a new style of dress and so on. For some, the *shahādah* is the beginning of a process of learning about Islam, both in theory and practice; conversion is commonly not just preceded, but also followed, by much reading and discussion on Islam, converts often taking to heart the

---

[112] Joseph, 'A Career Path for Tomorrow'; Fareena Alam, a born Muslim, makes a similar point ('Why I Reject the Anarchists Who Claim to Speak for Islam'), commenting that '[We have] few poets, painters or calligraphers. And we all know what such an imbalance can do to the psyche of a people.'

[113] Rambo, *Understanding Religious Conversion*, p. 119.

[114] See, e.g., Compton, 'The New Face of Islam', and McCall, 'Window on My World'.

Prophetic instruction to 'seek knowledge, even if it be in China'. In adopting the new religious identity converts tend to begin with the more private aspects of Islamic practice, or with practices that they only carry out with other Muslims, such as praying, while delaying the more visible changes, such as wearing the ḥijāb, until they feel ready to present themselves as Muslims to non-Muslims (and to answer the inevitable questions that will ensue).[115] A possible exception to this is abstention from alcohol, which most converts implement immediately, and which may entail revealing their new faith to non-Muslims.

Some people hesitate to convert out of fear of not being able to cope with the magnitude of the changes that they feel are required, especially the five daily prayers. Among Na'ima Robert's interviewees, Claire said: 'I could see Islam was the truth but I couldn't get away from seeing all the restrictions that it entailed as well'; Umm Muhammad was 'loath to give up her party lifestyle', whilst at the same time feeling that 'Islam came with a lot of obligations and I was afraid I wouldn't be able to fulfil them'.[116] Joe Ahmed-Dobson tells a reporter: 'I didn't want to say I was Muslim until I was sure I could live by it.'[117] This seemingly all-or-nothing approach to adopting a new religious identity may be illuminated by the concept of 'liminality', to which Hermansen draws attention in her study of American women converts, defining it as a transitional, anxiety-ridden state between detachment from the old and attachment to the new. She finds that those converts who make a complete change in lifestyle and a radical break with their past experience less liminality than those who do not.[118] Halima, an interviewee who converted at sixteen, described a phase of her life which illustrates both the experience of liminality and the need to take decisive action in order to go beyond it:

> Although I say I was Muslim when I was sixteen, when I went to university I was like any other teenager away from home for the first time. I wanted to go out and I wanted to have fun and I wanted to enjoy myself, and so that was difficult because after a while I started thinking, why am I saying I'm Muslim when I'm living a double life? If I was not wearing Islamic clothes, if somebody Muslim was coming towards me

[115] Bourque, 'Being British and Muslim', p. 9.
[116] Robert, *From my Sisters' Lips*, pp. 47–8.
[117] Petre, 'My Dad Buys me Books about Islam'.
[118] Hermansen, 'Two-Way Acculturation', p. 191.

I'd want to hide. Similarly if I was wearing Islamic dress and someone non-Muslim was coming I'd want to hide again, wondering what will they think and what will they say, so that was difficult. There came a point where I had to just say no and cut off, and just not answer the doorbell because if I answer the doorbell I'm going to end up going with them to the pub or something and I don't want to do that.

Some scholars draw attention to the personality changes that may occur as part of the conversion process.[119] In the social scientific literature, religious conversion is often seen as a decisive step entailing radical changes not just in personality but also in beliefs and values, both in the converts' own perception and in reality.[120] Of my interviewees, almost all felt that they had changed since their conversion in ways they attributed to their Islamic faith rather than to the natural process of maturation (although one or two acknowledged that it was difficult to tell the difference). They were asked an open question along the lines of: 'Do you feel that you've changed as a person as a result of your conversion, and if so, in what ways?'; the following categories are therefore overlapping and not mutually exclusive. Eight felt that they had become calmer, more patient or less angry, while six felt that they had become a better person in some way, for example less selfish, less materialistic and more altruistic or responsible. Fatima said that she had been a very angry person prior to her conversion, but that Islam had helped her to manage her anger. When I asked her how this had happened she said that it had 'sort of evaporated', and related it to the Qur'anic verse in which God says: 'He will remove the anger from their hearts' (9:15). Six people referred to changes in outlook or values, while four referred to changes in lifestyle, including abjuring drugs, violence, swearing, drinking and flirting. Several said that their basic personalities had not changed, but one of these drew a distinction between 'personality' and 'character' (in the sense of moral character), and felt that the latter had changed but not the former. A few said that they had become better sons or daughters (or in one case sister) as a result of their conversion. Kavindra was one such, but she felt that there were limits to personality change: 'We have a lot of family anger. I've tried to change that but I think some things in personality whether you change religion or not

---

[119] See, e.g., Parrucci, 'Religious Conversion'.
[120] See, e.g., Greil and Rudy, 'What Have we Learned from Process Models?', p. 317; Barker and Currie, 'Do Converts Always Make the Most Committed Christians?', p. 305; Gillespie, *The Dynamics of Religious Conversion*, p. 67.

are never going to change. I try my best, you do try and improve yourself, [but] you may not always achieve it.' Six of the interviewees felt that their awareness and understanding of other people had deepened; one of these was Rachel, who combines several of the more common responses: 'I'm much, much calmer than I used to be, probably a much better daughter, partner and sister than I would have been before, because I feel that I'm just more considerate, more aware of other people's emotions and feelings, and that comes from having a spiritual side to you I think.' Several others also mentioned spiritual changes – in particular, awareness of God was cited as a key difference between the pre- and post-conversion periods – while one said that she had lost her fear of death, which she experienced as 'an enormous sense of relief'. One or two were reluctant to comment on improvements in their character as they felt that to do so would be tantamount to boasting, and contrary to Islamic *adab* (etiquette or way of behaving).

Interviewees were also asked about changes in their Islamic faith or practice since their conversion, and only two felt that this had not changed at all. Not surprisingly, many (eleven) said that they had become more knowledgeable, or better able to distinguish between different scholars or factions in Islam, or more confident in deriving their own interpretations from the sources. Two of the women, with reference to the difficulties of being a convert, said they had become more confident vis-à-vis the wider Muslim community, and felt less need to justify or defend themselves on Islamic issues. Thirteen interviewees mentioned that they had become more tolerant, especially of other Muslims. One of these was Sulayman, who had been a Muslim for almost twenty years: 'I'm probably more willing to accept people for what they are and Muslims for what they are. If I'd met somebody Sufi a few years ago I just didn't want to talk to them because I just didn't like Sufis and that was it. But now I've just met too many nice Sufis, and I realized that that's just not how it works. So I just take people for what they are and if you can influence them fine and if you can't it's okay.' It was not only the longer-standing converts who reported such changes; one woman who had only been Muslim for four years felt that she had become 'a lot more tolerant of other people's views and it being okay that I have a different view'. Amin said that he used to get into a lot of arguments but was now more prepared to let things go, while Yaqub said that his attitude towards mainstream society had softened: 'I thought that you had to be completely apart from society, wrongly, incorrectly, and that the Muslims had to be on their guard against all these evils coming in. Then I realized of course that if one has that message [i.e. Islam] then one has to pass that message as much as possible and go about your life in the real world which means not hiding or cocooning yourself.' Two interviewees said that they had become surer of their faith and had fewer doubts as time progressed, while three said that they had become stricter, more disciplined or more 'orthodox' in the application of their faith. One of these gave an example: 'If I've got one hair showing, Allah will account me on that so I'm always checking my hair because we don't wear *ḥijāb* for fashion or any other reason, this is a *farḍ* [obligatory act]'; she mentioned almost in the same breath that her love for her Creator had grown.[121] Another woman, who was affiliated to a Sufi order, said that she had been granted a love for the Prophet and that her faith had become more 'inward'.

Some converts emphasize the discontinuity with their former lives and selves, as does a convert writing on a New Muslims Project website as a Muslim of almost two years. He describes the period immediately after his conversion in the following terms: 'In the space of a week my whole character shifted, it was quite uncanny and scary to kind of watch yourself change so much in such a short period of time.' He writes a poem which portrays the change in dramatic terms: 'Who was that man I remember?/ He disappeared when I was born in cold November./ ... I continue wearing his clothes still, / as a small remembrance of him,/ though he has gone and his body I now fill/ ... will he ever return, is there anything to fear?/ No! He won't return no matter how hard he tries!'[122] American convert Abdul-Lateef Abdullah, contributing to the *Islam for Today* website, also paints a picture which seems to emphasize discontinuity: 'Every piece of "us" must change, must undergo examination and renewal to arrive at truth ... It is nothing less than the total renewal of the person, from top to bottom.' However, when he speaks of his own change, the picture is more nuanced: 'Although I am still very much the same person as I was three years ago, how I experience the world and how I view it and life has completely changed. Life is the same, yet different ... When I look at myself today as opposed to three years ago, I see two

[121] In Islam, and especially in Sufism (although this woman is not a Sufi), it is not uncommon for scrupulous adherence to the law to accompany the idea of the love of God, while in Christianity the two have sometimes been seen as antagonistic.
[122] Mannion, 'Dawud's Story'.

different people. No, rather I see two people with many of the same attributes, but in completely different places.' He goes on to liken his self three
years ago to being 'in a badly damaged shelter', while today it is 'in a much
better shelter, one that protects me as long as I stay in it and don't leave it'.[123]
Both of the above examples are relatively new converts, and it may be that
they would have a different view a few years down the line.

Others take a different view of the past. Timothy Bowes, an English
Muslim convert of eight years, writes in an article on his blog entitled 'The
Legacy of my Christian Upbringing':

> Much of who I am, how I act and what I think are a legacy of my
> Christian upbringing. I am not ashamed of this and do not think I
> should be. This upbringing taught me good manners and modesty
> after all, both of them perfectly admirable Islamic characteristics. And
> there is more: concerns about global justice and social responsibility . . .
> I do not consider Islam a negation of my upbringing, but a continua-
> tion of it . . . a perfection of it.[124]

Contributors to a *Meeting Point* discussion on the subject of 'Conversion –
Rejection or Continuation of my Upbringing?' by and large emphasize continuity.[125] One man highlights the positive lessons he drew from his
upbringing: 'Certain basic ethical values of my parents have stayed with me
. . . Doing the "right thing" whatever others may think of you, respecting others, that love was worth more than anything and that we all have a responsibility to do what we can to promote better social justice . . . I saw coming to
Islam as a change of way and not a rejection of my past'. A female contributor expresses a similar sentiment, saying that her parents would never have
dreamed of cohabiting before marriage: 'I am really closer to my original
upbringing than I had previously thought.'[126] Another man describes how

---

[123] Abdullah, 'Understanding Conversion'.
[124] Bowes, 'The Legacy of my Christian Upbringing'.
[125] Continuity seems to prevail over discontinuity as a discursive strand among al-Qwidi's
sample too. Most said that their conversion was a return to their real selves rather than a transformation, and saw themselves as the same person. For most, Islam was seen as a culmination
of previous knowledge and outlook, rather than a break or diversion (al-Qwidi,
'Understanding the Stages of Conversion to Islam', pp. 233, 203 and 211).
[126] Allievi observes that for some Italian converts, the cognitive dissonance arising from the
culture gap between their original Italian identity and the adopted Muslim identity can be
minimized if they come from a traditional family; for example, they may have had a strict

he has taken more interest in the various Muslim cultures than his own English culture in recent years, but says: 'I no longer think that it is very easy to escape one's upbringing . . . In other words, one's rejection is also just another kind of continuity. My observation over the years is that converts to Islam retain many elements of our class roots and other types of social distinction, as well as our formative experiences once we enter the huge world of Islam.'[127]

The last two contributions hint at what seems to be a common trajectory among converts, an initial degree of rejectionism followed by greater integration and acceptance of the past life, and therefore past self. Roald, studying Scandinavian converts, observes that 'as time goes by, the social structure into which one is primarily socialised tends to resurface', and that converts may experience a desire to return to their original roots, having perhaps already progressed from a parochial to a more universal form of Islam.[128] Some converts express regret that they felt the need to make such drastic changes, and look on their former selves as overzealous. Sarah Joseph, who converted at the age of sixteen, says: 'I was very forceful in my wanting to be a Muslim – maybe too forceful in many ways. I could have been more tactful and that would have been better.'[129] Batool al-Toma writes in a *Meeting Point* editorial about her mother's dying and the regrets it precipitated in her:

> Long before she became ill . . . I knew I had much to seek forgiveness for from my Mother – not least the fact that I had put so much emphasis on issues like Halal food and the wearing of a scarf in those turbo charged days of early conversion not fully realizing the words of the Prophet Muhammad 'Make things easy, don't make them difficult. Speak gently and with wisdom not with confrontation and catastrophe.' Perhaps if I had gotten the priorities like the concept of *Tawhid* – One God, and matters relating to the inwardly spiritual rather than the outwardly visible right, things might have been different.

upbringing, or their mothers or they themselves may have worn long clothes when they were children (*Les Convertis à l'Islam*, p. 262). Dissonance is reduced too when a certain moral ethos obtained in the family of origin, as in the case of the convert just quoted.

[127] 'Point of View', in *Meeting Point*, 26, June 2002.
[128] Roald, *New Muslims in the European Context*, pp. 282 and 257–9.
[129] Internet discussion, 'My Journey to Islam', 27 January 2004, http://www.islamonline.net/livedialogue/english/Browse.asp?hGuestID=s3WmL5 (accessed 09/06/05).

She regrets in particular not having discussed with her family either her conversion or her sudden marriage, and that both 'were landed on them with the subtlety of a sledge hammer and followed by those awfully long and painfully tense years'.[130]

The initial tendency of some converts to effect extreme and sudden identity changes is parodied by an American convert who writes about the disease of 'convertitis': 'We see that Jane has changed her name to "A'isha", is wearing full niqaab (black only), buying everything (even potato chips – which she may stop buying as it is "imitation of the kufar"[unbelievers]) from the halaal market, getting into interfaith debates at her job . . . and considering accepting a marriage proposal to be a co-wife.'[131] Abdal-Hakim Murad, who initially coined the term 'convertitis', describes this mindset as absolutist: 'Everything going on among pious Muslims is angelic; everything outside the circle of faith is demonic. The appeal of this outlook lies in its simplicity. The newly rearranged landscape upon which the convert looks is seen in satisfying black and white terms of Them versus Us, good against evil.' He finds this phenomenon understandable given the speed with which the convert has to establish a new identity, unlike for example the Indian Muslim immigrant who over time gradually adopts a British identity. He adds that 'fortunately, it [this condition] almost always wears off'.[132] A letter from a convert to *Q-News* illustrates the difficulty of integrating such sudden changes:

> I began practising Islam after the events of September 11th . . . I grew a beard, put on a *topi* [Muslim cap] and raised my joggers above my ankles. Since the change in lifestyle, I have encountered one obstacle after another . . . I am 17 and have my whole life ahead of me but what is the point of studying so hard when no employer will hire a bearded man wearing a *jubbah* [Muslim overcoat]? Is it wrong for me to expect to be hired for my knowledge and skills, rather than my appearance? I feel like it is just going to get worse and the only remedy is to exclude myself from everything and just keep myself engaged in the remembrance of my Creator.[133]

---

[130] Al-Toma, 'Your Mother, your Mother, your Mother . . .'. Batool said that she received many phone calls from converts with similar misgivings after the publication of this editorial (interview with the author, 13 December 2006).

[131] Saraji Umm Zaid, 'Convertitis – or the Case of the Insta-Scholar', http://www.islamfortoday. com/ummzaid02.htm (accessed 04/08/04).

[132] Murad, 'British and Muslim?'   [133] Letter in *Q-News*, 352, December 2003.

Given this person's youth and the relative newness of his conversion, it may be that he will achieve more of a *modus vivendi* with the society in which he grew up in the future; which is not to justify the prejudice encountered.

CONCLUDING REMARKS

Most Muslim converts experience substantive and lasting change in many areas of life. Hermansen describes four options which are available to converts with regard to expression of identity: not to express overtly their Muslim identity; to express it in certain (e.g. Islamic) contexts; to express it in all contexts but to continue to be involved and integrated in Western society; and finally, to modify their lifestyle totally.[134] Köse and al-Qwidi found that converts' Islamic identity is central to their dealings with the Muslim community but not to their dealings in mainstream society, suggesting conformity to the second option.[135] This is illustrated by the use of Arabic-Islamic and Western names in Muslim and non-Muslim contexts respectively; the same applies to men who wear Western dress in one context and Muslim/Islamic dress in another. However, for women who wear the *ḥijāb* the situation is different, since their appearance marks them out as Muslim in all public contexts, so they would not fall into either of the first two of Hermansen's categories. In my own study of British Muslim converts I found only one who conformed to the first option, none to the fourth option, with the vast majority falling into the second and third categories: expressing their Islamic identity, but not necessarily in all contexts, with a continued involvement in British society. The extensive changes in the lives of most converts did not generally result in them becoming alienated from the wider world, although there was often a degree of separateness with regard to social activities.[136] As Roald points out, many converts, like second-generation Muslims, develop 'integrated plural identities'.[137]

---

[134] Hermansen, 'Two-Way Acculturation', p. 193.
[135] Köse, *Conversion to Islam*, p. 134; al-Qwidi, 'Understanding the Stages of Conversion to Islam', p. 215.
[136] This is also the finding of Köse (*Conversion to Islam*, p. 134) and al-Qwidi ('Understanding the Stages of Conversion to Islam', p. 177).
[137] Roald, *New Muslims in the European Context*, p. 285, citing S. Ostberg, 'Islamic Nurture and Identity Management', *British Journal of Religious Education*, 1, 2000, pp. 91–103.

Adolescence is often regarded as a crucial stage in identity formation, and conversion studies in the past have often found it to be the stage of life when most conversions to Christianity occur, thus highlighting the close link between religious conversion and identity achievement. As discussed in chapter 1, converts to Islam in the European and North American contexts are generally well past adolescence at the time of conversion, and this suggests that for these converts identity formation does not go hand in hand with religious conversion in the same way.[138] Al-Qwidi finds that the transition to Islam is not about identity achievement but rather about consolidating 'realistic long-term commitments'.[139] It does seem however that for some converts, becoming a Muslim facilitates the integration of aspects of their identity, and that this may be a motivating factor in the conversion.[140] For example, Emira Topham had a child with a long-standing convert (who was lapsed at the time), married him, and then converted (in that order). She describes her own conversion as a step which 'married up the inside and outside'. She felt that her family benefited too, and it was 'easier to establish Islamic guidelines in the home'.[141] Hilary Saunders, speaking four weeks after converting, says: 'I would almost describe it as "coming out", because a part of me that has been important, but always very private, is now out in the open.'[142] Abd-ul-Waahid Bruce Paterson describes the integration in more cognitive terms: 'The Qur'an is like a text book guide to life. In it you will find answers to all questions. For me, everything I had learnt about all the different religions, everything that I knew to be true, fitted together like pieces of a jigsaw puzzle. I had all the pieces all along but I just did not know how to fix them together.'[143] These examples suggest a dialectical relationship between conversion and identity change: someone who is drawn to convert is, almost by definition, seeking to change, integrate or validate some aspect or aspects of their identity, whilst at the same time, conversion itself may lead to changes in their identity which were unforeseen.

---

[138] Köse suggests Erikson's 'moratorium' period, a time when the religious quest is dormant during young adulthood, as a useful concept with regard to conversion to Islam (*Conversion to Islam*, p. 66).
[139] Al-Qwidi, 'Understanding the Stages of Conversion to Islam', pp. 139–40.
[140] This aspect of conversion is strongly emphasized by Wohlrab-Sahr in 'Conversion to Islam' and 'Symbolizing Distance'.
[141] Berrington, 'Islam Sheds its Image'.
[142] Saunders, 'Why I Took the Hijab'.
[143] Paterson, 'My Journey to Islam'.

It is worth reflecting on the extent to which converts to Islam maintain their Islamic identity over time. In pre-modern societies, and in some contemporary societies (notable among them Muslim ones), the social structure supports and affirms a religious worldview; clearly this is not the case in modern secular societies, in which the maintenance of a religious identity requires a certain effort. It has been famously said by Berger and Luckmann that 'to have a conversion experience is nothing much. The real thing is to be able to keep on taking it seriously; to retain a sense of its plausibility.'[144] The encouragement, guidance and 'sponsorship' of the receiving religious community is said to be vital in order for the convert to remain converted.[145] No doubt this is true of many converts to Islam, but al-Qwidi's study finds some evidence to the contrary. Although most of her interviewees expressed disappointment with the level of support they received from the Muslim community, all had successfully maintained their commitment to their religious faith and practice in spite of that.[146] One of my own interviewees was so thoroughly disillusioned by his experiences of the Muslim community, including converts, that he had very little interaction with Muslims at all, apart from his wife; yet he maintained a strong commitment to Islamic theological beliefs, in particular *tawḥīd*, and was still a practising Muslim several years after his conversion. It is difficult to give an accurate picture of religious staying power in the absence of any empirical study of those who relapse; it is not always easy to identify and locate such people.

To observe the degree to which Islamic religious identity is transmitted to the next generation is beyond the scope of this study. I did ask my interviewees whether they were optimistic about bringing their children up as practising Muslims in a non-Muslim society such as Britain, and many felt that it was (or would be, in the case of those who did not yet have children) a struggle; several expressed a desire to bring their children up in a Muslim country if possible. Between them, the interviewees had a total of six children who were eighteen or over, and of those, only one (unlike his/her three adult siblings) was not practising.[147] Hermansen has observed the

[144] Berger and Luckmann, *The Social Construction of Reality*, p. 145.
[145] Fowler, *Stages of Faith*, pp. 286–7; cf. Rambo, *Understanding Religious Conversion*, p. 170.
[146] Al-Qwidi, 'Understanding the Stages of Conversion to Islam', pp. 212–13.
[147] I am not including here the adult children of one of the male interviewees, as these children had stayed with their non-Muslim mother when their parents divorced following their father's conversion.

transmission of Muslim female identity in a study of eleven American convert women (in their late forties and above) and their daughters (nineteen in all) aged fifteen or over. Although she describes the Muslim identity of the daughters as 'strong', with most of them choosing to marry Muslim husbands, she also found that three of the daughters had 'left Islam', and a further nine were considered by their mothers to have 'less Muslim identity' than they themselves. Only a quarter wore the *ḥijāb*, compared to three-quarters of the mothers. However, Hermansen also points out that changing circumstances, such as demographic shifts and wider availability of Islamic education, mean that this finding may only hold true for that particular age cohort.[148]

National identity does not figure prominently in converts' discourse, although some converts have challenged exclusive concepts of Britishness which potentially marginalize Muslims.[149] Overall there was little evidence of Islamic ideological influence on ideas of Britishness (hardly any, for example, made a point of saying that they were 'Muslim first, British second'), despite the fact that converts generally have strong views on British foreign policy. Partly due to colonial history (and current events), it was difficult for converts to feel much sense of pride in being British, whereas Irish, Scots, Welsh and to some extent English belonging did not have the same stigma. Overall, convert views on Britishness do not seem dramatically different from those of born Muslims; however, the latter are more likely to have suffered racism and discrimination, leading to a sense of exclusion and a decreased likelihood of identifying with 'Britishness'. Ethnicity (e.g. Irish, Asian, Caribbean) seems to be something that can be accommodated within the cultural diversity of Islam, and is therefore not generally seen by converts as problematic.

For converts to Islam, as well as for many born Muslims, religious identity is a public as well as a private matter. Women who wear the *ḥijāb* are, as observed by Badran, 'assertively putting religion back into public space'.[150] Allievi lists some of the main functions of the *ḥijāb* for converts as follows: 'It helps women to convert . . . to keep to the new choice, to "enter" it in a radical way . . . It helps them to be accepted by the new "significant others" . . . It

---

[148] Hermansen, 'Keeping the Faith', pp. 266, 265 and 272–3.
[149] See, e.g., Seddon, 'Locating the Perpetuation of "Otherness"' and 'British Muslims or Muslims in Britain?; Joseph, 'The Future of our History'.
[150] Badran, 'Feminism and Conversion', p. 204.

helps them to establish and maintain the *haram/halal* frontiers: which in themselves, in the Western context, are shifting, unclear, and not at all stable';[151] many of these points were borne out by my interviewees. The hostility encountered by women who wear *ḥijāb* usually has the effect of reinforcing their Islamic identity,[152] in much the same way as the Rushdie Affair had the effect of strengthening the Islamic component of British Muslim identity. For some of the minority of women who choose to cover their face, *niqāb* is on a continuum with *ḥijāb* and represents a further strengthening of their Muslim identity; it can also be associated with an enhanced spirituality, or with reinforcing sexual or gender boundaries.[153]

With regard to lifestyle changes, a question might arise as to the causal relationship between Islamic tenets and cultural practice: to what extent do converts reorganize their lives in accordance with Islamic teachings, and to what extent do they interpret Islamic teachings in such a way as to accommodate their cultural preferences? One convert might, for example, choose to see Christmas and birthdays as harmless cultural phenomena because of their importance to family members and to themselves, while another might give up such celebrations despite their emotional attachment to them, because they believe that this is what Islam requires.[154] It is not always easy to tell the difference, but it does seem to be the case that religious or spiritual considerations sometimes transcend or supersede personal preferences, so that there may be an element of 'sacrifice', even though Muslim converts would be unlikely to use that term, for reasons explained earlier. On more than one occasion, interviewees told me that they had hesitated to accept the most lenient scholarly opinion on a particular issue for fear of doing so out of their own selfish desires (based on the Qur'anic condemnation of 'those who follow their own desires [*ahwā'*]'). Several interviewees

---

[151] Allievi, 'The Shifting Significance of the *Halal/Haram* Frontier', p. 145.

[152] However, a few do take it off; see, e.g., ibid., p. 144.

[153] In late 2006, heated public debate followed comments by Jack Straw (then Leader of the House of Commons), and then Tony Blair, which strongly implied that the *niqāb* represented an obstacle to the integration of British Muslims. I did not find any evidence that wearing the *niqāb* was accompanied by a general rejection of, or unwillingness to 'integrate' into, British society. Of course, accusations of failing to integrate are rather more likely to be directed at Muslims who constitute ethnic minorities than at converts.

[154] These examples are intended to indicate a spectrum; in reality, of course, every individual is influenced to a greater or lesser degree, consciously or unconsciously, by their personal experience, preconceptions, inclinations, etc.

mentioned 'reward' (i.e. in the afterlife) as a motivation for obeying God or doing good deeds, even if this went against their personal inclination.[155] One of these was Sakina, who spoke on the subject of the comprehensive guidance available to Muslims:

> Whenever you have a problem, you just go to the books or you go to Qur'an or you go to a Shakyh, and they will tell you what you do in this situation, and if you fear Allah, you love Allah and you want the best for your *ākhirah* [Hereafter], you might not think it's the best thing for you in the *dunyah* [this life] . . . The reward that you're going to get in the *ākhirah*, that's what counts and that's what will make you do the right thing in the *dunyah*.

Like the belief in the Hereafter, the belief in a God who is active in the world has an impact on choices and behaviour; such a belief encourages converts to take steps which they find daunting. A few of the interviewees who had at first found it difficult to take on the *ḥijāb* said that Allah had 'made it easy' for them. One of these recounted how she had prayed: 'Allah please, do I have to? Do I have to?' before putting it on the following day; another felt at first that she looked like 'an old granny', but said to herself: 'I'm doing this for Allah, I'm doing this for Allah, I'm doing this for Allah.'

Many Muslims would say that the question of music is one in which there are allowable differences of opinion (*ikhtilāf*) between religious scholars. It is interesting, in the light of this, that the majority of my inter-viewees chose to abstain from listening to secular or instrumental (as opposed to purely vocal or percussive) music, although I found relatively little tendency among those who abjured music to condemn those who held a different opinion.[156] As Allievi observes, converts are often stricter on the subject of music than born Muslims.[157] I believe this would still be the case even if one were to compare them exclusively to *practising* born Muslims; this may reflect the fact that there are no major Muslim cultures in which

---

[155] Interestingly, Franks's study of Muslim and Christian revivalist women found that while the Muslim women were quite comfortable with the idea of 'reward' and sometimes cited it as motivation for doing good deeds, the Christians felt it was inappropriate to do things in expectation of reward, even if it be otherworldly: *Women and Revivalism in the West*, p. 106.

[156] An exception to this was the interviewee who said: 'There's a lot of converts who go in for this Islamic poetry, Islamic comedy and Islamic music, it's just like, what do they know about Islam?'

[157] Allievi, *Les Convertis à l'Islam*, p. 210.

music (including instrumental music) does not play a part. Converts are generally conscientious in following religious precepts as they understand them, and tend to avoid anything that might be doubtful. There is evidence to suggest that for some young Muslims in the UK, music is becoming a way in which to enhance their Islamic identity, with the rise of Islamic rap-groups or 'boy bands' providing an alternative to the Western secular music scene. While some of these groups confine themselves to *nashīd*, many use instruments other than percussion.[158] Mecca2Medina, an Islamic rap group who are all British-born converts, give a possible explanation for the increasing popularity of such groups in an interview with *emel*. One of the group members, Ismael, tells how Muslim audiences were apprehensive at first, being unsure as to the Islamic permissibility of the music, but talks of a change of mood since 9/11: 'Many Muslims felt it was necessary to show the world we're not members of a religion which enslaves its followers but in fact are part of a beautiful faith that allows them to celebrate their culture and be proud of who they are. Our music is a way of doing that.'[159] Judging by convert attitudes to music described in this chapter, it would seem that the function of this music in enhancing Islamic identity applies more to born Muslims than to converts.

I found little correlation between attitudes to music, Christmas and birthdays and factors such as length of time since conversion and Islamic orientation. Predictably, the four interviewees who could be regarded as *salafī* in orientation did not listen to secular music or celebrate Christmas, but then the same was true of the majority of the interviewees as a whole. Although Sufism tends to be accommodating of cultural diversity and the arts, almost half of those with Sufi tendencies abstained (or endeavoured to abstain) from listening to instruments other than percussion; this may be explained by the fact that some Sufis are strongly *sharīʿah*-oriented and associate piety with a fairly strict adherence to its provisions. Perhaps the most significant variable is personal experience and disposition, which is not quantifiable, though one can cite examples like that of Peter Sanders, a

---

[158] As shown in the BBC documentary *Boyz Allowed: The New Voices of Islam* (BBC1, 24 October 2006), the controversy which follows these groups revolves not just around the issue of instrumental music but also around the issue of what may be seen as Islamically inappropriate behaviour at concerts, with young and teenage girls in particular expressing their enthusiasm for the band members.

[159] Hafeez, 'Mecca2Medina', p. 87.

prominent Muslim photographer whose grandfather, whom he much admired as a boy, was also a photographer.

On cultural issues there seems to be something of a tension between a vocal minority, with relatively liberal and inclusivist views (as seen for example in the more progressive Muslim media such as *Q-News* and *emel*), and a quieter majority, who are occupied with applying religious precepts as best they can and trying to avoid 'doubtful' areas, as recommended in a well-known *ḥadīth*. To describe this as a polarization would probably be an exaggeration, given the popularity of Hamza Yusuf (when interviewees were asked about which Islamic scholars or thinkers they respected, he was easily the most frequently mentioned individual).[160] Yusuf's integrationist and inclusivist approach, illustrated below, coexists with a deep respect for traditional Islam.

The paradox that Muslims in some ways perceive greater continuity with their former lives and selves than do Christians, despite the fact that they usually effect greater changes in their external lives, may be partly explained by the prevalence of different discursive patterns in Christianity and Islam, rooted to some extent in the contrasting teachings of the two faiths. While in Christianity (especially among Evangelicals) there is an emphasis on the convert as a repentant sinner who needs to be 'born again', in Islam there is a sense of returning to a natural, God-given identity with which the convert was born (thus the concept of 'reversion').[161] The issue of continuity is also discursively related to attitudes to Western or British society: those wishing to emphasize the compatibility between Islam and the West, and to highlight the desirability of the integration of Muslims into mainstream society, are likely to see their upbringing in terms of continuity.[162] In the following passage by Hamza Yusuf, this connection is explicit:

[160] As mentioned in chapter 1, eight people mentioned Hamza Yusuf, compared with a maximum of three for any other figure. Although one or two mentioned Tariq Ramadan, some others felt that he compromised too much with Western values in his approach.

[161] Some scholars of religious conversion have found a tendency among converts to denounce their pre-conversion lives as sinful (see, e.g., Ullman, *The Transformed Self*, p. 15), but this is generally not the case with converts to Islam. See Köse, *Conversion to Islam*, p. 128; al-Qwidi, 'Understanding the Stages of Conversion to Islam', p. 207.

[162] As Moll points out, some converts describe their conversion as a direct function of the compatibility of Islam with Western civilization, as in the following quote: 'Islam and the West are highly compatible. I don't think you would have so many people converting to Islam otherwise' ('"Beyond Beards, Scarves and Halal Meat"').

We Muslims are unpersuaded by many triumphalist claims made for the West, but are happy with its core values. As a Westerner, a child of civil rights and anti-war activists, I embraced Islam not in abandonment of my core values, drawn almost entirely from the progressive tradition, but as an affirmation of them . . . never have the universals [of Islamic law] come into conflict with anything my progressive Californian mother taught me. Instead, I have marvelled at how most of what Western society claims as its own highest ideals are deeply rooted in Islamic tradition . . . Not only can our civilizations co-exist in our respective parts of the world, they can co-exist in the individual human heart, as they do in mine.[163]

[163] Yusuf, 'Islam Has a Progressive Tradition Too'.

Chapter 4

Society and politics

Muslims have been vocal critics of Western civilization and society for several generations now. Sayyid Qutb's description of life in America, where he stayed from 1948 to 1950, sounds curiously modern, as if it might be more applicable to today's America than that of half a century ago. Anticipating many subsequent critiques of Western society, Qutb describes America as a country of 'extreme wealth, and indulgent pleasure', relating his impressions of Americans as follows:

> I saw them there as nervous tension devoured their lives despite all the evidence of wealth, plenty, and gadgets that they have. Their enjoyment is nervous excitement, animal merriment. One gets the image that they are constantly running from ghosts that are pursuing them. They are as machines that move with madness, speed, and convulsion that does not cease. Many times I thought it was as though the people were in a grinding machine that does not stop day or night, morning or evening. It grinds them and they are devoured without a moment's rest. They have no faith in themselves or in life around them.[1]

Qutb was also dismayed by the sexual mores of mid-twentieth-century America. In *The America I Have Seen*, he describes what he witnessed at a dance in a provincial church hall: 'They danced to the tunes of the gramophone, and the dance floor was replete with tapping feet, enticing legs, arms wrapped around waists, lips pressed to lips, and chests pressed to chests. The

---

[1] Quoted in Rippin, *Muslims*, p. 236; original source Sayyid Qutb, *Fi'l-Tarikh: Fikrah wa-Minhaj.*

atmosphere was full of desire.'[2] The same themes – a loss of spirituality, and the resulting materialism and permissiveness – continue to resonate with Muslim commentators on Western societies today.

Qutb was describing life in America as an 'outsider'; some of his con-temporaries, however, were converts engaging in cultural criticism of the civilization in which they grew up. These included the Austrian-born Muhammad Asad (1900–92) and the American Jewish Maryam Jameelah (b. 1934), both of whom spent (or, in Jameelah's case, has spent) most of their adult lives in Muslim countries.[3] Some of the most sophisticated and sustained critiques have come from the 'perennial philosophers' who include many high-profile converts among their number, such as the French philosopher René Guénon (1886–1951)[4] and the Englishmen Martin Lings (1909–2005) and Hasan Le Gai Eaton (b. 1921). The perennialists lament the decline of traditional societies (seen as repositories of the eternal wis-dom), and the loss of spirituality in the Western, modernized world. They view the European Renaissance as a retrograde step, presaging a movement away from Christianity and towards humanism and paganism.

In *The Eleventh Hour: The Spiritual Crisis of the Modern World in the Light of Tradition and Prophecy,* Lings laments the fact that religion and belief in God have given way to agnosticism and atheism in Western soci-eties. He describes rationalism and scientism as constituting 'the pseudo-religion of the modern world', with their mistaken belief that 'man has progressed throughout the ages and that he will inevitably continue to progress in the future'. According to Lings, Islamic civilization and modern civilization are incompatible.[5] Similarly, Eaton sees modern Western civi-lization, like Islamic civilization, as an organic whole, denying that it is pos-sible to take the good from it and leave the bad. He sees those Islamic modernists who wish to demonstrate Islam's compatibility with contempo-rary thought and 'the moral and philosophical norms of European civiliza-tion' as 'the "Uncle Toms" of Islam'.[6] It is not made clear, though, what it

[2] Quoted in R. Siegel, 'Sayyid Qutb's America', http://www.npr.org/templates/story/story. php?storyId=1253796.
[3] For their critique, see, e.g., Asad's *Road to Mecca* (London: Max Reinhardt, 1954) and *Islam at the Crossroads* (Lahore: Arafat Publications, 1975), and Jameelah's *Islam versus the West* (Lahore: Sh. Muhammad Ashraf, 1962).
[4] See, e.g., Guénon, *The Crisis of the Modern World* (Varanasi: Indica Books, 2002).
[5] Lings, *The Eleventh Hour*, pp. 17 and 51.
[6] Eaton, *Islam and the Destiny of Man*, pp. 25–6.

would mean in practice to reject modern civilization as a whole, and matters are hardly clarified by Lings' suggestion that a small group of intellectuals (i.e. those in sympathy with the perennial philosophy) might 're-establish a traditional framework for themselves and have the spiritual benefits it offers, while keeping the modern world at bay by all sorts of compromises which only they would know how to make'.[7]

Although the perennial philosophers may sound similar to Qutb in their radical rejection of Western civilization, they are far removed from his brand of political radicalism and religious exclusivism, and believe that all religions contain within them the seeds of the eternal wisdom. According to Eaton, the divide that emerged over the Rushdie Affair is not between two cultures, but between an 'uncompromising religious world-view' and a non-religious one: 'The distinction between religion and irreligion has become blurred in the West. In the Islamic world it cuts like a knife.' In his view, 'religion cannot survive, whole and effective, when it is confined to one single compartment of life and education. Religion is either all or it is nothing; either it dwarfs all profane studies or it is dwarfed by them.'[8] Eaton speaks of the 'degeneration' that has taken place in his lifetime, and feels that there is a marked contrast between the values of Muslims and modern Western values. He is not optimistic about the direction in which Western society is going, and sees in its contemporary manifestation the signs of civ- ilizational breakdown: 'I find it difficult to believe that this culture can go on as it is, all that much longer . . . Where we are going I do not know.'[9] Lings is reported to have felt, in his last years, that the world was 'on the brink of some great purification'.[10]

One person who stands out in the British context in terms of taking an oppositional stand vis-à-vis Western society is the Scottish convert Shaykh 'Abd al-Qadir as-Sufi (also known as Ian Dallas), founder of the now global Murabitun movement. Initially part of the 1960s counter-culture, 'Abd al- Qadir converted to Islam in Morocco in the 1960s and returned to London where he began to acquire a following which at that time consisted almost entirely of converts. According to Köse, a critical attitude towards Western civilization was a precondition for joining the movement.[11] 'Abd al-Qadir's

---

[7] Lings, *The Eleventh Hour*, p. 52.
[8] Eaton, *Islam and the Destiny of Man*, pp. 42 and 4.
[9] Rahman, 'The Talented Mr Gai Eaton'.
[10] Hamza Yusuf, 'A Spiritual Giant'.   [11] Köse, *Conversion to Islam*, p. 184.

ideology has been described as 'a radical Islam tinged with elements of classic European anarchism, moderate feminism, refined anti-Semitism, and dense Heideggerian phenomenology'.[12] Along with some of his followers, in the mid-1970s he set up an experimental self-sufficient Muslim community near Norwich in order to implement a true Islamic society. Believing that such a society did not exist in the Muslim world, he and his followers distanced themselves from born Muslims and thus embodied a wholly indigenous form of Islam. 'Abd al-Qadir attempted, for a while at least, to disengage from Western society, requiring his followers at different times to avoid such things as Western dress, electricity and modern technology in general, and state schools for their children (not wishing them to be assimilated into '*kāfir* society').[13] His critique of Western civilization, as expounded in various booklets and publications, is eclectic, radical, and even anarchistic at times. His writing is highly intellectualized and shows a certain (albeit selective) familiarity with the history of Western thought and philosophy. In an early publication 'Abd al-Qadir speaks of the need for *jihād* (in the military sense) against unbelievers, but without specifying a particular target; he also advocates polygyny on political and economic grounds, arguing that 'multiple wives is the necessary condition to end the basically bourgeois family group on which totalitarian modern statism is based'.[14] 'Abd al-Qadir's radicalism notwithstanding, much of his critique of Western societies is on a continuum with Islamic discourse in general, if at an extreme end of it. The interest of his thought stems partly from the fact that it is not purely theoretical, but has inspired practical experiments such as the 'e-dinar' project which attempts to dispense with paper and plastic money and return to the use of gold and silver as a medium of exchange, in order to avoid speculation and financial interest.[15]

In his early publications, 'Abd al-Qadir regards Western civilization as having no future: 'It is a goalless society without direction, like a mouse which chases its own tail in terror, turning on itself.'[16] He sees the breakdown of law and order in Western societies as the result of people 'rejecting the industrial work-nexus', and feels that such unrest signals 'the death-throes

---

[12] Dibbell, 'In Gold we Trust'.   [13] Köse, *Conversion to Islam*, p. 177.
[14] As-Sufi, *Jihad*, pp. 39–40 and 18.
[15] For more details see Dibbell, 'In Gold we Trust'.
[16] Cited in Köse, *Conversion to Islam*, p. 185 (from *Jihad*, p. 18 – I was unable to locate the quote in the original source).

of northern techno-culture'.[17] Ahmad Thomson, a British barrister and long-standing follower of 'Abd al-Qadir, has produced a sustained exposition of the latter's ideology in his book *Dajjal: The AntiChrist*. The prevailing mode of expression is reminiscent of the far left, with its talk of the way in which Western capitalist societies keep people enslaved by keeping them in ignorance, and its vision of a (Muslim) society which has no need for a police force or prisons (Thomson often talks of 'systems', especially 'the *kafir* system'). There is an emphasis on economic matters, with repeated references to 'the producer consumer process', the pernicious effects of interest, debt, and the accumulation of capital, and the inordinate power of the world banking system. He believes that Western civilization is in a state of 'total collapse'.[18]

As mentioned above, sexual morality is an area of concern for contemporary Muslim critics of Western society. Classical Islamic scholarship has not been shy of addressing sexual matters, and the sexual needs of both men and women are taken into account in Islamic law and teachings. Be that as it may, there is a disjuncture between Islamic teachings and the norms of contemporary Western societies which is potentially problematic for Muslims wishing to uphold Islamic standards and socialize their children into an Islamic way of life. This chapter includes a section on sexual morality, partly because in the course of the interviews this was frequently mentioned as one of the most difficult aspects of living in a Western society. Also, I anticipated that the issue of homosexuality in particular would provide an opportunity to observe the interplay between the Islamic and Western influences on converts, since same-sex activity is clearly prohibited according to mainstream Islamic teachings but increasingly accepted in contemporary Western societies.

The second half of this chapter addresses politicial issues such as participation, voting patterns and general political attitudes and ideology, and also looks at how converts situate themselves in relation to the Muslim world or the *ummah*. Such issues need to be seen against the backdrop of the rise of political Islam internationally and the growing politicization of

---

[17] As-Sufi, *Jihad*, p. 20.
[18] Thomson, *Dajjal*, p. 19; on the subject of the imminent collapse of Western civilization, Murad remarks that 'the wider world of unbelief... despite the breathless predictions of some of our coreligionists, continues to grow more powerful and prosperous' ('British and Muslim?').

British Muslims as a result of recent developments in international and domestic politics. The global dimension of this politicization includes a growing concern over the past decade and more with the plight of Muslims in different parts of the world such as Palestine, Bosnia, Chechnya, Kashmir, Afghanistan and Iraq. At first I hesitated to include political issues in this study, being unsure as to whether converts would be distinctive in their political views vis-à-vis born Muslims. In the end, however, these matters could hardly be avoided: such is the level of Muslim preoccupation with political developments and the high profile of Islamic issues in both domestic and international politics at the time of writing, that it would have been a glaring omission not to have given space to them. Also, there is an inevitable interplay between political and other factors. There can be little doubt that the Iraq war is, or will ultimately prove to be, at least as significant as the Rushdie Affair in terms of its impact on British Muslim identity, although the effects are still being played out and the resulting changes cannot yet be described or analyzed in detail.

British Muslim converts have a tradition of political activism and involvement, from Abdullah Quilliam and Marmaduke Pickthall, who supported Muslim causes overseas in the late nineteenth and early twentieth centuries, to the Murabitun in recent decades. In the late 1980s a group of Muslims, mainly converts, founded the Islamic Party of Britain; their aims included combating media prejudice against Islam and encouraging interest-free banking. However, they had little success at the ballot box, even in areas of high Muslim concentration such as Bradford, partly because they had no natural constituency (South Asians relating more to their own ethnic groups than to white converts).[19] The highly politicized fringe group Hizb al-Tahrir has attracted its fair share of converts. Some of these are quoted in an *Independent on Sunday* article as saying such things as: 'I can see a lot of good from the terrorism going on today – terrorism that is approved by God' (citing the wave of conversions since 9/11), and: 'People want us to condemn 9/11 and terrorism. We don't. They are our Muslim brothers and sisters.'[20] Hizb al-Tahrir does not officially advocate violent methods, and one suspects that there may be an element of bravado on the part of those who talk in this way to a journalist in the knowledge that they

---

[19] On the Islamic Party of Britain see Köse, *Conversion to Islam*, pp. 21–4.
[20] Stanford, 'Preaching from the Converted'.

will be quoted in a major national newspaper. Nevertheless, such statements can be distressing for Muslims as well as non-Muslims to hear, not least because they contribute to an image of Islam which many work hard to counter. In the light of recent British legislation making it an offence to 'glorify terrorism', it is conceivable that statements of this nature could lead to prosecution.

The active, armed involvement of British Muslims in international Muslim causes and terrorist activities is a relatively new phenomenon. High-profile cases such as those of the 'shoe bomber' Richard Reid and the 7/7 bomber Germaine Lindsay have highlighted the role of converts in terrorist actions, and have given rise in some quarters to a view of converts as traitors to their country.[21] Although the percentage of Muslims involved in such activities is very small, the presence of converts among them is deserving of comment. New converts are sometimes vulnerable, often going through a period of flux, heightened excitement and openness to the new. Their relative ignorance (in many cases) of Islamic teachings leaves them open to manipulation, especially if they feel that they have to prove themselves. Batool al-Toma suggests that they may also be 'seeking respite in Islam from a troubled past', as in the case of the Belgian convert-turned-suicide bomber Muriel Degauque, who had reportedly been on drugs prior to her conversion.[22] Furthermore, radical groups often deliberately target converts both because of their susceptibility and because they are usually less easily identifiable as Muslims.

While a relatively small minority of converts are attracted to militant or confrontational styles of political activism, there are many who are seeking to combat extremism, especially in the wake of the July 2005 bombings. Converts are prominent contributors to a British Muslim discourse which emphasizes the need for the full engagement and participation of Muslims at all levels of British society (without excluding the need for constructive criticism of it). This is a common theme in Sarah Joseph's *emel* editorials. Writing prior to the 2005 elections and reflecting on the Iraq war and its

---

[21] See Birt, 'We Muslim Converts are not Traitors in your Midst'. Three out of twenty-four people arrested on suspicion of plotting to blow up trans-Atlantic aeroplanes in August 2006 were converts, sparking further speculation on converts' susceptibility to extremism.
[22] Ford, 'Why European Women are Turning to Islam'; see also Lyall, 'Hungry for Fresh Recruits'. Mohammad Siddique Seddon suggests that people such as Reid are 'disenfranchised before they come to Islam' (Petre, 'My Dad Buys me Books about Islam').

aftermath, she expresses her extreme disillusionment with the British political process, but at the same time insists that it is not just a right but a duty for Muslims to participate: 'We have a civic responsibility to fully participate in the processes of the country that God, in His Divine Wisdom, placed us in . . . Make this country a better one by your active engagement, and in so doing fulfil your obligations as God's steward on this Earth.'[23]

In summary, this chapter will observe converts' attitudes to British society, laying particular emphasis on their beliefs regarding the role of religion in public life and on their opinions about issues of sexual morality. It will also examine attitudes to domestic and international politics (the two are difficult to separate in view of Britain's involvement in Iraq), while attempting to assess the impact of conversion on political orientation. Much of the chapter deals with discourse and ideology, but, as elsewhere in the book, practical and embodied aspects of converts' experience will be taken into account where appropriate.

VIEWS OF BRITISH SOCIETY AND WESTERN CIVILIZATION

Asaf Hussein, a former tutor in race education at the Open University, has argued that Islam enables Westerners (i.e. converts) to speak out about the problems in their own society: 'If they want a faith which gives them a participatory and active role, the choice is Islam. It places a very strong emphasis on social justice and empowers westerners to say: "This is not correct".'[24] As described above, Muslims in general and converts in particular have been active in critiquing Western civilization for generations. Abdal-Hakim Murad, in various essays published on the internet in recent years, puts forward a searing critique of Western culture alongside calls for moderation and loyalty to the British state and government. In an essay entitled 'Seeing with Both Eyes' (an implicit reference to the one-eyed *dajjāl* which in Islamic cosmology ushers in the end of the world), he sees the present time as characterized by 'a loss of perspective': 'Once the old were respected and admired more than the young; today it is the other way around. Once unnatural vice [i.e. homosexual activity] was despised, now it is the only practice

[23] Joseph, 'Count Yourself In'.
[24] Berrington, 'Islam Sheds its Image'.

that cannot be criticised in the films or in polite society. Once humility was praised, and pride was a sin; today there has been a complete inversion. No longer are we asked to control ourselves, instead we are urged to "discover" ourselves.' He describes the overriding ethos of modern civilization as follows:

> Modernity holds out lifestyle options centred on the self, and on the lower, agitated possibilities of the human condition. Every word of every magazine now breathes the message of the *nafs* [self, ego]: explore yourself, free yourself, be yourself ... The result, of course, is a society which pursues happiness with great technical brilliance but which puzzles over spiralling rates of suicide, drug abuse, failed relationships, and ever more aberrant forms of self-mutilation. It is a society in denial, a society in pain.[25]

Although Murad does not seem to pull his punches when criticizing Western society, in a talk addressed to American Muslims post 9/11, pointedly entitled 'Tradition or Extradition?', he stresses the need for measured criticism rather than 'wild denunciations of Great Satans or global Crusader Conspiracies', which are in his view 'not only dangerous, but . . . also discourteous – scarcely a lesser sin'. This is in the context of a feared backlash against immigrant Muslims, for he suggests that 'in the long term, the choice is between deportment, and deportation'.[26]

In an essay entitled 'Passing Between the Clashing Rocks: The Heroic Quest for a Transcendent Identity', Jeremy Henzell-Thomas, an English convert and educationist (with training in linguistics and psychology), is similarly pessimistic about the evolving ethos of the modern (or postmodern) world:

> The language of technology, military strategy, corporate efficiency, quantification and managerialism increasingly dominates our view of things in the West, and it articulates the de-souling of our culture and society ... Governments of 'developed' countries ... are obsessed with the need to exercise stringent control and demonstrate higher productivity, perpetual growth and improvement in standards of living, so that they can maintain their position in the first division in the great competition for materialistic supremacy.

---

[25] Murad, 'Seeing with Both Eyes'.   [26] Murad, 'Tradition or Extradition?'.

He adumbrates the tools of 'micro-managerialism' now ubiquitous in Western society: 'testing regimes, performance indicators, strict "commercial disciplines", "best practice" . . . league tables, inspections, targets'. By contrast, he argues, what is needed is 'connectivity, wholeness, and meaningfulness'.[27] Henzell-Thomas speaks of the 'frenetic hyperactivity' that is characteristic of modern societies, a theme which was taken up by Dawud, one of my interviewees, in a description reminiscent of Qutb: 'Life is basically built around entertainment, so you're constantly being entertained, and you're constantly consuming so you're being consumed. You're going around. Billboards never stop, the gimmicks never stop, the sports never stop.' Ahmad Thomson describes the end-result of the constant exposure to the media that is characteristic of modern life:

> Having been shocked or lulled by the news you can then be excited by sports time, or entertained by music and drama time, or captivated by competition time, and suddenly another precious day has gone . . . 'Reality' is indeed virtual . . . The result of being plugged into the media system for too long is that in the end you will accept almost anything, without actually doing anything about it, provided that your stomach is full, your bed is warm, and your home is comfortable.[28]

As discussed in chapter 2, disillusionment with Western society is a significant (though often not the prime) motivating factor in conversion to Islam. Interviewees were asked whether there was anything that they liked about British society; they were also asked whether there was anything they disliked about it. These questions preceded other questions about politics, religion and sexual morality in order to avoid possible distortion. By far the most commonly mentioned positive feature (cited by seventeen people) about British society was its tradition of pluralism, diversity and tolerance, and in particular the freedom to practise Islam (a few contrasted this with the situation in some Muslim countries); two of the black interviewees mentioned anti-racism as a positive feature of British society. Sulayman commented: 'It's probably the best place in the world to live as a Muslim because you can live pretty much as you want,' while Ali felt that London had the 'least amount of xenophobia' in Europe, and possibly in the world. The

[27] Henzell-Thomas, 'Passing Between the Clashing Rocks'.
[28] Thomson, *Dajjal*, p. 74.

next most frequently mentioned theme was good manners or common decency, and this was not infrequently contrasted with negative experiences among born Muslims; Rahima mentioned a number of social virtues including social justice, politeness and the system of queueing, and added: 'These are Islamic virtues – it's just that the Muslims seem to forget them most of the time!' Only one or two interviewees had difficulty thinking of anything positive to say about British society. Prabha mentioned several things that she liked about British society, and implied that the very existence of converts in a society made it difficult to condemn it: 'This is the place that has brought you up and you went through the education system here and you didn't come out half bad, do you know what I mean?'

When interviewees were asked whether there was anything they disliked about British society, four themes emerged most prominently: the prevalence of alcohol and/or drugs (mentioned by sixteen people); a lowering of standards of sexual morality (e.g. in the form of permissiveness, pornography, or simply women being scantily dressed – thirteen people); the prevalence of violence and crime (ten people); and the low level of religion or spirituality, or the fact that religion is 'unfashionable' in Western society (ten people). Three of the last group contrasted British attitudes to religion with those of other countries (both Muslim and non-Muslim) that they had visited or lived in. One of these commented that people in Jamaica were quite happy to talk about God, whereas in Britain: 'If you went up to someone and started talking about God they'd think you were a nutter, they'd run away ... The people who are religious are just seen as being cranks.' Eight people spoke of the decline of the family or family values; other themes that recurred were individualism (seven) and materialism (six). On the last subject, one woman commented: 'For British people and British society the *dunyah* [the present life] is everything, they'll work everything for the *dunyah*, they'll work all the hours Allah sends them.' Similarly, Na'ima Robert says of herself and her convert friends that Islam freed them 'from seeking fulfilment and happiness with the fleeting, transient things in this world ... We are not victims of the materialist brainwashing that has consumed so many in the world.'[29]

Economic issues did not figure prominently in interviewees' comments on British society, apart from a few references to consumerism. However,

---

[29] Robert, *From my Sisters' Lips*, p. 235.

since many Muslims believe that financial interest is prohibited in Islam (unlike modernists, who tend to say that the *ribā* condemned in the Qur'an refers only to usury, i.e. lending money at exorbitant rates), I asked interviewees about mortgages. Of the twenty-three people who were asked, only three had a conventional mortgage and all of these saw this as undesirable, justifying it with reference to the Islamic juristic principle of 'necessity' (*ḍarūrah*).[30] A further three said that they would take out a mortgage if it was absolutely necessary, while an overwhelming majority (seventeen) said that they would not consider a conventional mortgage under any circumstances. This figure may be partly explained with reference to the new availability of 'Islamic mortgages' (one person already had one and another was about to take one out), but in fact many interviewees expressed scepticism about these, along the lines of: 'They still take interest, but they don't call it interest.' As mentioned in the introduction, 'Abd al-Qadir as-Sufi and his followers place considerable emphasis on economic issues. Aside from the 'e-dinar' project, Murabitun members based in Norwich set up an organization called PAID (People Against Interest Debt) to combat interest, which 'Abd al-Qadir and the movement see as responsible for many of the world's social and economic ills.[31]

Some interviewees expressed the view that British society had been more compatible with Islamic values in the past. Mahmud spoke of looking at some albums belonging to his grandparents, which contained dedications and quotes as well as photos: 'The attitudes portrayed are very Islamic, in terms of religion, and in terms of purpose of life, talking about the Day of Judgement, it's very very far away from the modern kind of society, and it's much closer to Islam.' David drew attention to the similarities between Islamic morality and that of the England of the 1950s, and Yaqub spoke of a need for Britain to go back to 'Victorian or very British family values'. Abdal-Hakim Murad expresses a similar sentiment, drawing attention to the impact of social change on Muslims:

> The country to which many of us [Muslims] migrated no longer exists. Back in the 1950s and early 1960s, British family values were still recognisably derived from a great religious tradition rooted in the

---

[30] The *ḍarūrah* argument has been made by eminent Muslim scholars including Yusuf al-Qaradawi.
[31] Köse, *Conversion to Islam*, pp. 182–3.

family-nurturing Abrahamic soil. While the doctrinal debates between Islam and Christianity remained sharp, the moral and social assumptions of the 'guest-workers' and their 'hosts' were in most respects reassuringly and productively similar. That overlap has now almost gone.

He therefore constructs Muslims as 'the sole defenders of values which would be recognised as legitimate by earlier generations of Britons'.[32]

Almost every interviewee responded enthusiastically when asked whether they thought Islam had something to contribute to British society. Predictably enough, most spoke in terms of morality, guidance, family ties or spirituality (the word 'respect' came up in five people's answers). Fatima's answer combined several of these themes: 'Islam can offer back to Western culture basic lessons in how to be a human being which we've forgotten. How to share, how to be kind, how to be a community, how to be a spiritual being, to have your spirituality integrated into your everyday life, not to have it boxed off at home while you go to the office, how to have self-respect.' Na'ima Robert claims that 'the Islamic lifestyle is one that protects those who live it from many of the most harmful aspects of today's society. We are safe from addictions, alcohol and drug abuse, sexually transmitted diseases, unwanted pregnancies, abortions, sexual harassment, among so many other things.'[33] Jeremy Henzell-Thomas comments on government plans to get Muslims to subscribe to 'British values', which include 'taking responsibility for others' (understood as an attempt to get the Muslim community to take responsibility for dealing with the problem of extremism). Fresh from reading newspaper reports documenting teenage delinquency, eating disorders, bullying in schools, abuse of the elderly, attacks on teachers and nurses, huge credit card debts, alcohol-related problems, and addictive gambling, he suggests that 'the best Muslim social values can properly be invoked as a solution to many of the problems in wider society . . . the great majority of Muslims, through their strong family ties, socially responsible behaviour, and ethical values, can offer many lessons to the community at large'.[34]

When asked about the state of religion and spirituality in British society generally, most interviewees felt that it was either moribund or very weak, and many, like Fatima, commented on the detrimental effect on society of

[32] Murad, 'The Fall of the Family (Part I)'.
[33] Robert, *From my Sisters' Lips*, p. 237.
[34] Henzell-Thomas, 'Taking Reponsibility for Others'.

this decline: 'A lot of people are really lost in this society, and don't know how to find their way back to anywhere – it's quite scary, it's quite worrying. Depression is on the rise, young people don't know what to do with themselves.' Dawud lamented the decline of the authority of religion: 'I long for a society where you see the spiritual people are the celebrities and you aspire to them ... I'm so fortunate I've found that among Muslims.' He went on to talk about Muslim societies where people are 'mentioning God in their speech all the time, so you don't feel alien, where here you feel conversation is spiritually suffocating'. Several people said that they thought many people were looking for something, perhaps without really knowing what they were seeking. Of those who commented on New Age-type spirituality, most, like Fatima, thought that it was 'faddish' or superficial: 'I know there's a lot of people who say they're spiritual but it's a very individualistic kind of spirituality, so it's only effective in society in little pockets, there's not a coherent spiritual movement.' Not surprisingly, the criteria for measuring the effectiveness of religion or spirituality were for many based, implicitly at least, on the Islamic paradigm. According to Kavindra: 'Religion isn't just about doing your own stuff in the house, it's not about that. It's about the *ummah*, it's about the society, it's about providing and protecting the society, all these new religions don't cater for any of that.' Halima commented: 'You can't just fit spirituality into an hour on a Friday, it's got to be all-inclusive,' while another woman felt that the churches were not doing a 'proper job', explaining this simply by saying: 'They have no dress code.' Rahima saw New Age spirituality as 'sort of part-time religion, religion on the go', and added: 'Actually religion is something that's more time-consuming, sorry, and difficult . . . That's not very appealing to people these days because they want instant gratification and instant nirvana, and it's not like that.' Similarly Abdal-Hakim Murad opines that New Age spirituality deceptively implies that 'the gifts of the spirit may be had without paying a price, or changing one's treasured "lifestyle"'.[35] Two or three interviewees, however, felt that New Age spirituality might hold some value. Peter, for example, said he was glad that there were people with New Age beliefs in society: 'I think a lot of people are Muslims without knowing it, they've got a good attitude, they've got good hearts.'

Three of my interviewees contrasted the present-day situation with the past when religion played a more prominent role in people's lives, and these

---

[35] Murad, 'Seeing with Both Eyes'.

(as well as a few others) seemed to attribute a positive value to Christianity. One of these was Sulayman, who was concerned about the rise of secularism and anti-religious feeling in society and said that he would like to see 'a stable Christianity' in Britain: 'I think a lot of people could benefit from finding their Christianity in a very simple and meaningful way . . . This country has a very strong Christian tradition, and if you look at communities in the past that were very basic, very simple, they supported each other, they had Christanity as the focus, they had their jobs, and you can tell they had a real happiness.' Kavindra felt that in the past Christianity had kept people 'on the straight and narrow, as much as Islam keeps us on the straight and narrow', while Hafsa felt that she would rather send her children to a Church school than 'a secular school being run by lesbians and occultists', because at least the Christian teachers 'have values that are very close to Islam'. Diana was another person who saw religion per se as a good thing: 'I'm not saying everyone should be Islamic, but I think if everyone had a religion, the world would be a lot better.'

Muslims tend to take a negative view of 'secularism', seeing it as inherently hostile to religion rather than as providing a safe space for people of differing beliefs. This negative view is partly for historical reasons (secularism having been imposed on many Muslim peoples from above, sometimes accompanied by aggressive Westernization), and partly because of the centrality to Islam of the *shari'ah*, which includes rulings pertaining to public as well as private life.[36] Several British converts have evolved intellectual critiques of secularism, insisting that religion has an important role to play in society. According to Abdal-Hakim Murad, 'religion is indispensable to the nurturing of a true humanism because it . . . insists that humanity has a telos, and that the soul is therefore sacrosanct'.[37] In his view, the privatization of religion 'abandons the world to the morality of the market leaders'.[38] While acknowledging that religion is often misused, he feels that religion alone, not secularism, provides a basis for ethical values and a motivation for upholding them. Murad's scepticism about the Enlightenment is reminiscent of the perennial philosophers' attitude to the Renaissance. He argues that Muslims have good cause to be uneasy about the Enlightenment, since

[36] For a fuller exposition of Muslim attitudes towards secularism, see Zebiri, 'Muslim Anti-Secularist Discourse'.
[37] Murad, 'Bombing without Moonlight'.
[38] Murad, 'Faith in the Future'.

it has 'produced so much darkness as well as light', and he attributes to it the rise of rationalism ('the Enlightenment . . . would propose that the mind is already self-sufficient'), whereas before the world had taken spirituality as 'the precondition of philosophical knowing'. According to Murad, the current state of Western society bears witness to the failure of the Enlightenment, which is an indication that 'the solution must be religious'.[39] Jeremy Henzell-Thomas sees modernism and secularism as 'ideologies which are essentially inimical to the spiritual quest'. He observes that 'secular fundamentalism', as he calls it, has its own dogmas: 'that religious faith is a "construction" of the human mind, that there is no conscious design, purpose or ultimate meaning in the life of man or the universe', and points out that 'secular' does not mean 'ideologically free'.[40]

Those who argue in favour of a public role for religion often call for a restoration of its central place in education. As a schools inspector and former teacher, Henzell-Thomas places some emphasis on this. In his view, 'the absence of any truly coherent moral and spiritual perspective' results in a 'deadening utilitarian agenda . . . geared to turning children into cogs in an economic machine, children who are dependent, conforming, materialistic, and lacking in curiosity, imagination, self-knowledge and powers of reflection' – a description which ironically echoes some secularist fears about faith-school education.[41] Ibrahim Hewitt, who is the headmaster of a Muslim primary school in Leicester, also highlights the importance of religion and spirituality in education. He is not impressed by the prevailing multicultural approach to education, which in his view marginalizes religious education and 'trivialises the beliefs and practices of billions of people and reduces them to superficial celebrations devoid of spirituality'. In the wake of the northern England riots of 2001 and the aspersions cast on religious schools in the aftermath, he argues that young people need *more* religion, not *less*: 'Take religion out of the equation, and we have seen what can happen; young people growing up with a diminishing sense of who and what they are, and an increasing sense of alienation.' He regrets that faith has become 'the forbidden f-word, with little or no role to play', and observes that 'young people are increasingly rootless . . . the faith of their parents and grandparents, ritualised and denuded of understanding, holds little

---

[39] Ibid.
[40] Henzell-Thomas, 'Passing Between the Clashing Rocks'.   [41] Ibid.

attraction for young people educated in a system which treats all faiths as equal and, by extension, equally worthless and open to question'.[42] Like Henzell-Thomas, Hewitt does not see secularism as neutral: 'The secularist approach is not a value-free space within which people of all faiths and none can mix freely; it is a conscious decision to remove religion from public life. For sincere people of faith, especially Muslims, this is unacceptable.'[43]

SEXUAL MORALITY

The issue of sexual morality is undoubtedly an area of concern for Muslims, even if it is currently being upstaged by political issues, and even if, as one interviewee suggested, Muslim protests are sometimes muted (especially on homosexuality) because Muslims themselves, like gay people, benefit from the tolerance afforded by pluralistic societies. In a two-part essay entitled 'The Fall of the Family', Abdal-Hakim Murad observes that 'never before has there been a society in which men and women mingle so casually, and where radically increased opportunity for temptation and unfaithfulness is so patent ... The eroticising of public space has become part of our culture.' He describes a scenario of middle-aged men being tempted by younger women, 'a superabundance of flesh reminding them painfully at every turn of what they are missing'. Murad goes so far as to suggest that the rights of spouses should be protected in the workplace by avoiding situations of 'illegitimate seclusion' (khalwah) in the office, and that politicians should have to justify their choice if they have personal assistants of the opposite sex. In his view, 'pornography and sub-pornographic advertising should be carefully censored as intolerably demeaning and as incitement to marital infidelity, the task of censorship being entrusted to those feminists who so rightly object to such portrayals of their sex'. Although he realizes that many would pour scorn on such suggestions, he is sanguine: 'The time must ultimately come when the decadence will be recognised for what it is and radical solutions will be considered. Then, quite possibly, the principled Muslim conservatism that is so derided today will come into its own.'[44]

---

[42] Hewitt, 'Alien Nation, or Alienation?'.
[43] Hewitt, 'Schools of Good Faith'.
[44] Murad, 'The Fall of the Family (Part I)'.

As mentioned above, thirteen interviewees mentioned issues related to sexual morality when asked an open question about what (if anything) they disliked about British society. Specific comments included: 'A loss of modesty and chastity'; 'sex in your face'; 'the obsession with pornography'; and 'people running around half naked'. Many expressed concerns about their children growing up in a sexualized society. Yaqub observed that if people living in Britain fifty years ago could have been shown present-day society, they would have been 'very shocked'. He also felt that Muslims would simply be dismissed if they tried to tackle these issues alone, so stressed the importance of cooperating with Jews, Christians and 'all the decent honourable people in this country who don't have a religion'.

Sexual morality is potentially a source of cognitive dissonance for Muslims living in Western societies. On the one hand, Islam upholds certain standards and regards sexuality as a private matter; on the other, a Muslim living in Britain can scarcely leave his or her house without seeing evidence of a very different approach to sexuality. Several interviewees mentioned the 'visual assault' to which they were subjected on a daily basis, in the form of billboards, pornographic material in shops, and women in revealing clothing. A few people referred to the impact these things had on their lives, speaking for example of the difficulties of trying to protect their children's 'innocence'. One man found it hard to maintain his spiritual concentration (*dhikr*) in the face of 'women walking past wearing little or nothing', while another said that he found it very difficult to handle the 'ever more blatant' presence of pornography on the lower shelves in shops. Some interviewees, such as Sulayman, expressed a degree of (sometimes resigned) acceptance of the state of affairs in Britain, on the grounds that there is not much that one can do much about it: 'You have to sort of accept that these things are going to be happening . . . I say to Muslims, if you can't cope with it, then go, go to Sudan . . . but you'll probably come back after three weeks because it's that tough. So you just have to accept that that's the way it's going.' Similarly, Michael Young argues that 'short of moving to an Islamic country, it appears there's no escaping sex in advertising', and urges Muslims to just come to terms with that fact.[45]

The commodification of sex is not infrequently decried by converts. Na'ima Robert says of the Western world: 'Where once, for better or for worse, religion, culture, family and community regulated human sexual behaviour, there is now a vacuum. And that vacuum is being filled by the interests of industry and capital – sex sells'; by contrast, 'Islam . . . considers sex to be something wonderful, an expression of love and intimacy between two people.'[46] One interviewee spoke of her personal experience of being treated as a 'sex object' in her teenage years. She described the attitude she had encountered from men at that time thus: 'That you're here for my pleasure and entertainment, [I was] just completely taken advantage of really, but sort of groomed in such a way, that that's what you've got to do to be loved. You've got to exploit yourself to be loved, so you exploit yourself, but you're still not loved.' She felt strongly about issues of sexuality in society: 'I was duped. I really feel duped by the messages that are given by this society about how you're meant to be as a woman . . . I'm deeply critical of this society's "grooming" of pubescent girls to be sexy and available, and the pressure on women to torture themselves in an attempt to be beautiful, to undergo surgery to stretch the skin on their faces in a desperate attempt to remain young.' Anas Sillwood, a British convert living in the Middle East, sees the decline in moral standards in the West as an inevitable consequence of the decline of religion and spirituality and the corresponding rise of secularism and materialism. He argues that 'no society has ever been confronted by such open, flagrant displays of nudity and sexuality', and comments that 'those happily participating in the sexual feast do not realise the spiritual and psychological damage they are doing to themselves, and those, whether Muslim or otherwise, that try to abstain, have to undergo a truly Herculean task to try and keep their eyes, thoughts and actions pure'. He sees this as a 'great infringement on the individual freedom of a person', and regrets that 'those that object, whether Muslims or non-Muslims, to the sexualisation of society, are simply considered neolithic prudes'. He talks of the need for Muslims to adopt strategies of persuasion vis-à-vis mainstream society, for example by drawing on the Judaeo-Christian tradition, invoking the moral codes of previous generations, or referring to academic studies that demonstrate the pernicious consequences of permissive sexual activity.[47]

Several interviewees expressed the view that Muslims could not expect non-Muslims to uphold Islamic standards of sexual morality; in some cases

[46] Robert, *From my Sisters' Lips*, pp. 176–7.
[47] Tufail and al-Zoubeir, 'Anas Sillwood'.

at least a relatively non-judgemental stance towards non-Muslims had arisen out of their own experiences. One woman, for example, asked: 'How can you condemn someone for something they don't know? Because I did a hell of a lot of things before I became Muslim, but I didn't know.' Another woman talked about how both she and her fiancé (a born Muslim) had had liberal upbringings; both had experienced getting drunk and having pre-marital sex. She felt that her own children would have to make their own mistakes: 'If my children choose to be in a relationship without being mar-ried, and choose to have sex before marriage, that's their choice and they have to deal with that with God.' One man who described himself as 'liber-tarian' in matters of sexual morality believed that 'people should be able to do what they want, sexually and in private', as long as they shouldered the consequences. However, he placed great importance on the public–private divide: 'If you live in a Muslim country, there are certain things which, whilst they may be going on, they are not in the public domain, they are not in your face … If you want pornography, fine, go behind the curtains of a sex shop, go on the internet, fine, but you don't have to have this lewdness in your face.' Ali felt that some Muslims failed to recognize that Muslim views applied only in an Islamic state: 'When we live in a secular democracy, we will not apply our opinions and our views, so we respect the law of the land.' Two of the men expressed a certain ambivalence about upholding strict Islamic standards, one saying that seeing lightly clothed women in the street was 'a source of huge delight', adding: 'I freely admit that's absolutely not in accordance with the teachings of Islam.' The other felt that it could be diffi-cult to 'retain some kind of degree of spirituality' in the face of such phe-nomena, but added: 'Sometimes there's nothing better than a woman without *ḥijāb* in a summer dress walking down the street … Sometimes I like a pretty girl to walk past, it makes my day.'

Four interviewees expressed the view (without being asked) that con-verts' attitudes to sexual morality may differ from those of born Muslims. On being asked whether he found it difficult to live in a society with stan-dards of sexual morality very different to those of Islam, Andrew replied: 'It's different for us, because we were born and raised with it, even though we're trying to be strict Muslims, we've kind of experienced it in a way.' Lisa felt something of a conflict: 'When we're brought up to be very free, it's very difficult to think that there's something wrong with it … I think I probably have a different understanding because I'm a Westerner, I've spent all my life surrounded by Western culture . . . I guess I'm as anaesthetized to a lot of it as most Western people are because it's in my blood almost.'

On the subject of sexual morality, interviewees had most to say on homosexuality, perhaps partly because it was so topical – several interviews took place around the time when civil ceremonies or 'gay marriages' were introduced, in December 2005. A few had also seen a Channel 4 television documentary entitled *Gay and Muslim* which was aired in January 2006.[48] In the Islamic sources, homosexual activity is condemned and incurs severe punishment (the death penalty, according to some schools of law). According to the vast majority of scholars (both Muslim and non-Muslim), the Qur'an condemns homosexual activity and upholds male–female sexual relations (within prescribed legal relationships) as the norm. There are several *ḥadīths* that harshly condemn same-sex activity; one of these stipulates that 'both the active and passive agent must be killed'.[49] However, the classical scholars were concerned with acts rather than desires or orientations, and attitudes towards homosexuality were tempered by the juristic principle that one should not expose the sins of another (or for that matter, one's own).[50] Moreover, in Islamic societies historically there has been a degree of tolerance of homosexual activity, alongside the celebration of homo-erotic desire in certain literary and poetic traditions. The tolerance was, however, conditional on the discretion of the parties concerned, with a prevailing attitude of 'don't ask, don't tell'.[51] As Kecia Ali points out, the emphasis on not discussing such issues 'creates a safe space for transgression to occur without challenging the normative view that such relations are forbidden'.[52]

In the light of Islamic teachings on this subject I fully expected that most or all of my interviewees would uphold the view that homosexuality is wrong or sinful, as do most Christians (and almost half British people generally, according to recent social research);[53] however, over and above this, I

---

[48] It can be difficult to ask direct questions on such a sensitive issue, but the recent legislation and the documentary provided an opportunity to ask exploratory questions about whether it is possible to be both gay and Muslim, and how people felt about the introduction of civil ceremonies.

[49] Bearman et al., 'Liwāt'.

[50] Ali, *Sexual Ethics and Islam*, pp. 83–4 and 78.

[51] See on this Murray, 'The Will Not to Know'.

[52] Ali, *Sexual Ethics and Islam*, pp. 88–9.

[53] Evans reports that in 2000, 47% of people thought that homosexuality was 'always/mostly wrong', while 33% felt that it was 'not wrong at all' ('In Search of Tolerance', p. 218).

was interested to see whether converts' attitudes and views on this subject were in less obvious ways at variance with mainstream Islamic teachings.[54] In fact, three of the interviewees said (without being asked) that they felt that born Muslims did not always handle the issue of homosexuality very well. Yaqub thought that there was a need for open discussion of such issues, and that converts would be better equipped than born Muslims to communicate with gay and lesbian people (in the context of debate, discussion or *da'wah*), and that they would be more subtle in their approach. Most people felt (in accordance with mainstream Muslim jurisprudence) that although homosexual activity was a sin, one could not pronounce someone a non-Muslim on that account. Three people drew a distinction (again, based on classical Islamic law) between committing homosexual acts, on the one hand, and denying that homosexuality was wrong, on the other, implying that in the latter case a person could no longer be considered a Muslim.[55]

In common with most Muslims past and present, many interviewees emphasized the public–private divide when speaking of homosexuality.[56] According to one of my male interviewees: 'It's not possible to be a gay Muslim in public because homosexuality is anathema to Islam. Now if you're of that disposition, if you keep it quiet, if you're in the closet, there's not a problem, because in theory Islam sets great store on privacy. You're not supposed to pry into other people's affairs.' He pointed out that a person could only be condemned for forbidden sexual activity, whether heterosexual or homosexual, if they are physically caught in the act by four witnesses, adding that this is 'virtually impossible'. He did not feel it appropriate for a gay Muslim to belong to an organized group, because 'by proclaiming yourself as a gay Muslim you are confessing and therefore leaving yourself open

---

[54] It is not difficult to find online *fatwās* by respectable scholars which mention the death penalty (as advocated by certain classical scholars) as a punishment for homosexual acts (in order to emphasize the gravity of this particular 'sin').

[55] The classical jurists drew a distinction between commiting a sin or omitting something obligatory (such as the daily prayers), on the one hand, and denying that the sin or omission in question is wrong, on the other.

[56] Three of the interviewees were not asked about homosexuality. In one case my female Muslim research assistant did not feel comfortable asking a male interviewee about it; I too found it difficult to ask some of the more socially conservative male interviewees about it, although I was sometimes surprised by the degree of openness with which they spoke. In the other two cases it did not seem appropriate to broach the subject because the interviewees' children were present.

to a death sentence ... I mean it's don't ask, don't tell. What I don't know can't hurt me.' The distinction between the private and public spheres meant that even those who expressed sympathetic views towards gay people were not happy about the recent legislation concerning civil partnerships.

Various other distinctions made by interviewees had the effect of miti-gating the Islamic condemnation of homosexuality. One woman, for example, drew a distinction between feelings and actions: 'Islam teaches that you can't help how you feel, but you can help how you behave'; she felt that Muslims in general needed to be more subtle and nuanced in their approach to homosexuality: 'Some men could probably live in a committed relationship, but then actually doing the act is forbidden in Islam ... There might be circumstances in which it might be overlooked if it wasn't being made too explicit.' Diana said that she had talked a lot about the issue of homosexuality with other Muslims; she felt that 'you can be gay and Muslim, because you can have the belief and still have those feelings', adding: 'It's got to be so hard for them.' Peter expressed a degree of admiration for homosexual Christian priests who remain celibate: 'I respect anyone who's going through some kind of internal struggle, whether they're practising or not. Even if they're practising, Allah's mercy is bigger than their sin'; he spoke of the need for 'compassion and understanding' rather than condem-nation. Several people expressed opinions about appropriate behaviour towards people who were homosexual. Only two of these expressed a need to distance themselves socially – one saying that it would be a 'barrier to close friendship', and the other saying that 'if you sit with any group of people long enough you'll become like them' (echoing a *ḥadīth* to that effect). Some of the interviewees expressed the view that any verbal abuse or violence towards homosexual people was wrong, and that knowing that someone was homosexual would not affect their behaviour towards that person.

Religious believers who subscribe to the view that homosexuality is a 'sin' tend to see it as being the result of socialization, a question of nurture rather than nature. This is contrary to the view of most gay and lesbian people that their sexuality is innate. To see it as inborn could be problematic for believers, raising questions about God's justice in creating a person who could not legitimately seek to fulfil their natural human and sexual needs. Three or four interviewees accordingly saw homosexuality as a psychologi-cal problem; one thought that a lot of gay people had been sexually abused as children or indirectly influenced by gay role models, whilst others felt that they 'needed help' or were 'confused'. Other theologically oriented opinions expressed by interviewees included the following: that a homosexual orientation is a 'test' for a Muslim; that a gay non-Muslim might become a Muslim in the future (as an argument against being judgemental); and that a gay Muslim might one day repent and ask for forgiveness (as an argument against ostracizing them or considering them to be non-Muslims).

It was clear that for several interviewees, personal experience or knowledge of gay or lesbian people had affected their attitude. Five people spoke of knowing or having known homosexual people; of these, two had one or more gay or lesbian friends in the present, and one had a close colleague who was a lesbian. One woman pointed out that it was her open-mindedness that had led her to look into Islam in the first place. She said that prior to being Muslim, she used to have 'huge arguments' with her father, who felt that homosexuality was wrong. She had had a bisexual friend at university, which was 'not a big thing', and she currently had a lesbian colleague at work with whom she said that she got on very well and with whom she often had a 'good laugh'. Condemning homosexuality was not high on her list of priorities: 'Obviously we have to have a certain viewpoint on it because of Islam, and it's not the natural way that we're intended to be. However if there are people that are gay and they're not affecting me and my life, I'm not about to go and start making things difficult for them.' Perhaps most striking was a woman whose empathy and understanding on the subject of homosexuality contrasted with her robust political views (against democracy and in favour of an 'Islamic state'). She had a non-Muslim lesbian friend whom she had met through attending a class when she herself was already a Muslim. She had got to know this friend as a person before finding out about her sexuality, and this had made it easier for her to accept it. She had advised her friend (who was a yoga teacher) not to make a point of telling a new class that she was lesbian, 'the same as I wouldn't go into a room and say: I'm so-and-so and I'm heterosexual'; at the same time, she acknowledged that her friend should not always have to hide her sexual identity or feel afraid of it being discovered. As with others, invoking the public–private divide helped this convert to be more accepting: 'She knows we [i.e. Muslims] don't accept that [i.e. homosexuality], but I would say to her: your sexuality is not the sum total of who you are, it's something which should be kept private.' This interviewee seemed to be influenced by a hope that her friend might one day become Muslim, for she mentioned that she had heard of a lesbian who had converted to Islam, and she described her friend as 'very interested in Islam and a very spiritual person'. Another woman said that she had 'gay friends', and drew a connection between 'gay' and 'Muslim' in terms of them both being oft-misunderstood minorities: 'I can identify with them because they also suffer the same as we do, that sense of stereotype and that sense of alienation, that sense that people don't understand you properly – so they have lots of similar problems.' In fact, she felt that because of this she now had a closer connection to her gay and lesbian friends than before she converted, two years earlier. She spoke of the need not to judge, as she herself did not want to be judged, and of the need to respect other people's choices, as she would want her own choices to be respected. However, she was also very aware of Islamic teachings on homosexuality, and felt that there was no such thing as a (practising) gay Muslim, 'because it's completely forbidden to be in a homosexual relationship if you're a practising Muslim . . . because at the end of the day it's against the natural norm. The natural norm is that you produce children.'

Attitudes before and after conversion showed a relatively high degree of continuity (although interviewees were not specifically asked about pre-conversion attitudes). As Diana said: 'Before gay people never bothered me, and they still don't bother me now', adding that she knew that Islamically it was 'not right'. Two of the men expressed a sense of visceral disgust at the idea of men having homosexual relations. One of these admitted to having 'double standards' in that he was 'a lot more relaxed about heterosexual goings-on than homosexual', adding: 'I'm really an uptight prude when it comes to homosexuality.' Both men said that they had felt the same way before becoming Muslim. Despite their feelings of disgust, both also expressed relatively lenient views on this subject. In fact, of the eight people who expressed a view that homosexuality was 'unnatural', 'against nature' and/or had potentially adverse medical consequences, all but two made some kind of mitigating comment or expressed relatively liberal views (vis-à-vis classical Islamic law) on the appropriate treatment of, and behaviour towards, gay and lesbian people. This suggests an implicit distinction between the 'sinner' and the 'sin', along the lines of 'loving the sinner but hating the sin'.

An internet search yielded two very different treatments of the subject of homosexuality by converts, one by Abdal-Hakim Murad, and the other by Yakoub Islam, the author of the progressive *Tasneem Project* website.[57] Murad provides a brief but interesting theological treatment of the subject in his essay 'The Fall of the Family'. Like most Muslims, he is adamantly opposed to any public or legal recognition of homosexual relationships, because such recognition would undermine the divinely mandated institution of marriage. He argues that 'human sexuality is an incarnation of the divinely-willed polarity of the cosmos', and that the 'biological sterility' of homosexuality is evidence of 'its metaphysical failure to honour the basic duality which God has used as the warp and woof of the world'. Unlike many traditionalists, he acknowledges that homosexuality can be inherent rather than acquired, and that therefore homosexuality as an 'innate disposition' cannot be a sin, since it is not chosen.[58] However, he draws an analogy with criminal tendencies, which are to be resisted (God 'tests some of us by implanting moral tendencies we must struggle to overcome'). He sees same-sex relations as destructive of the social fabric and as 'the most extreme of all possible violations of the natural order'.[59] It is worth remembering that all these arguments could have been (and surely have been) advanced by evangelical Christian thinkers.

In an internet article entitled 'Dissident Sexualities: Muslim and Gay in the UK', Yakoub Islam (referred to below as Yakoub rather than Islam, to avoid ambiguity) has a very different approach. He sidesteps the issue of the legality or otherwise of homosexual activity in Islamic law on the grounds that he is 'not an expert in *sharīʿah*', though he regards homophobia as largely a European invention. Yakoub draws attention to some of the admirable qualities of gay Muslim people and organizations, describing one such organization as non-judgemental and non-confrontational in its ethos, and finding that gay Muslims in the UK have forged 'a community and identities that are compassionate, insightful and bursting with a passion for our faith'. Approaching the issue from a human rights point of view, he shows considerable empathy with Muslims who have 'dissident sexualities', describing their struggle against 'homophobic hatred and rejection' (particularly in the Muslim community), the threat of physical and emotional violence they face from family or spouses, and the way in which they are forced

---

[57] See http://www.bayyinat.org.uk.
[58] Ali points out that this is problematic from the point of view of divine justice, since Murad recognizes sexual fulfilment as a human need, and rationalizes Islamic sexual segregation as a way of avoiding putting temptation in people's way (*Sexual Ethics in Islam*, p. 88).
[59] Murad, 'The Fall of the Family (Part II)'.

to live a lie. He goes so far as to suggest that these Muslims are among the *mustaḍʿafūn fiʾl-arḍ*, (the 'oppressed in the earth'), a phrase used in the Qurʾan to denote those who are marginalized and oppressed through no fault of their own. He argues that sexuality is not a matter of choice, 'because the extraordinary level of suffering experienced by gay Muslims makes no human sense if you assume human choice is involved'.[60] Throughout the article, Yakoub does not distinguish between celibate and non-celibate gay and lesbian Muslims, but argues simply that Muslims in general are duty-bound to defend such people because of the level of persecution and suffering that they experience.

A rare example of a sustained theological treatment of the subject of homosexuality and Islam is provided by an American convert, Scott Siraj al-Haqq Kugle, who holds an academic post in the study of religion at an American college. Kugle is one of a small but growing number of scholars addressing this issue and questioning the blanket condemnation of homosexuality in Islamic teachings.[61] In an article entitled 'Sexuality, Diversity, and Ethics in the Agenda of Progressive Muslims', he calls for a reassessment of the traditional Islamic teachings on homosexuality in the light of advances in modern knowledge in the spheres of biology and sociology. He sees this as an interpretive project, akin to the Islamic feminist and liberal projects. Like feminists and liberals, he privileges the Islamic principle of justice over certain dominant Islamic discourses, and he proposes to use the same hermeneutical methods as they do, in particular semantic and thematic analysis of the Qurʾan. He embarks on an analysis of Qurʾanic passages in which some of the prophet Lot's male contemporaries appear to be condemned for engaging in homosexual acts, arguing that what is being condemned is the violent manner in which these men behave rather than the sexual aspect of the actions in question. Kugle points out that there is no record of Muhammad actually punishing any man or woman for same-sex activity, and suggests that the *ḥadīths* detailing specific punishments are later fabrications, in view of the fact that after Muhammad's death, the

---

[60] Islam, 'Dissident Sexualities'.
[61] Other examples are A. Jameel, 'The Story of Lot and the Qurʾan's Perception of the Morality of Same-Sex Sexuality' (*Journal of Homosexuality*, 41, 2001, pp. 1–88), and A. AbuKhalil, 'A Note on the Study of Homosexuality in the Arab/Islamic Civilization' (*Arab Studies Journal*, 1993, pp. 32–4).

Companions did not seem sure of the appropriate punishment. He also deconstructs some of the classical scholarship, saying for example that the medieval scholars did not address homosexuality in the abstract, but only specific acts in specific contexts. In a more general sense, he argues that if, as he believes, sexuality is innate, then sexual diversity is simply a natural part of creation and therefore willed by God. Citing examples of contemporary Muslim societies which seem to turn a blind eye to various forms of sexual violence and abuse, he asks: 'What kind of society would denounce consensual sexual [i.e. homosexual] activity while protecting violent sexual abuse?'[62] Since changes have been effected in Muslim attitudes to monarchy, slavery and women's inferiority to men, he sees no reason why a similar change should not occur in the area of sexuality.

DOMESTIC AND INTERNATIONAL POLITICS

Although converts do not usually attribute their conversion to political factors, there can be no doubt that high-profile political events can attract a level of interest in Islam which may then have an impact on conversion rates (as is commonly said of 9/11). One of Köse's interviewees was impressed by the American hostage-taking in Iran in 1979 and wanted to find out 'what sort of religion can make America come down on its knees'; he liked the thought of joining a religion which was 'obviously so hated by the people in the West'.[63] In Allievi's study, political motives seem to figure quite prominently in conversion to Islam; he argues that for those who are already politically active, conversion can be a way of sacralizing politics.[64] The fact that Islam (in contrast to Christianity) is perceived as reconciling the political and the religious is, in his view, part of its appeal to potential converts. He points out that the marginalization of many Muslims on both the domestic and international levels attracts some who incline to the left; in view of the impossibility of taking either the nationality or race of the underdog, 'one can at least take the religion, which symbolically subsumes the other two'.[65]

---

[62] Kugle, 'Sexuality, Diversity, and Ethics', p. 225.

[63] Köse, *Conversion to Islam*, pp. 55–6; Köse sees this as an example of a 'rebellion conversion', but adds that this motive was not sufficient to cause the man in question to *remain* Muslim; in other words, other factors also came into play.

[64] Allievi, *Les Convertis à l'Islam*, pp. 129 and 328. [65] Ibid., pp. 137 and 135.

While the political 'motif' was not prominent in my own interviewees' accounts of their conversion, most said that they had become more politically aware since their conversion; although this could be partly attributable to growing older, many felt that this increased awareness was related to their Islamic affiliation. Fatima said that she had been quite politically naïve before her conversion, so becoming a Muslim had been a steep learning curve for her: 'It was literally another world opening up, and then realizing: oh my God! These countries have been colonized and they're so bound up with our history, British history ... Why wasn't I told about this? Why didn't we learn about this at school?' One young woman who had only been Muslim for just under a year, and who had not previously taken any interest in politics, told me: 'Before I was quite oblivious and didn't really care because it didn't really affect me in my little world. Now it does affect my world a bit because it affects Islam,' citing as an example the *ḥijāb* controversy in France. It was clear that she had been influenced by other Muslims in her evolving attitude to politics: 'There was a lot – a part – of me, even being Muslim, that didn't care [about the Iraq war] ... A lot of people would go on about it ... It's almost like I didn't care what was going on. It's like, let's concentrate on this country first, like your own community, before thinking about that. But now as I've got a bit more older and a bit more wiser with it as well, I've thought, you have to think about other countries.' An Irish man who had had socialist leanings prior to his conversion, and who felt that he had inherited the 'strong sense of justice that a lot of Irish people have', commented: 'You kind of just transfer to all the Muslim issues, issues of Palestine and political problems, so yes, I think I'm politically aware but in a different way, it's just with different criteria, it's just a different agenda.'

As some of the above quotes indicate, there are many ways in which the former political values or attitudes of converts can be accommodated within an Islamic framework. Allievi identifies both a right-wing and a leftist tendency among European converts and finds, as do Rocher and Cherqaoui, that such affiliations tend to survive conversion.[66] In my own study, twelve interviewees said that they had already been relatively politically aware at the time of their conversion, and six of those (20% of the sample as a whole) had had socialist or left-wing leanings, while two had had

[66] Ibid., p. 138; Rocher and Cherqaoui, *D'Une foi l'autre*, p. 128.

Conservative or right-wing sympathies.[67] Of the six who had been on the left, four were still more or less left-wing while two considered the category 'left-wing' to be no longer relevant to them. The two who had been on the right remained on the right. One of these said that he was right-wing on matters of public policy, including immigration, taxation and privatization of health care; he was the only interviewee to express such views. The great majority did not consider themselves to be either right- or left-wing; the failure to identify clearly with one or the other is not surprising given that Muslims may feel more in sympathy with the right on moral issues and family values, while inclining to the left on matters such as immigration and asylum. Some interviewees did not relate to these categories at all, or did not understand them. One woman said that she did not identify with either, 'because I don't believe it has any relevance for Muslims at all because it's not from a Muslim society, it's not got a basis in Islam'. Another reason for interviewees' failure to identify with the left–right spectrum is the blurring of these categories in British politics in recent years; as one woman who was asked about her political inclinations commented: 'Well if I could find a left wing or a right wing I would tell you [which I would support] but at the moment I don't think there is one!'

Muslims in Britain have traditionally been Labour supporters, as Labour has generally been seen as more sympathetic to Muslim concerns than the Conservatives, particularly in their policies concerning immigration and asylum, anti-racism and working-class interests. However, support for Labour has been declining since the 1970s, due to a combination of factors. These include that party's failure to support Muslims in the Rushdie Affair while in opposition, and more recently its anti-terror legislation, whilst the Conservatives have attracted support with their emphasis on private enterprise and family values.[68] This decline in support for Labour dramatically accelerated as a result of the Iraq war, with a marked swing among Muslim voters away from Labour and towards the Liberal Democrats (who, unlike the Conservatives, opposed the war) in subsequent local and national elections. In the national election of 2005, constituencies with high Muslim populations saw an average swing away from Labour of 9%, and George

---

[67] It should be borne in mind that the term 'right-wing' has pejorative connotations in some contexts and circles (including among ethnic minorities), making it less likely that Muslims would describe themselves as such.

[68] Ansari, *'The Infidel Within'*, p. 240.

Galloway of the newly formed Respect Party won the 'safe' Labour seat of Bethnal Green and Bow. The swing away from Labour was not confined to Muslims, who were, in McRoy's words, 'simply the vanguard of a crest of national disillusion with both Tories and Labour over the war'.[69] The aftermath of the Iraq war has also seen the emergence of tactical bloc voting among British Muslims, with organizations, notably the Muslim Association of Britain (MAB), offering specific guidance on which candidates to vote for.

The resonance of some traditionally conservative values with Islamic norms is highlighted by Abdullah Stockton, a contributor to *Q-News*. He describes himself as 'conservative-with-a-small-c', and highlights the areas of commonality between Muslims and 'middle Englanders': 'We do not support the promotion of homosexuality . . . we believe that morality ought to play a more important role in family life, we believe in abortion in only specially defined cases; disagree with adultery; are anti-drugs and pro-capital punishment'.[70] Abdal-Hakim Murad (appearing on *Shari'ah TV* as Tim Winter) has expressed the view that Muslims should seek to make alliances not with the left wing, whose social policies may be in conflict with Islamic teachings, but with those who are more socially conservative and religiously inclined such as 'orthodox Jews or traditional Catholics'.[71] Not surprisingly, converts of a traditionalist persuasion, such as Daoud Rosser-Owen and Rasjid Skinner (who stood as a Conservative candidate in the 1997 election) are more likely than others to identify as Conservative with a large 'C'.

In recent decades Muslim political participation in terms of both voter registration and involvement in local (and more recently national) government has steadily increased. However, a vocal minority of Muslim youth have argued that it is wrong to actively participate in the political life of a non-Muslim country. Already in the 1990s various groups or organizations such as the Muslim Parliament (which has since changed its stance), Hizb al-Tahrir and Jihadist groups were calling for Muslims to abstain from voting.[72] During the 2005 election, some of these mounted high-profile campaigns and lobbies in an attempt to dissuade Muslims from participating. The arguments in favour of non-participation are that it is wrong to be

[69] McRoy, *From Rushdie to 7/7*, pp. 48–9.
[70] Stockton, 'Halal Middle Englanders?'.
[71] *Shari'ah TV*, Channel 4, 4 April 2005, Series 2, Programme 1: 'Politics and Leadship'.
[72] Hussain, 'Muslim Political Participation', p. 384.

involved with a '*kāfir* state' (which by definition implements some policies that are anathema to Islam), that democracy itself is *kufr* or *shirk* (associating partners with God), and that it is a Western invention and nothing to do with Islam.[73] Others, including Hamza Yusuf, Tariq Ramadan and national Muslim organizations such as the MCB, have argued that it a duty for Muslims to participate, as failure to do so will perpetuate their marginalization. A counter-discourse has evolved to oppose the rejectionists, appealing to examples from the Qur'an, the life of Muhammad and Islamic history. These examples include that of the prophet Yusuf, who according to the Qur'an held high office in a non-Muslim government; the case of the Christian Abyssinian ruler (the Negus), who gave refuge to a group of Muslims fleeing persecution in the Meccan phase of Muhammad's mission; the *ḥilf al-fuḍūl* ('alliance of excellence'), a pact involving pagan Arabs in which Muhammad participated as a young man; and the Constitution of Medina, a formal agreement in which Muslims, Jews and pagans were all considered to be part of the same community (*ummah*). Others invoke the Islamic juristic principle of 'the lesser of the two evils' (*akhaffu'l-ḍararayn*), arguing that the damage to Muslim interests resulting from non-engagement exceeds the 'harm' of participating in an unIslamic system.[74]

All the interviews took place within the fourteen months following the May 2005 general election in which the Labour Party under Tony Blair won a third term. Of the twenty-seven interviewees who were asked about how they had voted in that election, nine had not voted, though in two cases this was for practical reasons. Four had refrained from voting out of cynicism or indifference, and implied that there was not much to choose between the parties, and three of the non-voters felt that it was wrong on principle to vote; two of these made reference to British foreign policy, suggesting that their views were strongly influenced by current events. One said: 'I don't believe it's right, because you're voting for something which is going to be against Islam ... Say if I voted for Labour, and Labour then goes and bombs Iraq and bombs Afghanistan, I'm responsible for that because I voted in this party who's done those things.' This woman went on to say that she would vote in case of

---

[73] Ibid., p. 380.
[74] Ibid., p. 385. For an academic treatment of intra-Muslim discussion of participation, loyalty and related issues, see Shadid and van Koningveld, 'Loyalty to a Non-Muslim Government'.

'obvious necessity', where a greater evil would result from not voting, for example to keep out an extremist party such as the British National Party (BNP). Another interviewee simply said: 'I wouldn't vote for any of them now, if they said you have to vote or else, I would take or else, I wouldn't vote. I can't vote and say I agree with your policies when they are fighting Muslims.' However, another person felt that it was wrong to abstain on the grounds that 'if you don't vote then your vote is counted as a vote to whoever's in power at that time, so my vote would have been counted as a Labour vote'. Sulayman drew attention to the difficulties facing Muslim voters; he felt that to vote Labour was unacceptable because of the Iraq war, but in view of the limited choices he found it hard to argue against those who advocated abandoning the political system, even though in principle he was opposed to that idea.

With regard to voting patterns among this particular sample of converts, the 'swing' away from Labour was even more marked than among Muslims nationally. Of the eighteen who had voted in the 2005 election, only one, a lifelong Labour supporter from a family of Labour supporters, said that she had voted Labour. Seven had voted Liberal Democrat, five voted Respect, three Conservative, and two were unsure how they had voted. Two said that they had voted tactically, one of these taking his lead from the MAB. No fewer than eleven people explained that they could not countenance voting Labour (which they otherwise might have done), because of the Iraq war. One of these was Amin, who acknowledged some of Labour's achievements and said that he was 'inclined to vote for Tony Blair last year but I just couldn't bring myself to do it because of what he's done in Iraq, which is basically disgraceful'. In fact, the number of people who actually voted might have been smaller but for the fact that several had voted purely in order to try and dislodge Labour from power.

As will have already become apparent, feelings ran high with regard to Iraq; the adjectives people used to describe their reactions to the war included 'disgusted', 'devastated', 'horrified' and 'furious'. Iraq was often seen not as an isolated event, but as part of a chain of events which included the invasion of Afghanistan and the threats against Iran and other countries. Halima spoke of her feelings on the invasion of Afghanistan: 'I remember sitting on a bus and going over a bridge and feeling at that time, I cannot see the beauty of London anymore. Normally I'd think, oh this is so nice, this is my city. But I thought, no, it's all rotten, it's all disgusting, it's all just a veneer and I hate it.' One man simply said: 'Tony Blair's got blood on his hands. It's a terrible, terrible, terrible thing.' Three people saw the war as a continuation of colonialism, including one man who said: 'What I believe we're witnessing is another wave of empire-building and a play for world domination by the Americans and whoever will be allied to them, which is mainly us.' Two or three interviewees saw recent events as adding up to a war against Muslims. As one man put it: 'No one can blame Muslims for feeling that America and their allies are aggressing against Muslim nations, because you just have to look at it on paper. What countries have they gone into? What countries are they threatening? They're all Muslim.' One woman said that although she felt there was nothing she could do about the situation in Iraq apart from giving charity, she drew consolation from the Qur'anic verse that says of the unbelievers who are conspiring against Muhammad and the Muslims: 'They plot and they plot, but they do not know that Allah plots better' (8:30). On the whole, though, people did not couch their objections to the war in specifically religious terms.

Although interviewees were not asked directly about British anti-terror policies, several expressed strong concern or anger about some of the new laws. Particular policies which were mentioned were stop-and-search; wrongful imprisonment and imprisonment without trial of terror suspects; the prospect of extradition to countries with dubious human rights records; and raids and arrests on insubstantial evidence. Comments in this context included: 'It's them and us'; 'It's a war on Islam at the moment'; 'Muslims are being done some terrible wrongs in this country right now . . . The government is abusing its powers against innocents. Draconian laws are affecting us all.' One woman expressed a strong sense of being besieged: 'There's no public–private divide. The police can just burst into your house any time, bug your telephone, tape your conversations, there's no privacy at all. There are so many raids happening now, and you have to think: what do I have to do in order to be a suspect? They can dig up anything, they'll dig around and around and around until they've found something.' Two other women expressed similar fears. One of these knew a man who had been imprisoned without trial, and the other commented: 'It's really scary, you might be invited somewhere where someone goes, I mean I've actually been sitting in a room and Abu Hamza was in the back garden.'[75]

---

[75] Muslims' general sociability combined with the relative numerical smallness of the Muslim community in Britain enhances fears about police harassment or persecution, since there

With regard to political ideology, interviewees were not asked about this as a matter of course, but it sometimes came up naturally in the course of the conversation or in relation to questions about other matters such as voting patterns or the Iraq war. Caution needs to be exercised in evaluating political discourse and rhetoric, a case in point being the common invocation of the 'Islamic state'. Polls that ask Muslims whether they would like to live in one are of limited value, since the 'Islamic state' is emblematic, and may simply represent people's aspirations for social justice or a harmonious society (this was one reason why I did not generally ask for interviewees' views on democracy or the Islamic state). In any case almost all Muslims agree that there is no model worthy of emulation currently in existence.

As mentioned above, certain Muslim groups such as the Hizb al-Tahrir perpetuate an anti-democratic discourse. This discourse does not appear to be confined to members of organized groups, however, and is arguably gaining currency among non-affiliated disaffected Muslim youth in contemporary Britain.[76] Four interviewees expressed political views to the effect that democracy is wrong on principle and/or that the Islamic state offered a better solution. Perhaps surprisingly, the three people with the most radical views were neither particularly young (all were over thirty) nor were they recent converts. The one with the most militant style was a woman who described herself as being affiliated to Hizb al-Tahrir. She spoke of a conspiracy to integrate Muslims in the West 'so they don't yearn for the Islamic state, they don't yearn to live under *sharī'ah* law', and of the West's fear of Islam and its determination to defeat Muslims, because 'the Muslim army, they have no fear of death. We're not like the *kuffār*, we have no fear of death. When a Muslim goes into battle, it's either death or martyrdom, so either way the Muslim wins.' She also spoke of the evils of living in a non-Muslim society: 'A true Muslim will never tolerate living in this city [i.e. London],

might easily be only one or two 'degrees of separation' between an ordinary Muslim and, say, Abu Hamza, as in this example.

[76] An ICM opinion poll conducted in February 2006 found that 40% of British Muslims were in favour of introducing *sharī'ah* law in parts of Britain (P. Hennessy and M. Kite, 'Poll Reveals 40% of Muslims Want Sharia Law UK', *Daily Telegraph*, 19 February 2006). The Gfk NOP survey for the Channel 4 *Dispatches* programme *What Muslims Want*, broadcast 7 August 2006, found that 34% of Muslims in the 18–24 age group would prefer to live under *sharī'ah* law (with lower figures for older age groups). It should not be assumed that *sharī'ah* law and democracy are mutually exclusive, but the figures do suggest a certain disillusionment with British democracy.

because we feel like a fish out of water, we're living in a *kufr* country under a *kufr* state of law. We're not living under Islam, we're not living under Qur'anic law, we feel something's wrong, we should never feel comfortable to live in this situation.' She felt that Muslims needed to realize that the West is aggressive and that they also needed to fight the regimes in their own countries. Interestingly, this woman showed less inclination to move to a Muslim country than most other interviewees, considering all Muslim countries to be unIslamic. Another woman who spoke of the need for an Islamic state was cynical about Western forms of democracy, which she felt consisted of 'making people think they have a say, but keeping people focused on minor issues and not the global issue, which is that the whole system needs an overhaul'. Although she was not formally affiliated to Hizb al-Tahrir or al-Muhajiroun, she felt that it was incumbent upon Muslims to establish an Islamic state or the *khilāfah* (caliphate). She believed that one could only be 'partially Muslim' in the West, citing as an example the difficulty or impossibility of avoiding insurance or financial interest: 'It's not that Islam wants to make our lives difficult, but it operates within a system and if you try and implement bits of that without the rest you get conflict and chaos.' One man, who was *salafī* by inclination, was accustomed to debating with non-Muslims about many issues in the course of his *da'wah* work. He had clearly devoted a certain amount of time and energy to elucidating his own position on democracy, as he spoke at some length and without hesitation on the subject. He argued in essence that in a truly democratic system, every single policy would be voted on by everyone, but since this was a practical impossibility, and 'a lot of people are not intellectually set up to choose', democracy was not viable. Furthermore, he argued, it was a democratic system that produced Adolf Hitler.

Criticism of democracy is not confined to Hizb al-Tahrir/al-Muhajiroun and those of *jihādī* or *salafī* persuasion. The traditionalist and Sufi-oriented Abdal-Hakim Murad speaks of the weakness of liberal democracies which have 'no fail-safe resistance to moving in a totalitarian direction', and regrets the passing of 'religious autocracy and sacred kingship'.[77] In a publication dating from 1981, 'Abd al-Qadir as-Sufi sees Western democracy as an embodiment of 'the colonial system in all its ruthless irrational power'. He argues that 'it does not lead to people's rule but rather it is

---

[77] Murad, 'Faith in the Future'.

a device to install an all-powerful bureaucratic elite who can carry out policies without further interference due to the mythic "franchise" that has been
granted them at the polls'. In his view, democracy has resulted in 'a quasi-
fascist state' in almost every European country.[78]

The interviewees with radical opinions may be viewed as falling at one
end of a spectrum of Islamic political thought. At the other end are those
who expressed concerns about the politicization of religion (several complained about fiery or political sermons in mosques), or who were sceptical
about the viability of an Islamic state. One man said: 'If we're cheating and
lying amongst ourselves there's no way we can have an Islamic state, it's
ridiculous'. Another man was very critical of 'groups like Hizb al-Tahrir
who say you can't do anything, life is suspended, until we have the *khalīfah*
[caliph]; if you're doing anything that's not connected in some kind of 100%
way to establishing the *khalīfah* tomorrow, you're not one of us, you're just
out of it, you're just one of these sleeping doped-up Muslims who's lost'. By
contrast, he emphasized the need for a grassroots approach to change.
Questions remain about the extent to which those with radical views were
influenced by recent British government policies – for example, two of the
three people who were most disenchanted with 'democracy' cited the fact
that the Iraq war happened despite the strength of public opposition to it as
evidence of the inadequacy of democracy in general or of British democracy
in particular. Globally, Islamic anti-democratic (or pro-Islamic state) discourse is related to political contingencies, and the British context is no
exception.

The events of 9/11, and more recently the July bombings, have given rise
to much intra-Muslim discussion and debate on the problem of extremism.
Converts (most prominent among them Hamza Yusuf), have been active
contributors to this debate and to the attempt to combat on theological
grounds those who undertake acts of terror. This fight against extremism is
very much a joint effort with born Muslims. The scholars featuring on the
website of the Radical Middle Way, a network formed in 2005 with the aim
of engaging theologically with British Muslim extremism, are born Muslims
and converts in almost equal measure;[79] the same is true of the contributors
to an edited volume (likewise dedicated to grappling with the issue of

[78] As-Sufi, *Letter to an African Muslim*, pp. 27–8.
[79] See http://www.radicalmiddleway.co.uk.

extremism, as well as public policy) entitled *The State we are in: Identity, Terror and the Law of Jihad*.[80] The refutation of radical Islamism in general and terrorism in particular are recurrent themes in Abdal-Hakim Murad's writings,[81] and several British converts, including Ahmad Thomson and Hasan Le Gai Eaton, have argued (as does Hamza Yusuf) that suicide bombing is not sanctioned in Islam.[82]

A NEW GEOPOLITICAL ORIENTATION?

Hilda Reilly in her book *Seeking Sanctuary* writes about converts (albeit a relatively small number of them) who feel they can only live a fully Islamic life by moving to a Muslim country.[83] Such people meet with a certain suspicion on the part of Westerners who find it hard to believe that they could prefer to live in a place like Sudan (where Reilly conducted her study), given that this entails a significant drop in their material standard of living. Historically, a number of prominent converts have chosen to live in Muslim countries, in some cases making a radical break with their past. Maryam Jameelah, a well-known American Jewish convert to Islam and author of many books on Islamic topics, moved to Pakistan in the early 1960s, not long after her conversion, to become the second wife of a prominent scholar; she still lives there in *purdah*. Muhammad Asad chose to become a Pakistani citizen and was the first Pakistani ambassador to the United Nations. In an age of cheap travel and easy communications, converts have more flexibility in their lifestyle choices, and many like the idea of spending some time in a Muslim country rather than moving permanently. Some, including Hamza Yusuf and Imam Zaid Shakir (another prominent American convert), spend (or have spent) quite extended periods of time in Muslim countries in order to immerse themselves in Islamic scholarship and/or a spiritual tradition, often studying under a particular teacher or spiritual guide. Others

---

[80] Edited by Aftab Malik.
[81] See especially 'Recapturing Islam from the Terrorists'; 'Bin Laden's Violence is a Heresy against Islam'; 'The Poverty of Fanaticism'; 'Bombing without Moonlight'; and 'Faith in the Future'.
[82] See Thomson, 'Martyr or Murderer?' and Eaton, 'The Radical Middle Way'. See also Young, 'The Islamic Rules of Warfare', which argues against the killing of non-combatants.
[83] Reilly, *Seeking Sanctuary*, p. 1.

may become involved in the life of a Muslim country (often the country of origin of their spouse) without necessarily moving there.[84]

Although none of my interviewees converted directly as a result of visiting a Muslim country, at least four had been to one at some stage prior to their conversion, and only seven had never visited one at all.[85] Five people had lived in a Muslim country for a period of a year or more since their conversion. Interviewees were asked about their future intentions or preferences with regard to living in Britain or moving to a Muslim country. The question was intended to be heuristic and exploratory, since an expressed aspiration to live in a Muslim country is of limited significance in itself; such an aspiration could merely indicate a desire to escape the pressures of living in London, for example, or a romantic vision of a harmonious Muslim society which may be more imagined than real. Nevertheless, some interviewees had given some serious thought to the possibility of moving, partly because the subject of future living arrangements often comes up in marriage negotiations. Four people expressed a definite intention to move, and in three of these cases the plan was to move to the country of origin of the spouse (one has since done so). In only one case were religious reasons given as a motivating factor. This was a woman who strongly felt that Western Muslims, including converts, who were relatively privileged, should make a contribution to poorer Muslims in other parts of the world: 'I just feel it's our duty ... There are still people begging, and you just think, how can I go back home and forget about people here? I think if Western Muslims have the advantages of wealth, education and job opportunities, then that needs to be recycled, utilized and put back into the Muslim community.' Seven others expressed a strong desire to move to a Muslim country, using expressions such as 'definitely' when asked if they would consider such a move. A further eleven said that they would consider moving or would quite like to. Of the rest, five strongly felt that their home was in Britain.

In general, interviewees acknowledged that there was no 'ideal' Muslim country. Several made comments to the effect that there was no truly Islamic

---

[84] Abdul-Hakim Murad and Jeremy Henzell-Thomas have both fostered a special connection with Bosnia, for example; the latter founded a charity called Bosnia Music Aid in 1998 to help reconstruct the war-damaged Primary Music School in Sarajevo.

[85] The most frequently visited country was Saudi Arabia (visited by nine people, in some cases for the Hajj or 'umrah (minor pilgrimage)), followed by Egypt (eight people), and then Morocco and Jordan (four each); a further twenty or so countries had each been visited by at least one person.

state or even Muslim society, and many were sharply critical of specific Muslim countries, saying that cultural practices had often become confused with religion. However, some had had positive experiences of visiting or living in a Muslim country. One of these was Halima, who had a strong intention to move to a Muslim country, and had already visited one: 'You appreciate the simpler things in life, even like catching water from a well and washing your clothes by hand, and all these things that would be a nuisance here. There it didn't matter because the pace of life was different.' Sulayman, now settled in Britain with his family, had lived in the Yemen[86] and had found the people 'delightful': 'I lived in a community where people were just very friendly. They shared, were easygoing, neighbours looked after each other, people gave each other lifts and it was just a breath of fresh air.' He had particularly enjoyed the full and spontaneous social life, and returning to Britain had been quite a culture shock: 'I phoned somebody and said I'd love to come and see you, and then they'd get the diary out and they'd try and fit me in for a week Tuesday, and I thought, what is this?'

Four people used the word *hijrah*, an Arabic-Islamic term which denotes the act of moving or fleeing from a place where one cannot fully practise one's religion to another place where one can. The use of this word implied two things: first, that an explicitly religious paradigm was being invoked, privileging religious motivations for moving; and second, that London, Britain, or perhaps any non-Muslim country, were not places conducive to living a good Muslim life. One woman who had never visited a Muslim country said that she would definitely like to move to one (her grown-up son was in fact living in one at the time): 'I would prefer not to be in this country if I'm honest, I'd like to do *hijrah* to any Arab country, even if it's Morocco. I know they're all *jāhil* [ignorant, unIslamic] there, but at least they're all wearing the same, you don't feel like an outcast.' Another woman, who could not countenance leaving Britain while her parents were still alive, nevertheless felt that *hijrah* was compulsory in principle. One man felt that it was 'highly recommended' rather than obligatory, and that it was less than ideal to live in a non-Muslim country. Abdal-Hakim Murad, on the other hand, speaks against *hijrah*, drily observing that 'most scholars don't teach that globalisation obliges us to make *hijrah* to a neighbouring planet'. He feels that despite 'a deep scepticism about the ability of a consumer society

---

[86] The name of this country has been changed to protect anonymity.

to increase human fulfilment and to protect the integrity of creation . . . Muslims are not committed to jumping ship'.[87] Similarly, Hamza Yusuf argues: 'If people don't want to live here they should go and live in certain Muslim lands and see how long they last before this country starts looking more like dar al-Islam.'[88] Speaking for himself, he says: 'I would rather live as a Muslim in the West than in most of the Muslim countries, because I think the way Muslims are allowed to live in the West is closer to the Muslim way.'[89]

The majority of the interviewees who expressed a desire to move did not attribute this to their disillusionment with British politics; in fact, most of those who were asked if British foreign policy made it difficult for them to live in Britain gave a negative answer, arguing that no country is perfect, or that Britain was still a relatively tolerant society. However, it is interesting to observe that in al-Qwidi's study based on interviews conducted in 1999 and 2000, most converts saw themselves as remaining in Britain.[90] Some of my interviewees expressed a desire to move in connection with a wish to bring their children up as practising Muslims and the fear that it would be difficult to do so in a non-Muslim society such as Britain. One woman had recently married a convert (who was living in a non-Muslim African country at the time of the interview), and hoped to find a Muslim country where they could live together and have children: 'I wouldn't bring them up here, because the whole society is calling to something else.' Another woman was home-educating her children: 'Everything is just a battle bringing them up in a *kufr* society, because everything is inimical to Islam. You can make your house as Islamic as you like but the minute you step outside you see half-naked women, you have loud music playing, you have people smoking and drinking in the streets, and this is all anti-Islam. So it's very, very difficult.' However, this woman felt that she was better off living in Britain rather than any of the Muslim countries 'because none of them are ruled by Islam and they're all oppressive to women, and if they're not oppressive to women they're very cultural and the Islamic laws have been so relaxed that there's all this free mixing, and all this *fitnah* [temptation, discord] is happening'. Other parents spoke of the need for their children to be integrated into society, though one of these felt conflicted, saying of her young son: 'I want him

---

[87] Winter, 'Muslim Loyalty and Belonging', p. 19.
[88] Yusuf, 'Just Enough Religion to Hate'.
[89] O'Sullivan, 'If you Hate the West'.
[90] Al-Qwidi, 'Understanding the Stages of Conversion to Islam', p. 234.

to be integrated and be part of this community, but I also want him to be a practising Muslim. It's difficult, and the two aren't always very compatible'; she thought that she and her family might spend a few years in a Muslim country while the children were growing up.

In the wake of events such as the Northern England riots, 9/11 and the July 2005 bombings, and the resulting backlash, there has been some talk among British Muslims of contingency plans in the event that things deteriorate. In a letter to *Q-News* (ironically published shortly before 9/11), one convert expresses the sense of impending danger, referring to the 2001 riots: 'As the Oldham and Burnley debacles demonstrate, Muslims in this country cannot guarantee to themselves that this is a safe country to live in. We don't know when things here will blow up . . . Whoever has an escape route, even if they would be less well-off materially, should use it.'[91] Even Sarah Joseph (writing in late 2004), a strong advocate of the need for integration and the creation of a British Islam, admits to having considered 'exit strategies', drawing parallels with the Jews in 1930s Germany.[92] However, only one interviewee explicitly linked the possibility of moving with the current climate of hostility against Muslims, saying that she and her husband and child would move 'if the situation gets worse'. One can only assume that such fears are at least as strong if not more so among born Muslims, who as first-, second- or third-generation immigrants, are likely to feel even more vulnerable to attack.[93]

The concept of the *ummah* is one that resonates with Muslims throughout the world. In a well-known *ḥadīth*, Muhammad says that 'the *ummah* is one body: when one part hurts, the entire body suffers'. There is a steadily expanding global Muslim discourse on the *ummah*, strengthened by the perceived injustices done to Muslims, and fed by the Qur'anic emphasis on God's justice and the struggle between good and evil; in the political context, the discourse of religion is often felt to be more effective than that of 'ethnic politics'.[94] Historically, the *ummah* was never a unified political entity, but always a powerful symbol of Muslim unity, the expression of a religious identity that was, and still is, seen as transcending national or ethnic

---

[91] Letters, *Q-News*, 334, August 2001.
[92] Joseph, 'Surmountable Obstacles'.
[93] An ICM poll conducted soon after the July 2005 bombings found that 63% of Muslims had considered leaving Britain (V. Dodd, 'Two-Thirds of Muslims Consider Leaving UK', *The Guardian*, 26 July 2005).
[94] Geaves, 'Negotiating British Citizenship and Muslim Identity', p. 71.

boundaries. Muslims may understand the concept in minimalist terms, as a vague sense of belonging which does not entail any duties or obligations, or, at the other end of the spectrum, in terms of an aspiration for political unity among Muslims; for most it is something in between. In the contemporary Western context, the reality of the *ummah* becomes more tangible as a result of immigration; in the more cosmopolitan mosques, for example, one finds Muslims of many different races and ethnicities worshipping together.[95] Some argue that globalization, especially the internet, has brought the potential for the *ummah* to be realized without the need for a single pan-Islamic polity.[96] Allievi observes that one of the attractions of joining Islam is that it opens 'vast horizons' in terms of personal and professional development and activities, and the new affiliation constitutes a kind of 'communal capital' from which converts can benefit as well as other Muslims.[97]

The sense of belonging to the *ummah* is potentially as real and powerful for Muslims as any sense of affiliation to a national or ethnic group. In fact, Jacobson argues that the *ummah* is analogous to an ethnic group in its provision of a 'sense of belonging and continuity', whilst its 'sacred history' provides a 'sense of kinship . . . [and an] emphasis on sacred places'. According to her, for British Muslims, who constitute a relatively small minority, the idea of the *ummah* provides a sense that 'their religious beliefs and practice traverse the globe and history and are, thus, components of what is a vast and (potentially at least) powerful force'.[98] Jacobson argues that this concept has the potential to strengthen the plausibility structure in which Muslim identity can flourish;[99] if so, this must be all the more true for converts, who need to forge an Islamic identity without the benefit of a Muslim family of origin. Birt finds that 'the insistence upon an overriding attachment to the umma and its suffering' has become central to British Muslims' identity, partly as a result of their feelings of exclusion in relation to the wider society.[100] The growth of the Muslim media in Britain has further enhanced this sense of belonging to a global *ummah*.[101]

---

[95] As Sayyid puts it: 'This juxtaposing of various Muslim populations has the effect of producing the conditions for the articulation of a Muslim *Umma*' ('Beyond Westphalia', p. 36).
[96] See on this Mandaville, 'Reimagining the *Ummah*?'.
[97] Allievi, *Les Convertis à l'Islam*, pp. 282 and 280.
[98] Jacobson, *Islam in Transition*, p. 149.   [99] Ibid., p. 148.
[100] Birt, 'Between Nation and Umma', p. 6.
[101] Ahmed, 'Reading Between the Lines', p. 119.

Converts tend to have Muslim friends from diverse ethnic backgrounds; this, combined with the fact that Muslims are often very sociable, interacting with each other in private gatherings, meetings or in the mosque, heightens the awareness of the *ummah*. As one woman pointed out, when there is a crisis in a part of the Muslim world: 'We tend to know people [connected with the crisis], so it makes it more real to us.' Not surprisingly, almost all my interviewees felt that the concept of the *ummah* was meaningful to them, saying that they had a sense of connection (to varying degrees) with Muslims globally. Some described this connection in specific ways. One black woman felt that the solidarity she had previously experienced with other black people had been replaced by a sense of solidarity with Muslims. Whereas before in any given social situation she had been used to gravitating towards a black person over a non-black person, now 'if there was a *ḥijābī* and a non-*ḥijābī*, I'd gravitate towards the *ḥijābī*, because I'd feel like maybe we'd have the same thing, have the same mindset or something like that'. One woman from an Asian background observed that in Britain 'you can go to any wedding, any mosque, anywhere in the country, and if there's a Muslim they'll talk to me and I'll talk to them, even if we have nothing in common. I never had this before I was Muslim. Because even as an Asian ... I wouldn't automatically talk to any Asian, but now I will automatically talk to any Muslim.' A woman of Irish origin said: 'If Muslims are getting hurt in Iraq or Palestine or Afghanistan, your blood is boiling, it's like it's your country,' adding: 'If someone attacked Ireland I would have the same feeling.' Sulayman felt that the *ummah* was not just a fellow-feeling with other Muslims but also a living social reality manifested in a tangible way: 'You have little pockets of communities working very nicely thank you very much, they're doing very well, and you have mosque committees distributing *zakāh* [Muslim alms tax], neighbours helping each other out. And Eid, everyone prays. You think actually, in many subtle ways this is working very, very well.' However, he did feel that governments in the Muslim world tended to obstruct this 'connecting up of communities'.

Several interviewees contrasted the ideal of the *ummah* with the disappointing reality; Mahmud, for example, had thought of the *ummah* as 'an extended brotherhood and sisterhood', but felt that that was disappearing: 'Everything's got much more difficult. People are at each other's throats, denouncing each other and finding fault with each other.' The theme of Muslim disunity is echoed by Mohammad Siddique Seddon, who observes that paradoxically, 'Muslim identity is defined by its universalism but the inability to realize this practically, beyond the Hajj, has left Muslims staring at each other like strangers'.[102] Four interviewees had concerns about the concept of *ummah* being hijacked or misused by extremist Muslims for political ends,[103] and several others expressed reservations of one kind or another about the *ummah*. One of these was Andrew: 'It's not the be-all and end-all of being a Muslim, I'm not going to jump up and down about it . . . you just do whatever you can do in your own sphere of influence.' Peter said that the concept was 'a bit abstract' for him, although he did feel a connection with other Muslims and was concerned at the plight of Muslims who were suffering. He was frustrated at the state of affairs in the *ummah* because 'some Muslims are making trouble for the rest of us'. Amin acknowledged that it was part of the faith 'to feel for people wherever they are', but since he did not have any control over what happens in the Muslim world, he felt that British Muslims should focus on their own problems, such as lack of unity.[104] Some converts point out the dangers of 'tribalism', or an attitude of 'my people right or wrong'.[105] On the subject of the *ummah*, three interviewees specifically mentioned the need to be concerned for non-Muslims as well as Muslims.

Roald found in the course of her research that converts sometimes felt overwhelmed by the problems of Muslims globally and so needed to find 'relief from the sheer weight of the burden of the Muslim Umma'; she argues that such converts may gravitate back to their original culture as an anti-dote.[106] This point is illustrated by Michael Young in his article 'Frustrations of a Muslim Convert': 'When I became a Muslim, I did NOT adopt an alien culture . . . Nor did I sign up as a supporter of a variety of nationalistic

---

[102] Seddon, '"Some Thoughts on the Formation of British Muslim Identity"', p. 187.

[103] Yahya Birt feels that the politicized notion of the *ummah* which has gained currency in recent years is 'reductive', and not 'rooted in transcendent values'. While understanding the temptation to see in globalization an opportunity to realize the *ummah* in an unprecedented way, he believes that the nation-state holds out more hope for the enfranchisement of Muslims and other minorities ('Between Nation and Umma', pp. 1 and 6).

[104] Overall, Shi'i inteviewees were slightly more reserved about the *ummah* than Sunnis. One Shi'i convert I spoke to (not part of my sample) said: 'Shi'is don't really have that concept [*ummah*] because they were always excluded from that.'

[105] See, e.g., Scott, letter to *Q-News* (November 2001) and Birt, 'Islamic Citizenship in Britain after 7/7', pp. 11–12.

[106] Roald, *New Muslims in the European Context*, p. 337.

independence or separatist struggles around the world . . . just because the protagonists happen to be Muslims.' He feels that some of the Muslim struggles, including the Palestinian one, are matters of geopolitics rather than religion: 'I genuinely feel that Muslims who fail to distinguish between the secular/political and the religious/theological in this regard do a great disservice to the religion of Islam.'[107]

Ideological opposition to 'nationalism' (variously defined, and often undefined) is a fairly common motif in Islamist discourse, and some converts participate in or contribute to this anti-nationalist discourse. One or two of my interviewees expressed views opposing nationalism or the nation-state, but most did not comment on (and were not asked about) such theoretical matters. In a booklet published in 1978, 'Abd al-Qadir as-Sufi's list of 'actions necessary for a return to Islam' include the following: 'Oppose nationalism. Do not permit nationalist mosques . . . Refuse to salute flags or respect national anthems.'[108] While some see nationalism and allegiance to the *ummah* as antithetical, appeals to the *ummah* do not necessarily downplay national belonging. In a study of the more progressive British Muslim media (*Q-News* and *emel*), Moll finds an extensive interest in the plight of Muslims suffering in different parts of the world, and that this is 'sacralized in the discourse, represented as stemming from the very "nature" of Islam as a borderless, organic entity'; however, she finds no suggestion that attachment to the *ummah* should replace or supersede British nationality.[109]

Murad, who is engaged in an attempt to retrieve a British Muslim heritage (for example by reviving traditional English Muslim songs originally composed by Quilliam and others),[110] goes further than most in harmonizing (British) nationalism with Islam. In his view, British national identity is not inimical to Islam because, unlike some of its European counterparts, it was not constructed in conscious opposition to an Islamic rival. As a 'founding epic' for British national identity he finds the Arthurian legend somewhat congenial as 'a religious story replete with an esoteric . . . symbolism', and suggests that the imagery of the Round Table, representing the zodiac, might be of Middle Eastern origin.[111] His reservations about multiculturalism

---

[107] Young, 'Frustrations of a Muslim Convert'.
[108] As-Sufi, *Jihad*, p. 38.
[109] Moll, '"Beyond Beards, Scarves and Halal Meat"'.
[110] See Murad, 'Muslim Songs of the British Isles'.
[111] Winter, 'Some Thoughts on the Formation of British Muslim Identity', p. 11.

('a country that accepts migrants ... has the right to expect that they engage in some form of cultural migration as well') are echoed by Hasan Le Gai Eaton.[112] One of my interviewees (who was scathing about 'the multicultural claptrap') spoke of his 'inherent sympathy with nationalism, whoever's nationalism it is', and he described it as his 'main guide in political philosophy'. On this matter, he referred to himself, appropriately enough, as 'a very untypical Muslim'.

Western commentators often raise the issue of loyalty in relation to British Muslims, positing a tension between allegiance to the *ummah*, on the one hand, and to Britain, on the other. Perhaps partly in response to suspicions arising from this alleged tension, one man reiterated several times in the course of the interview that Muslims were 'model citizens' who abide by the law of the land. Muslims have advanced several arguments to show that Islamic identity is not incompatible with citizenship of a non-Muslim country. Dilwar Hussain, for example, argues that different loyalties operate at different levels, and it is part of the human experience to be constantly balancing the various loyalties to family, work, nation and so on. He points out that the experience of conflicting loyalties is not peculiar to Muslims, and that the European or modern traditions of freedom of thought and human rights presuppose a certain latitude in negotiating such varying allegiances.[113] A common argument amongst Muslims (which invokes the importance of upholding contracts in Islamic law) is that by living in a Western country Muslims accept the 'contract' of citizenship and thereby agree to abide by its laws. Only in extreme cases (for example, if one was forced to do something against the *sharī'ah*) would there be a need to break the contract, and even then this would be done not by breaking the law but by moving to another country.[114] One woman of *salafī* persuasion who expressed a strong desire to perform *hijrah* rehearsed this argument almost exactly: 'I have to completely respect the country which I'm living in and follow the rules. Islamically that's what it says, if they have rules you don't like

---

[112] Murad, 'Tradition or Extradition?'; Rahman, 'The Talented Mr Gai Eaton'.
[113] Hussain, 'British Muslim Identity', p. 104. He further argues that Muslim grievances about British foreign policy need not be problematic, since many Muslim countries have perpetrated crimes against other Muslim nations without people feeling the need to denounce their national identity on that account (p. 110). Dilwar Hussain's argument that Islamic affiliation is a religious and philosophical matter while British identity is a matter of citizenship was described in chapter 1.
[114] See, e.g., Yusuf, 'Just Enough Religion to Hate'.

you can move out and do *hijrah* ... You signed a contract saying that you have to follow their rules.'

According to Abdal-Hakim Murad, the Islamic principle of *maṣlaḥah* (public interest) provides the basis for the duty to act according to the law. In his view, Islam 'supplies arguments for loyalty ... because it recognises that it is the point from which one needs to begin working towards the ideal'. Although Muslims hope to see the *sharī'ah* implemented eventually, he points out that in the British context at least that is an ultimate hope rather than an imminent reality. He also observes that in any case it is not currently implemented in any Muslim country: 'The fundamental object[ive]s, *maqāṣid*, of the *sharī'ah* ... are respected in the legal codes of the contemporary West. We may even venture to note that they appear to be better maintained here than in the ham-fisted attempts at creating *sharī'ah* states that we see in several corners of the Muslim world.' On the issue of loyalty, Murad draws a parallel between Muslims in Britain today and Muslims in British India in the past, arguing that most Muslims chose to stay and live under British rule. He also refers to the Muslim contribution to the British cause at different junctures in history, including the Second World War, in which 'to fight for the Allies was unquestionably a *jihād*'.[115] Hassan Scott brings similar arguments in support of Muslim loyalty to a non-Muslim government. He deplores the fact that Muslims who join the establishment are attacked for so doing, even if they engage in constructive criticism of it, and feels that young Muslims are given a false choice between loyalty to Islam and assimilation to ' "kuffar" society'. However, he also relates (in an article published in December 2003) that when he told a gathering of converts that Muslims should be grateful to Western powers for 'the defeat of Fascism and Communism', he was met with a resounding silence.[116] Such a view is evidently unfashionable in the current climate.

CONCLUDING REMARKS

As Gerholm points out, Western societies are characterized by a high degree of open debate and tolerance of disagreement, and they tend to have a

---

[115] Winter, 'Muslim Loyalty and Belonging', pp. 19–20.
[116] Scott, 'Right This Way'. It is not stated whether this occurred before or after the onset of the Iraq war.

strong tradition of criticism from within.[117] Muslim critiques of Western society are perhaps most akin to two particular strands of this criticism, one religious and one not. There is some common ground with evaluations of secularism advanced by evangelicals who call for religious faith to have a greater role in society and culture.[118] However, criticism of Western societies is on the whole higher on the agenda of Muslims than Christians, and the Muslim critiques tend to be more radical and oppositional. To that extent, they resemble the more explicitly political and economic approach of 'alternative' critiques, for example those of the anti-globalization and ecology movements.

From the mystical–philosophical approach of the perennial philosophers to the radical–revolutionary stance of the Murabitun to the traditionalist mode of Abdal-Hakim Murad, converts have been pioneering Muslim intellectual critiques of Western society from within for over half a century. Unlike many of these critiques, that of the perennial philosophers is something of a shared enterprise with both non-Muslims and born Muslims, Seyyed Hossein Nasr being the most prolific and widely read of the latter group. The Murabitun combine an intellectual radicalism with an activism which is manifested in community building and calls for 'financial *jihād*'. In its early phase in particular this movement (then known as the Darqawiyya) represented a unique manifestation of an indigenous Islam. Its emphasis on being a European movement (which for a time involved a dissociation from born Muslims) while rejecting Western social norms is somewhat paradoxical. The Murabitun's critique of Western society is very much one 'from within', as its members do not take the Muslim world as their reference point (seeing all Muslim states as *kāfir*), although they do hark back to the historical models of the early Medinan community (and the Maliki *fiqh* which originated there) and the *ribāṭ*.[119] The fact that Ahmad Thomson's book (*Dajjal: The AntiChrist*) continues to be reprinted by a well-known UK Muslim publishing house suggests that such writings appeal to a wider audience than just the Murabitun. As a traditionalist, Abdal-Hakim Murad, like the perennial philosophers, has a shared ethos with many born Muslims, though he has his own idiosyncratic style. He provides a more

---

[117] Gerholm, 'Three European Intellectuals', p. 272.
[118] See, e.g., the writings of Lesslie Newbigin; see also http://www.gospel-culture.org.uk.
[119] An outpost or centre dedicated to both military and religious training.

tempered critique than the Murabitun, arguing that Muslims cannot reject the whole of global modernity, but should instead introduce Islam as 'a prophetic, dissenting witness *within* the reality of the modern world'.[120]

Muslim converts' chosen marginality enables them to question the dominant ethos. Addressing Western liberals, Hamza Yusuf observes: 'Because you wish your values to prevail throughout the world, it doesn't always follow that the world wishes to adopt them.'[121] Na'ima Robert says unequivocally: 'As Muslims, we live by a different moral code from the society we live in.'[122] She speaks of the 'arrogance' of Western people, asking: 'How do you know that the Muslim woman walking down the street is not happier than you?'[123] However, the fact that British society provides an environment in which it is possible for people to become Muslim militates against any blanket condemnation or outright rejection of British life and culture. The following comment by one of my interviewees illustrates the way in which converts may differ from born Muslims in their attitude to certain 'unIslamic' features of society: 'For the sake of Allah, obviously I hate the pubs and the drunkenness and the clubbing thing on a Friday and a Saturday night, but to be honest I can't hate it too much because I know I was part of it and it made me what I am, and I became Muslim.'

Western and Islamic norms are inverse mirror images of each other with respect to both religion and sexuality. In Western society religion is considered by and large to be a private matter, while sexuality has entered the public sphere in many different ways and has become part of identity politics.[124] For most Muslims, on the other hand, religion is not just a personal and spiritual affair but also very much a social – and to some extent a political – phenomenon, while sexuality is a very private matter. Attitudes to religion and sexuality are therefore among the most counter-cultural aspects of being Muslim in Western society. However, the acknowledgement by one man that he was 'really an uptight prude when it comes to homosexuality' provides an interesting example of the way in which Western norms may continue to operate after conversion; even though this man agreed with the Islamic ruling that homosexuality was wrong, he still privileged prevailing

[120] Murad, 'Faith in the Future'.
[121] Yusuf, 'Islam Has a Progressive Tradition Too'.
[122] Robert, *From my Sisters' Lips*, p. 93.
[123] Gordon, 'That Muslim Woman Could be Happier Than you . . .'.
[124] See on this Modood, 'The Place of Muslims', pp. 125–6.

Western norms (at least in conversation with a non-Muslim interviewer) in his description of himself as 'an uptight prude'. I could find no clear correlation between sexual attitudes and either conversion age or chronological age. It might be expected that people who convert later in life would be more likely to bring their fully developed adult views and attitudes with them into their new Islamic identity (and thus to preserve views that were formed in a Western, relatively liberal, context). However, a countervailing point is that the younger converts grew up in an age of even greater liberalization (given the speed with which attitudes are changing in British society). Therefore, although their adaptation to Islamic norms might be more radical due to their greater impressionability, their starting point, as it were, is one of greater liberality. As no research has been done to date on British Muslim attitudes towards sexuality, it is difficult to make a comparison with born Muslims. However, some interviewees did feel that converts had a different approach to this issue based on their experience of growing up as non-Muslims. The emphasis on the public–private divide is common to all Muslims, but I did gain the impression that many converts have a more nuanced view of homosexuality than one would expect from most born Muslims.

In Western Europe and North America, attitudes to sexuality have changed dramatically in recent decades. On sexually related matters it must be acknowledged that the dominant Islamic (or for that matter Christian or Jewish) paradigm is very different from that of contemporary Western societies in which even to talk about 'appropriate treatment' or 'tolerance' of homosexuals would be politically incorrect and probably also offensive to gay and lesbian people. The Islamic emphasis on the public–private divide may seem hypocritical to some and is clearly at odds with the idea of homosexuality as an identity. This is a subject about which emotions run high and people can become polarized (witness the opposition to Yusuf al-Qaradawi's visit to Britain in July 2004, which focused largely on his views on homosexuality). Even if the Islamic paradigm is anathema to some, it is important to recognize nuances and diversity within it.

Converts are to be found at all points of the political spectrum, from the far left to the far right.[125] However, in many cases one person's opinions fall

---

[125] Roger Garaudy gave a boost to revisionist thought among Muslims in his 1995 book *Mythes Fondateurs de la Politique Israelienne*, which was translated into Arabic and Persian. In 1998 he was found guilty of Holocaust denial by a French court.

at different points on the left–right continuum, making it doubtful whether 'left' and 'right' are the most useful categories of analysis for Muslim political thought in contemporary Britain. Among my sample, political views or stances did not seem to be age-related; the more 'extreme' views were not necessarily promulgated by the younger or more recent converts, as one might have expected. On political matters there is a need for caution in drawing conclusions due to the difficulty of ascertaining how far convert discourse is influenced by contingent factors, given the rather dramatic events of recent years. As mentioned earlier, the Islamic state, the *sharī'ah* and the *ummah* are emblematic and often have an emotional resonance. They may be equally emblematic for non-Muslims, with the phrase 'Islamic state' conjuring up negative images of, say, draconian punishments for particular crimes. Again, due to the limited nature of research on British Muslims, it is difficult to compare convert and born Muslim reactions to recent political developments, including both terrorist actions perpetrated by Muslims and British foreign and domestic policy. It is clear that converts, like born Muslims (and, it bears repeating, many non-Muslims), have been deeply affected by these events, and that the Iraq war and the anti-terrorist measures in particular have led to a high degree of disaffection and disillusionment with the British government. In published and internet material converts are vocal critics of both British government policy and Islamic extremism. Given that converts probably constitute around 1% of British Muslims, it is fair to say that their representation in this discourse is disproportionate to their numbers, reflecting converts' relatively high level of participation in Islamic activities and debate generally. Converts participate in the same debates about political participation and loyalty as born Muslims; but the favourable disposition towards nationalism on the part of Murad and a very few others may be unique to converts.

The recent politicization of British Muslims, including converts, needs to be viewed in the framework of a diasporic attachment to the *ummah*, with the latter, as Birt points out, being defined as an *ummah* of suffering.[126] The potentially radicalizing effect of the Iraq war struck me most forcibly in the case of one male convert who I spoke to; he was very far from being an 'extremist' (he was not involved in or affiliated to any politically oriented organization or group, and he said that he had spent some time and effort

---

[126] Birt, 'Between Nation and Umma', p. 6.

trying to reason with radicalized young Muslims and dissuade them from any unwise actions). He told how after the invasion of Iraq he had seriously contemplated committing an act of violence against a person whom he deemed to have some responsibility for the war. He had experienced a considerable internal struggle. On the one hand, he was afraid that to do nothing would be wrong and that he would be answerable for that in the Hereafter; on the other, he acknowledged that such an act would have been a case of vigilantism or a 'crime of passion', and not sanctioned by Islam. Ultimately, he had taken a deliberate decision not to act.

Where a desire to move to a Muslim country was expressed, it seemed to spring from social rather than narrow political considerations, with interviewees evincing a strong desire to bring children up in a society where religion is accorded a positive value and where standards of public and sexual morality are more in keeping with Islamic norms. I would see the aspiration to move as the expression of a perennial urge to escape the stress of trying to uphold values and standards of behaviour that are so clearly at odds with those of society. It is worth remembering that there are plenty of non-Muslim Britons choosing to move abroad in search of a better quality of life, and perhaps in search of values they feel are being eroded in modern Britain. Many people, Muslim and non-Muslim alike, would agree that it is not easy to bring children up in cities whilst trying to protect them from social ills such as drug and alcohol use and criminal activity. Comparing my findings with those of al-Qwidi (whose interviews were conducted before 9/11), it seems that the appeal of living abroad may have increased among converts in recent years, whether due to perceived social decline, political developments or fear of possible persecution in the future.[127]

Many of the concerns expressed by Muslims resonate with traditional British 'conservative' values, particularly in the areas of the family and social morality. Wider concerns relating to the Iraq war and the 'war on terror', as well as consumerism, materialism and (perhaps to a lesser extent) the sexualization of society are also shared by many non-Muslims in Britain and Western societies. However, while the moral protests of so many fall prey to the forces of inertia and desensitization, converts find in Islam a support

---

[127] I would argue that unfortunately such fears are not unfounded. If further Muslim-perpetrated terrorist incidents were to happen on British soil, for example, the impact on public opinion could have serious repercussions, greatly strengthening the far right.

network which validates their concerns and their disenchantment with British society. The Islamic framework enables them to formulate a particularly cogent critique of Western culture. The step that converts take when they embrace Islam is, in a sense, a step sideways, a disengagement from many of society's values, not necessarily the core liberal values – but the excesses that flow from them.

Chapter 5

Women and men

Issues of gender and sexuality have a high profile in both Muslim and non-Muslim discourse on Islam. For non-Muslims, it is these issues rather than religious concerns in the narrower sense that epitomize Islam's 'otherness'; no doubt this is related to the fact that Islamic teachings on male–female relations are highly distinctive when set against the norms of contemporary mainstream Western society. The subject of women in Islam is highly sensitized (there is a long history of polemic and apologetic between Muslims and non-Muslims), and not without political overtones. In the colonial period, claims that Islam's teachings on women were evidence of its 'backwardness' provided justification for political intervention in Muslim countries, and some argue that the construction of Islam as 'oppressive' towards women continues to serve specific Western political interests, contributing to the construction of Islam or Islamism as the new 'enemy' to replace communism.[1] Apart from this aspect of 'oppression', another common motif informing the negative portrayal of Islam in the Western media and popular imagination is that of violence. The *ḥijāb* is widely read as a symbol of the former, but also, at times, of the latter, and so serves as a focal point for Western hostility to Islam in general. As Farhia Thomas of the Muslim Women's Resource Centre in Glasgow points out, describing reactions that she and her *ḥijāb*-wearing friends encounter: 'We're either oppressed or we've got Kalashnikovs under our coats.'[2] Women who convert to Islam sometimes find themselves on the receiving end of a particular type of hostility, being accused of being traitors to their sex, or of

---

[1] E.g. Bullock, *Rethinking Muslim Women and the Veil*, p. 227.
[2] See http://www.nujglasgow.org.uk/understandingislam.html.

10

having betrayed the cause of feminism for which women in the West fought so hard. Katherine Bullock, a Canadian convert and author of an academic study on perceptions of the *ḥijāb*, reports that she was told that she 'didn't belong' at an International Women's Day gathering, as it was felt that she represented the subjugation of women.[3]

Gender issues sometimes feature in conversion stories, particularly those of women. Converts not infrequently describe how they initially shared the 'prejudices' of mainstream society, and how these had to be over-come before conversion could take place. Many therefore make a point of informing themselves on the Islamic teachings in this area before taking the decision to become Muslim. For some, male–female role differentiation and the emphasis on marriage and the family is one of the attractions of conver-sion, as mentioned in chapter 2. The contrast between the Islamic emphasis on marriage and the family and the perceived breakdown of family values in Western society is a common theme among converts generally. As Fatima put it: 'I have discovered that Islam allows convert women not to compete in the workplace, or in the beauty-stakes. There are women who do actually just want to stay at home and have children. Islam makes it okay to do that. They are not seen as failures, as they might be by other Western women.'

The fact that some women are attracted to more traditional gender roles needs to be seen against the backdrop of the social upheaval of recent decades, and in particular the rapid and dramatic changes in gender roles and sexual behaviour since the 1960s. Harfiyah Ball-Haleem expresses the resulting sense of confusion: 'Society expects women to be both men and women, to be sexy and virtuous, beautiful and clever and everything else'; for her, Islam provides a counterpoint: 'In Islam you have your role shown to you. Your femininity is recognised and appreciated and valued but you are not restricted from working or doing anything else.'[4] Social changes will have impacted differently on different generations of converts, but the gen-eral state of flux is a common factor. Franks, in a study of Muslim and Christian revivalist women in Britain, observes that the fact that some Western women choose to join religious revivalist movements (despite living in liberal, democratic societies), implies that they must derive some advantage from their choice, and so cannot simply be seen as passive

[3] Bullock, *Rethinking Muslim Women and the Veil*, p. xv.
[4] Quoted in Petre, 'My Dad Buys me Books about Islam'.

victims.[5] She suggests that the appeal of such movements has grown with the increased pressures on women (who bear the 'double burden' of domestic duties and competing in the labour market), especially in the context of a diminishing welfare state in Britain.[6] According to Franks, although women who join such movements may not contest patriarchal relations directly, they may nevertheless gain a sense of empowerment through their religious involvement.[7] Hermansen also draws attention to the broader context, suggesting that research on women's involvement in New Religious Movements (NRMs) that revitalize traditional gender roles may provide a useful analytical framework for understanding female conversion to Islam; she points out that while some researchers see such involvement as a backlash against feminism and a return to patriarchal norms, others see it in terms of a critique of secular gender roles and as an example of female empowerment.[8]

Research on gender and conversion to Islam has looked at the extent to which women converts adopt or maintain traditional Islamic gender paradigms.[9] Roald suggests that new converts initially go along with these paradigms, but that as they become more confident in their knowledge of Islam they may challenge them and gravitate towards patterns which more closely resemble those of their culture of origin.[10] In her view, it is those who are more marginalized and who have less contact with majority society (including *salafīs*), as well as the less educated, who are more likely to accept the traditional Muslim gender pattern.[11] Badran describes how the element of critical thinking and investigation that initially brought a woman to Islam may be applied to the Islamic sources after her conversion, notwithstanding patriarchal forces which may attempt to dissuade her from such investigation.[12] Badran and Roald both feel that converts have a particular contribution to make to gender issues; Badran argues that converts are 'less likely [than born Muslims] to get stalled in repetitive debates over terminology, cultural imperialism, and authenticity', and so may be better placed to advance the debates on issues such as Islamic feminism,[13] while Roald feels

---

[5] Franks, *Women and Revivalism in the West*, p. 77.   [6] Ibid., pp. 116 and 121.
[7] Ibid., p. 185.   [8] Hermansen, 'Keeping the Faith', pp. 262–3.
[9] Much of this research is contained in van Nieuwkerk (ed.), *Women Embracing Islam*.
[10] Roald, 'The Shaping of a Scandinavian "Islam"', p. 59; cf. Badran, 'Feminism and Conversion', p. 201.
[11] Roald, 'The Shaping of a Scandinavian "Islam"', p. 63.
[12] Badran, 'Feminism and Conversion', p. 216.   [13] Ibid., pp. 195–6.

that converts are well placed to engage in cultural synthesis, bringing elements of both Western and Islamic culture together.[14] It is difficult to sustain a view of Muslim women converts as oppressed and disempowered given that, as Badran points out: 'In converting, women exercise agency, bravely and decisively, in going against the grain of their background, family, and culture and in opting for something strange and new.'[15] However, Badran also finds that 'converts often acquiesce in conventional patriarchal, so-called Muslim family practices, accepting a subordinate position, often euphemistically called a complementary position.'[16] Hermansen in her study of American women converts suggests that only a minority of converts follow a gender paradigm that reflects the norms of mainstream society.[17]

Converts to Islam have been described as the 'collateral damage' of feminism.[18] Among Muslims generally, Western feminism is often seen as too individualistic and as having failed even on its own terms, since women continue to suffer the double burden of domestic duties and work outside the home. Abdal-Hakim Murad claims that Western feminism has 'diminished the self-esteem available to wives seeking fulfilment in traditional roles'.[19] Similarly, Harfiya Ball-Haleem argues that 'feminism has robbed women of their right to be women. It has forced them out to work and fewer and fewer are getting married. This is something that Islam protects against. I feel that I'm more liberated now because I was terribly confused about the values that society held.'[20] Despite their rejection of Western feminism, converts' views on gender need to be seen against the backdrop of the rise of Islamic feminism in the early 1990s. The term 'feminism' in this context continues to be controversial, with many who could be described as having broadly feminist aims reluctant to accept the label because of its Western, individualistic connotations.[21] Islamic feminism aims at the empowerment

---

[14] Roald, 'The Shaping of a Scandinavian "Islam"', p. 68.
[15] Badran, 'Feminism and Conversion', p. 202.
[16] Ibid., p. 210. 'Patriarchy' is generally used as a pejorative term by feminists, including Islamic feminists; however, the term needs to be problematized since many if not most of the latter still hold to the idea of the husband being 'head of the household' in some sense.
[17] Hermansen, 'Keeping the Faith', p. 263.
[18] Haddad, 'The Quest for Peace in Submission', p. 34, quoting a convert.
[19] Murad, 'Diana and Dionysus'.
[20] Quoted in Petre, 'My Dad Buys me Books about Islam'.
[21] Badran draws a distinction between feminism as a term of identity and as an analytical term, pointing out that 'many Muslims identify *with* feminism as an analytical construct

of women through methods or sources derived from the Islamic tradition, in particular Qur'anic interpretation (*tafsīr*). Most Islamic feminists subscribe to an 'equal but different' view of male–female relations which stresses complementarity over strict equality; this is a point of contention with most Western forms of feminism, which tend to view the assertion of difference between the sexes as implying male superiority. While many Islamic feminists believe that Islam can be disengaged from patriarchy, most Westerners see Islam as an inherently patriarchal religion and are consequently sceptical about 'Islamic feminism', which may be dismissed by Western feminists as 'false consciousness'.[22]

When it comes to the position of women in Islam, converts frequently highlight the contrast between ideals and realities, and are keenly aware of the fact that the practice in Islamic societies often leaves much to be desired. Huda al-Khattab, for example, feels that many of the problems in Muslim cultures stem from the unequal treatment of boys and girls, with the boys being given more freedom and a better education.[23] Abdal-Hakim Murad observes that in countries such as Saudi Arabia where women are 'not even permitted to drive cars', they are 'the victims of an oppression which is not the product of a divinely-willed sheltering of a sex, but of ego, of the *nafs* [self, ego] of the male'.[24] Fatima Martin's article 'What Muslim Women Want' can be read as a catalogue of the failings of some Muslim cultures, as it includes the following headings: 'equal access to education'; 'the right to choose their husbands'; 'the right to work'; 'the right to visit the mosques'; 'the right to acquire religious knowledge'; and 'the right to the help and presence of the husband at home'. These headings draw attention to an implicit distinction between Islamic ideals (how things should be) and cultural realities (how things are), which is a common strategy of Muslim or Islamic feminists.

Women converts such as Amina Wadud in the US, Katherine Bullock in Canada and Anne-Sofie Roald in Norway have been prominent contributors to the 'Islamic feminist' enterprise, whether or not they use that term.[25]

---

and act upon this, but do not identity themselves *as* feminists' ('Feminism and Conversion', p. 201).

[22] Bullock, *Rethinking Muslim Women and the Veil*, p. 39.

[23] Al-Khattab, *Bent Rib*, p. 61.

[24] Murad, 'Islam, Irigaray, and the Retrieval of Gender'.

[25] See Wadud, *Qur'an and Woman* and *Gender Jihad* (Oxford: Oneworld, 2006); Bullock, *Rethinking Muslim Women and the Veil*; and Roald, *Women in Islam*.

There has been no comparable intellectual contribution in Britain, although some British converts such as Ruqaiyyah Waris Maqsood, Huda al-Khattab (now resident in Canada) and Na'ima Robert have written on women's issues.[26] Interestingly it is a male convert, Abdal-Hakim Murad, who comes closest to participating in the contemporary 'Islamic feminist' discourse on an academic level; his method resonates with the hermeneutical approach of such scholars as Amina Wadud and Asma Barlas in America (although in many respects his views differ from theirs), while also incorporating insights from the Sufi-oriented work of Sachiko Murata, which explores the mystical dimensions of gender.[27] Murad sees men and women as manifesting 'complementary aspects of the divine perfection', and holds that 'gender is not convention but principle, not simple biology – but metaphysics'.[28] Men and women will therefore 'naturally gravitate towards divergent roles which affirm rather than suppress their respective genius'.[29] He refers to certain aspects of Islamic theology which in his view distinguish Islam from the other Abrahamic religions, especially Christianity; foremost among these is 'the spectacular absence of a gendered Godhead'. He elaborates: 'A theology which reveals the divine through incarnation in a body also locates it in a gender, and inescapably passes judgement on the other sex. A theology which locates it in a book makes no judgement about gender.'[30] The fact that God is not seen as 'Father' in Islam is represented as a further step away from patriarchy and male dominance.[31]

African American convert Amina Wadud embodies a progressive strand of Islamic feminism in that she has been prepared to challenge taboos such as the issue of female *imāms* (prayer leaders) and the desegregation of prayer space in the mosque. As a result of her efforts, she has suffered much hostility from more traditionally minded Muslims.[32] As previously mentioned, there are no comparable studies by British Muslim authors (convert

---

[26] See, e.g., Maqsood, *The Muslim Marriage Guide*; al-Khattab, *Bent Rib* and *The Muslim Woman's Handbook* (London: Ta-Ha, 1994); and Robert, *From my Sisters' Lips*.

[27] See especially Wadud, *Qur'an and Woman*; A. Barlas, *Believing Women in Islam: Unreading Patriarchal Interpretations of the Qur'an* (Austin: University of Texas Press, 2002); and S. Murata, *The Tao of Islam: A Sourcebook on Gender Relationships in Islamic Thought* (Albany: State University of New York Press, 1992).

[28] Murad, 'The Fall of the Family (Part II)'.

[29] Murad, 'Islam, Irigaray, and the Retrieval of Gender'.   [30] Ibid.

[31] Murad, 'The Fall of the Family (Part II)'.

[32] Badran, 'Feminism and Conversion', pp. 224–5.

or otherwise), but the seeds of such an approach can be discerned on the *Tasneem Project* website created by a male convert, Yakoub Islam.[33] In a paper entitled 'Gender Jihad', he laments the fact that contemporary mainstream Islamic discourse is 'flooded by puritanical Wahhabi and Salafi rhetoric, which either derides Muslim women or promotes social structures that disempower them', and draws attention to the need to incorporate the findings of contemporary social theory and acknowledge that gender and sexuality are 'social constructs'. He proclaims: 'As a middle class, white, liberal-arts educated European Muslim, I also consciously reject masculine identities that celebrate social distance and dominance . . . I also embrace Muslim discourse forms which elevate the masculine beyond patriarchal behaviour patterns.'[34]

This chapter will look at the practical and embodied aspects of gender identity, examining patterns of gendered behaviour and dress which are adopted by converts, while also observing their gender-related discourse. It incorporates sections on female covering (*ḥijāb* and *niqāb*),[35] social mixing and/or segregation between the sexes, views and practices related to marriage (including arranged marriage and husband–wife relations), and polygyny, an issue to which many converts have devoted much thought. It will be interesting to observe the extent to which Islamic feminist discourse has influenced converts' thought and practice in these areas, and also to discern any ways in which converts' attitudes are distinctive vis-à-vis those of born Muslims. A further area of interest will be the degree to which the findings of other researchers, in particular those whose views have been referred to in this section, are borne out in the British context.

ḤIJĀB AND *NIQĀB*: ELUDING THE MALE GAZE[36]

The covering of the body goes directly against mainstream British (and Western) culture in a dramatic and visible way. Roald lists some of the

---

[33] For the *Tasneem Project* see http://www.bayyinat.org.uk.
[34] Islam, 'Gender Jihad'.
[35] While the identity-related aspects of *ḥijāb* and *niqāb* were covered in chapter 3, here the focus is on aspects related to gender and sexuality.
[36] The term *ḥijāb* is used in this chapter to denote Muslim female dress covering everything except the face and hands, while *niqāb* denotes the face veil. Some use the term *ḥijāb* in a broader sense, denoting a whole etiquette of male–female relations. I have generally preferred

reasons for the hostility encountered by the *ḥijāb*-wearing woman as follows:

> She may evoke anger from non-Muslim westerners because they believe her to be betraying the struggle for women's rights by submitting to her own oppression in wearing the veil. Furthermore, she is perceived to be displaying the fact that she is at odds with the prevailing social and religious norms. An extreme reaction might even see her as dangerous for she might support or participate in so-called 'Islamic terrorist organisations' that threaten social stability. The visibility of her religious commitment may be seen to signal a 'holier than thou' attitude and thus evokes resentment in the non-Muslim.[37]

Guardian journalist Natasha Walter illustrates the ambivalence felt even by liberals, who espouse ideals of tolerance and pluralism: 'A lot of our culture is just so bound up with the idea that we should be free to uncover ourselves, to express ourselves through our clothes and the look of our bodies.' Although she says that she does not like *ḥijāb* herself, she insists that 'it's something that a pluralistic society has to accept – that people make choices that may seem to others peculiar or irrational'.[38] There has been a certain amount of debate among British Muslims on the socio-political aspects of *ḥijāb*, and some anxiety that Britain might become more like France, which is notorious among Muslims for its robust brand of secularism and its restrictive policies regarding *ḥijāb*.[39] Such is the strength of feeling on this subject that an organization based in Britain, *Protect-Hijab*, has come into existence specifically in order to campaign for Muslim women's right to wear the *ḥijāb*.[40]

Another reason for the hostility encountered by women wearing *ḥijāb* is that it subverts a long-standing tradition in Western culture which assigns to women the role of being looked at, of being evaluated and enjoyed visually, by men in particular but also by other women. Franks refers to the long history of female nudity in Western art which has contributed to this, and

it to the word 'veil' which, as well as being ambiguous, has exotic/Orientalist and sometimes negative connotations in Western discourse.

[37] Roald, *Women in Islam*, p. 254.   [38] Deen, 'What Women Want'.

[39] See on the French 'headscarves affair' F. Burgat, 'Veils and Obscuring Lenses', in J. Esposito and F. Burgat (eds.), *Modernizing Islam: Religion in the Public Sphere in Europe and the Middle East* (London: Hurst & Co., 2003).

[40] See http://www.prohijab.net.

points out that although British society is liberal in many ways, it still has certain expectations of women, in particular that they be 'the object of the gaze':

> This pattern of 'male looking/female "being looked-at-ness"' has been reinforced by the cinematic images of Hollywood ... The disruption of this pattern of the masculine gaze is not taken lightly by many women or men ... The disruption caused by the *ḥijāb* to the established hierarchy of the gaze is especially apparent when a woman is entirely covered because, unsurveilled, she is able to claim the right of scrutiny.[41]

There is a substantial body of academic literature on *ḥijāb*, mainly written from an anthropological or sociological viewpoint, documenting its multiple meanings and the varied reasons women give for wearing it.[42] Motivation for wearing the *ḥijāb* can be religious (for example a desire to obey God, an affirmation of a growing sense of spirituality), political (to express anti-Western sentiment, or opposition to a regime), economic (to save money on dress, or hide one's class origins), practical or pragmatic (to gain greater freedom of movement, avoid the unwanted attentions of men, or improve one's marriage prospects) or cultural. It might also represent a stand against consumerism or the dictates of fashion, a response to peer pressure, or a way of reinforcing gender divisions in order for women to claim their Islamic rights, especially the right of a woman to be maintained by her husband and to keep her own wages. Most often, motivation is complex and incorporates more than one of these factors. For female converts living in non-Muslim societies, some of these factors are more relevant than others. For example, the religious motive is likely to be relatively more prominent since for them, wearing *ḥijāb* is not culturally sanctioned; it may also represent a stand against prevailing social or sexual morality, a rejection of secularism (or at least a statement that religion is not just a private matter) and, as discussed in chapter 3, a statement of identity and belonging.

---

[41] Franks, 'Crossing the Borders of Whiteness?', p. 920.
[42] See, e.g., Bullock, *Rethinking Muslim Women and the Veil*; F. El-Guindi, *Veil: Modesty, Privacy and Resistance* (Oxford: Berg, 1999); F. Shirazi, *The Veil Unveiled: The Hijab in Modern Culture* (Gainseville: University Press of Florida, 2001); S. Zuhur, *Revealing Reveiling: Islamic Gender Ideology in Contemporary Egypt* (New York: State University of New York Press, 1992).

The theme of the empowerment of women emerges particularly clearly in the discourse on *ḥijāb*, thus introducing a strong feminist element even if the word 'feminism' itself is avoided. There is a particular resonance with the Western feminist critique of the objectification and commodification of the female body in capitalist societies.[43] As mentioned in chapter 3, women often report a heightened sense of self-confidence and self-esteem as a result of taking on *ḥijāb*, arising in part from a sense that they are now treated as a person rather than as a 'sex-object', and also from the fact that they are no longer dressing to please men. Roald points out that while feminist theory associates female covering with patriarchy and the control of female sexuality, converts do not generally feel that the issue of covering is linked to that of male power.[44] Western feminism has a long history of seeing the veil as a sign of women's oppression, and as something that restricts their freedom of movement, whereas for Muslim women it is sometimes the opposite, actually facilitating their entry into the public sphere and interaction with the opposite sex. This is described by Kavindra, an interviewee: 'As a female who wears *ḥijāb*, that allows you to do some things that perhaps without *ḥijāb* you couldn't do . . . it allows you to then talk to your colleagues, in not a socializing, not a flirtatious, not a chit-chat way.'[45] The use of the veil as a means of participating in society challenges the common Western (and to some extent traditional Islamic) association of veiling with seclusion.[46]

As Franks points out, the power relations vested in the *ḥijāb* depend on context, and wearing it in a liberal democracy such as Britain is very different from wearing it in a Muslim country where it is commonplace (and in some cases obligatory): 'In Britain, wearing Islamic dress is a sign of difference and non-conformity. Contrary to the view that Islamic revivalist women who wear the *ḥijāb* are passive victims, in order to wear Islamic dress in Britain today, they have to be bold and intrepid.'[47] This boldness is reflected in the discourse of Muslim women who make a conscious decision to wear the *ḥijāb*, whether they be converts or born Muslims. This discourse is sometimes spirited to the point of defiance, as illustrated by one of

---

[43] Bullock, *Rethinking Muslim Women and the Veil*, p. 72.
[44] Roald, *New Muslims in the European Context*, pp. 239–40.
[45] Bullock also observes that women may feel freer to talk to men when wearing the *ḥijāb* (*Rethinking Muslim Women and the Veil*, p. 102).
[46] Bullock, *Rethinking Muslim Women and the Veil*, p. 103.
[47] Franks, 'Crossing the Borders of Whiteness?', p. 920.

Bullock's interviewees, a born Muslim, who says of her decision to wear *ḥijāb*: 'I'm doing this because I'm obeying God, and it's a free country and I can do what I want . . . I don't care if I'm accepted by them [i.e. non-Muslim society] or not, I'm going to do it anyway.'[48] The discourse linking the *ḥijāb* with female empowerment is often intertwined with criticism of Western or British society. Aisha Masterton, for example, writes: 'Before I was Muslim, I used to look at ladies in hijab, and I was struck by their strong, powerful, pure appearance and I wanted to cover as well . . . To cover yourself, especially in this culture, asserts more strength and power than to surrender to the plastic, superficial values that tell ladies to offer their beauty to the whole world.'[49] Like born Muslims, converts are highly sensitized to prevailing Western images of the *ḥijāb*, and have evolved a countervailing discourse. The logic of the pluralist Western society is sometimes deployed to refute Western objections to *ḥijāb*, as in the case of one of Bullock's interviewees: 'If people [have] the freedom to go out in public almost naked, why should a Muslim woman not also have the freedom to wear *ḥijāb*?'[50] Shahnaaz, an English convert speaking on the BBC television documentary *A Muslim in the Family*, similarly inverts the arguments of Western detractors: 'They feel that they have to dress a certain way and they have to conform to fashion and society. So if they think we're oppressed, they're just as oppressed as they think we are.'[51]

Linked to the theme of empowerment, and also embedded in the discourse on *ḥijāb*, is the theme of sexuality. Abdal-Hakim Murad sees Islamic dress, including the *ḥijāb*, as having the effect of 'desexualising' the public space, in contrast to modern societies which delight in 'random erotic signalling'.[52] Muslim women often speak of *ḥijāb* as a way of regaining control of their sexuality. Many converts refer to the common link between sexual attractiveness and self-esteem for women in Western societies; against this, Kawthar (an interviewee) argued: 'I think to cover up oneself is respectful for yourself . . . Why would you want a man or someone to slobber all over you or to have bad intentions over you, that's not free because you have to doll yourself up to make someone look at you to make yourself feel better.'

[48] Bullock, 'The Hijab Experience of Canadian Muslim Women'.
[49] Masterton, 'Think about This'.
[50] Bullock, *Rethinking Muslim Women and the Veil*, p. 83.
[51] *A Muslim in the Family*, BBC 1, 2 May 2004.
[52] Murad, 'Islam, Irigaray, and the Retrieval of Gender'.

This discourse is common to both converts and born Muslims. Mary Walker, who travelled to different areas of the Muslim world as a production coordinator on the BBC series *Living Islam*, spoke with Muslim women in different places. She was somewhat persuaded by the arguments she encountered in favour of *ḥijāb*, which included the following: 'It is not liberation where you say women should go naked. It is just oppression, because men want to see them naked'; some of the women she met claimed that men in the West are 'cheating women . . . They let us believe we're liberated but enslave us to the male gaze.'[53]

Aware that the female Muslim dress code leads many Westerners to think of Islam as repressive or prudish, converts sometimes emphasize the fact that sexual attraction or sexuality is a healthy phenomenon, but that it belongs in a certain context. As Katherine Bullock puts it: '*Ḥijāb* does not smother femininity or sexuality. Rather, it regulates where and for whom one's femininity and sexuality will be displayed and deployed'; furthermore, 'society is better served by keeping male and female sexuality in check, inside and outside the home, and especially in the public sphere'.[54] Na'ima Robert, who wears the *niqāb* as well as the *ḥijāb*, elaborates on this: 'I'm not a desexualised being. Just because we don't display ourselves outside, people presume we don't do it at all and, in a lot of cases, that couldn't be further from the truth.'[55] Her description of married life emphasizes the importance of sexuality: 'As a young man and woman, you can now interact with each other, freely and without limits, you can let down your guard, remove your *hijab*, laugh and cry, go out or stay home . . . What's more, the "pleasures of the flesh" are yours for the taking.' She accurately observes that the satisfying of sexual desire is 'one of the express aims of Islamic marriage'.[56] Reilly in her study of Western converts living in Sudan suggests that *ḥijāb* actually enhances a woman's awareness of her own sexuality, 'reminding her constantly of her potential attractiveness to men'.[57]

Taking on *ḥijāb* is often framed as taking a stand against Western culture's emphasis on external appearance and physical beauty, as Na'ima Robert illustrates: 'Our society teaches us to be obsessed with appearance.

---

[53] Walker, 'The Seeds of my own Re-evaluations'.
[54] Bullock, *Rethinking Muslim Women and the Veil*, pp. 199 and 209.
[55] Gordon, 'That Muslim Woman Could be Happier Than you . . .'.
[56] Robert, *From my Sisters' Lips*, p. 146.
[57] Reilly, *Seeking Sanctuary*, p. 210.

As long as someone is beautiful, thin, wealthy, fun-loving or talented, we are happy to accept him or her at face value . . . No matter how self-obsessed, egotistical, vain, greedy, vapid and shallow an individual "celeb" may be . . . as long as they look beautiful and smile for the cameras all is well and the audience is satisfied.' She goes on to say: 'On this scale, the Muslim cannot compete: no matter how intelligent, talented, kind, gener-ous or honest she is, she doesn't "look the part" and that is something she will not be forgiven for.'[58] Taking on the *ḥijāb* thus becomes akin to 'drop-ping out of the race', and according to Robert, this frees a Muslim woman from some of the pressures experienced by her non-Muslim counterparts: 'She has, in effect, taken her looks out of the equation. She does not feel the need to live up to society's changing expectations of women's bodies'; this offers some protection from such things as eating disorders, low self-esteem and anxiety.[59] Similarly, Sarah Joseph describes the modelling industry in which she was brought up: 'I had seen at first hand the superficiality of the way beauty was externalised. Nothing was what it seemed. Beauty was manufactured,' and she contrasts this with what the *ḥijāb* means for her: 'The hijab stood against that. It was authentic and wholesome. It meant the end of being judged according to the superficial and subjective criteria of beauty.'[60]

Some women refer to the fact that by covering, a woman changes the dynamic between herself and unrelated men. Prabha, who described herself as 'a hot-pants and crop-top type person' before her conversion, explained what she liked about wearing *ḥijāb*: 'I love the fact that my work colleagues wherever I've worked listen to what I'm saying, they're not checking me out, because it wouldn't even occur to them because I cover so much that there's nothing to check out.' She found it hard to understand why any woman would not want to cover herself: 'Girls are always talking about how they want to be with someone who loves them for their personality and their mind, not their looks, so why wouldn't you?' Many women say that when they began to cover, men (including non-Muslims, sometimes) treated them with greater respect. Na'ima Robert describes the impact that taking on the *ḥijāb* had on her behaviour and that of her friends towards men: 'When it came to the opposite sex, we no longer felt comfortable having

[58] Robert, *From my Sisters' Lips*, p. 100.   [59] Ibid., pp. 123–5.
[60] Joseph, 'More Than Just a Scarf'.

conversations that were too personal or familiar and the *ḥijāb* made flirting a definite no-no.'[61] She also illustrates the potential of the *ḥijāb* to affect the power dynamic between men and women: 'I changed how I dressed and how I interacted with men, keeping a certain distance between them and me ... *It meant that I called the shots* [my italics]: I shared as much of myself as I saw fit and no more – no man had any *right* to me. What can I say? It was empowering.'[62] Some women gain a feeling of protection from wearing *ḥijāb*. This theme is taken up by male convert Abdal-Hakim Murad: 'A woman who exposes her charms in public is vulnerable to what might be described as "visual theft", so that men unknown to her can enjoy her visually without her consent.' *Ḥijāb*, he continues, 'allows a vision of Islamic woman as liberated, not from tradition and meaning, but from ostentation and subjection to random visual rape by men'.[63]

Some of those who wear the *ḥijāb* also see it as changing the dynamic between women. A contributor to the Leeds New Muslims website comments on the effect of taking it on: 'I felt at ease in not competing with other women';[64] Hilary Saunders, writing of her conversion in the *Guardian*, feels that part of its rationale is to avoid 'causing envy'.[65] The potential role of the *ḥijāb* in strengthening solidarity among Muslim women is emphasized by Shahnaaz, an English convert featured in *A Muslim in the Family*: 'Amongst the sisters, when you're wearing the *burqah* no-one can judge you, you're all equal, no-one can judge you on the hair you have, the clothes you wear, nobody is superior to another person, no matter how much money or anything that they have. You are a Muslim sister and that is all that matters.'[66] Fatima, an interviewee, described how wearing the *ḥijāb* proved to be an unexpected source of support following 9/11 when she was feeling vulnerable: 'That was a really tense time, I remember you'd venture out on the street and see another *muḥajjabah* [woman wearing *ḥijāb*] and so you'd *salām* each other [say *al-salāmu 'alaykum* to each other], but it was a kind of *salām* as in, yeah, a sort of acknowledgement of the very tense situation you're in, so it's almost like you reassure each other with your *salām*.'

[61] Robert, *From my Sisters' Lips*, p. 114.
[62] Ibid., p. 11.
[63] Murad, 'Islam, Irigaray, and the Retrieval of Gender'.
[64] 'Personal Accounts', http://www.leedsnewmuslims,org.uk/new_muslims/personal.asp (accessed 17/03/05).
[65] Saunders, 'Why I Took the Hijab'.
[66] *A Muslim in the Family*, BBC1, 2 May 2004.

Seventeen of the twenty women in my sample wore *ḥijāb*, and of the three that didn't, two felt that they should, and hoped to do so in the future. The minority of converts who do not wear *ḥijāb* can be divided into those who believe that it is obligatory to do so and those who do not. The latter group, who are the minority, sometimes argue that inner sincerity is more important than outer appearance, or that the fact that it attracts attention in Western societies goes counter to the original intention behind it.[67] Those who believe that it is obligatory generally feel that they ought to wear it but have not yet mustered the courage to do so. Lisa, who had mixed feelings about wearing the *ḥijāb*, was one of the two interviewees who fell into this category. On the one hand, she wished she had the courage to wear it to work, but on the other, she feared it would adversely affect her relationship with her clients, as her work involved dealing with families and their emotional problems: 'I just think would it be a barrier in this current climate, because people have perceptions that you're not going to understand my world because you must be in a different world if you've got that thing on your head.' Eleanor was worried about hostile reactions and about offending her family, for whom it would be another 'slap in the face', the first one having been her conversion. Rachel was the only female interviewee who did not seem to regard the headscarf as obligatory; she took a broader view of the concept of *ḥijāb*: 'The word *ḥijāb* means modesty, so actually when I leave the house I'm in a state of *ḥijāb* anyway because I cover my arms, I wear modest clothes . . . Just because I don't wear a scarf over my hair doesn't mean I'm not in a state of *ḥijāb*.' She felt that observing *ḥijāb* in England would be very difficult 'because it isolates you so much from life'. She loved swimming, but because she lived in a rural area, there were no women-only facilities available to her such as single-sex swimming. She therefore compromised by going to the pool at very quiet times when there were hardly any men: 'It's all about minimizing the risk, making that effort to go at a time when the sin I'm committing is minimal.' While she acknowledged that what she was doing was 'sinful' according to Islamic teachings, she could not bring herself to give up certain activities (dance as well as swimming) which she felt were important to her well-being and her health.

It was when the women interviewees talked about *niqāb* that the concept of strengthening the boundary between men and women emerged

---

[67] See, e.g., the interview with Kristiane Backer in Paterson, 'Would You Swap?'.

most clearly. Of the twenty female interviewees, none thought it was obligatory, and this is in accordance with majority Islamic scholarly opinion in
the present day.[68] One said that she always wore the *niqāb* when she went
out; six said they wore it sometimes; two said they intended to wear it when
they got married; two said they would wear it if they went to a Muslim country; and one said she wanted to wear it but her husband was against it. Thus
twelve out of the twenty women interviewees had a positive attitude to the
niqāb.[69] Wearing it was not uncommon, but was mainly situational, for
example in the mosque, travelling to a party while wearing make-up, going
to a crowded place where there would be many men, or visiting a Muslim
country. Hafsa explained that when she wore only the *ḥijāb* she got stared at
by Asian men because of her white skin, but when she wore the *niqāb* 'not
one of them looked at me'. Halima felt that in a Muslim country, *ḥijāb* was so
common that it did not really fulfil the function of marking the wearer out
as 'religious': 'It's only if you wear *niqāb* that men will keep their distance
and be more respectful.' Sakina (the one whose husband was against the
niqāb) wanted to wear it despite the fact that it might be 'a bit impractical', as
she felt it would offer some protection in a morally decadent environment:
'Because there's so much *fitnah* [temptation, chaos] especially living in this
country, there's so much *fitnah*, with people looking, because the men have
no shame, the *kuffār* men have no shame, even the brothers that are not very
practising, they have no shame either.'

    Charlene was the only interviewee who wore the *niqāb* full time. She
described how this had come about: 'I was thinking, I'm not going to wear it,
and then one day I just walked outside and I got this really strong feeling that
my face was exposed, and I really did want to cover it up. So I came back
home after doing everything, and I read up on it and decided if the wives of
the Prophet did it and I feel like I really do want to wear it then I might as well
just do it – so I did.' As many of the women said about *ḥijāb*, she said that she
would now feel naked without it and that it felt 'really natural' to wear it.
Na'ima Robert gives a slightly different reason for taking on the *niqāb*: 'I had

---

[68] A minority of Muslims, from the *salafī* tradition and relying mainly on Saudi scholars, do
regard it as obligatory. According to Roald, three of the four classical Sunni schools of law
regard the face-veil as obligatory (*Women in Islam*, p. 267).
[69] One male interviewee and a female convert (not one of my sample) who runs a convert
support group both expressed very strong opinions *against* the *niqāb*, seeing it as detrimental
to the image of Islam and as impeding communication.

begun to feel uncomfortable with the fact that anyone, any man, could see my face – I felt that, although they didn't have a right to it, they were still able to take a curious look whenever they wanted to.'[70]

Some of the women who were not opposed to the *niqāb* per se did not feel comfortable about wearing it in Britain. One of these was Rahima: 'I've ... worn it in public places and I don't like it, I feel it creates a barrier ... I like that social exchange, I do think that part of giving *da'wah* is just being very nice to people in the street, which is hard to do in *niqāb*.' The aspect of seeing without being seen which applies especially to those who cover the face has an impact on power relations, as illustrated by Rabia, one of Franks's interviewees, who wore the chador when in Saudi Arabia: 'It was *wonderful*. That was the biggest sense of freedom I have ever had ... You are like a spy not taking part and you can pull faces, you can laugh and no one can touch you and you go out there really like Candid Camera' (italics in original).[71] One of my questionnaire respondents had worn it once when visiting a Muslim country, and commented: 'It gave me a feeling of power, because I could see everybody but no one could see me.' This feeling of 'empowerment' runs directly counter to common perceptions of the *niqāb* as disempowering and as symbolizing the oppression of women.[72]

Some interviewees made a connection between the *niqāb*'s role in strengthening the boundary between unrelated men and women and an enhanced spirituality. One such was Rahima, who wore the *niqāb* occasionally in order to avoid the attention of Muslim men whose curiosity is roused by her 'English' appearance. Like several of the women, she wore *niqāb* at particular times such as during Ramadan or when visiting the mosque, especially on Eid days when it was crowded: 'I see it as a kind of spiritual thing, for me it gives me a sort of distance or space ... It's very powerful actually, it really feels powerful to have that kind of space for yourself.' Prabha wore it whenever she went to study with her shaykh (who is himself a Western convert) in the Middle East, as did all of his female disciples. She

---

[70] Robert, *From my Sisters' Lips*, p. 120.
[71] Franks, 'Crossing the Borders of Whiteness?', p. 921.
[72] Bullock quotes a female Canadian journalist who describes her reaction to a woman wearing the *niqāb*: 'I see a premedieval spectre before my eyes ... her oppression, for oppression it is, becomes a symbol of the difficulty all women once faced and a startling reminder that the struggle for equality has not ended ... This woman is a walking billboard that proclaims public space is reserved for men' (*Rethinking Muslim Women and the Veil*, p. 129).

explained that although the shaykh did not advocate wearing the veil in Western countries, he felt there was a greater than usual danger of temptation or attraction between men and women who were on a similar spiritual path, and therefore a need to guard against it by having women wear *niqāb*.

SOCIAL CONTACT BETWEEN THE SEXES

'Free mixing' is a term used by Muslims to denote unrestricted social contact between men and women, as is commonly practised in Western societies. Huda al-Khattab explains that free mixing is not permitted: 'Islam takes the "prevention is better than cure" approach; when it forbids an act, such as adultery or fornication, it also forbids its followers from doing things that may lead to the forbidden act.'[73] In reality, the issue of social mixing between men and women (where at least one of the parties is a Muslim) is highly nuanced with many shades of grey rather than being a black-and-white, all-or-nothing affair. This reflects the different types of guidance found in the sources, in particular the Qur'an and the *ḥadīth*. There exists a whole etiquette of male–female relating which is subject to varying interpretations, and which includes not just the permissibility of face-to-face communication but also appropriate modes of behaviour (e.g. degree of eye contact, manner of speech)[74] and dress (as discussed in the last section), among other things. On each of these matters, there is a range of opinion and a diversity of practice among Muslims. It is relatively uncommon to find practising Muslims either completely abstaining from direct communication between unrelated men and women, on the one hand, or entering freely into individual friendships across the gender boundary, on the other. A *fatwā* produced by the European Council for Fatwas and Research expounds a moderate position; it advises that women are not forbidden to talk to men, but that 'this does not imply the lifting of all boundaries so that women start speaking to all men who come and go or that men start speaking to all women ... It is permissible for a woman to speak to a male relative, a teacher, a neighbour, a supervisor at work, and others according to the

[73] Al-Khattab, *Bent Rib*, p. 83.
[74] A Qur'anic verse (33:32) asks the wives of the Prophet not to be 'soft in speech' when talking to men, in case they provoke desire in them; this is often taken as a model for Muslim women in general.

requirements and needs of everyday life.[75] Yusuf al-Qaradawi stipulates that the contact should be for a 'noble cause' such as acquiring knowledge and doing charitable works.[76] One issue on which most Muslims agree in principle is that a Muslim man or woman should avoid being alone with a non-*maḥram* member of the opposite sex (this 'being alone' is known as *khalwah* in Arabic-Islamic terminology).[77] However, there is some disagreement as to whether this applies in all contexts, including the public sphere (e.g. in an office setting), or whether it only relates to the domestic sphere, where, it is argued, the man and woman in question are more likely to be led into temptation (and the woman's 'reputation' is more likely to be compromised).

Women's place in the public sphere is another common topic of debate among converts. Most take it for granted that a Muslim woman's domestic role does not necessarily preclude her from taking an active role in society. While Huda al-Khattab, for example, acknowledges that in Islam 'it is definitely recommended that women's lives be home-based', she feels that this can be taken too far, with the result that some women can't even go out to the local shop and are 'infantilized' in the name of religion; she also acknowledges that there will always be a need for some Muslim women to work.[78] Abdal-Hakim Murad goes further than al-Khattab in extolling the advantages of retaining a primarily masculine public sphere. He promotes a traditional view which is arguably only practised in pockets of the Muslim world: 'The public space is primarily that of men, who may valorise it over the private; but the latter is valorised by women, who may regard the public space as morally and spiritually questionable.' He contrasts this with the norm in modern societies, which 'make war on all remnants of gender separation', and further argues that 'the random intrusion of women into the public space' leads to 'patterns of conflict, marginalisation, the neglect of children, and spiralling divorce'.[79] This is a controversial view, not just in terms of mainstream Western or British norms, but also among Muslims generally,

---

[75] See http://www.islamonline.net/servlet/Satellite?pagename=IslamOnline-English-Ask_Scholar/FatwaE/FatwaE&CID=1119503546580.
[76] See http://www.islamonline.net/servlet/Satellite?pagename=IslamOnline-English-Ask_Scholar/FatwaE/FatwaE&CID=1119503544520.
[77] This is based on a *ḥadīth* which states that whenever an unrelated man and woman are alone with each other, Satan is also present (included in al-Tirmidhi's collection).
[78] Al-Khattab, *Bent Rib*, pp. 79, 75 and 82.
[79] Murad, 'Islam, Irigaray, and the Retrieval of Gender'.

many of whom (including most converts) do not see women's presence in the public space as problematic.

In Islamic discourse the case for separate spheres is often made in terms of 'closing the avenues that lead to evil' (*ṣadd dharā'i' al-fasād* – an Islamic juristic principle). Na'ima Robert takes this line, emphasizing the serious-ness of adultery in the Islamic view in contrast to its 'glamorization' in the Western media. She portrays a typical evening out for Westerners, involving 'free mixing', alcohol and dancing. The scene is portrayed as a potential minefield as far as fidelity (marital or otherwise) is concerned: 'Very often, where there are men and women, the seeds of desire are sown. Some seeds die before they can take root, others manage to produce shoots before they too fade; others grow into fully fledged blooms.'[80] However, the argument for segregation is often made in more positive terms. Mary Walker, an English documentary-maker, found her preconceptions challenged when she spent time in a segregated Muslim society: 'The invisible boundary between men and women was a welcome partition, and within this bound-ary womanhood reigned supreme . . . Now the men were excluded . . . I was now in a world where the men had no voice.'[81] The theme of women being more powerful than men in their own domain is taken up by Nouria, a con-vert who is quoted by *The Times* as saying that in a sense men are just guests in their own homes: 'My husband has to ask my permission before another man can stay in the house. This is my kingdom, my domain.'[82] Some con-verts speak in terms of the benefits of sisterhood and a much-reduced level of competitive feeling amongst women when they have a separate sphere. Yvonne Ridley, for example, found herself impressed by the female solidar-ity she found among Muslim women, who were 'always helping each other in matters such as childcare, fundraising and studying. They want each other to do well'; she contrasts this in a somewhat polemical fashion with her view of women in Western culture: 'In the west we're all too busy pinch-ing each other's boyfriends, and criticising each other's clothes or weight.'[83] Abdal-Hakim Murad speaks of 'a parallel space of the *entre-femmes*, a realm of alternative meaning and fulfilment, where men are the guests . . . which creates a sociability between women . . . which is lacking in the

---

[80] Robert, *From my Sisters' Lips*, pp. 93–4.
[81] Walker, 'The Seeds of my own Re-evaluations'.
[82] Berrington, 'Islam Sheds its Image'.
[83] Quoted in Napier, 'Articles of Faith'.

conditions of modernity or postmodernity . . . Some form of localised, informal sorority may provide women with the matrix of identity which a fragmenting modernity denies them.'[84]

Most of my interviewees practised some form of segregation of the sexes in their own home, the environment over which they had the most control. All of them seemed familiar with the concept of *khalwah*, and nearly all of them avoided it in practice. Men were slightly less strict than women overall, with two of the men for example agreeing to be interviewed in a domestic setting by a female interviewer with no one else present.[85] Some of the women spoke of the 'limits' to be observed when conversing with men. According to Diana: 'You can't really be just having a full-on conversation with someone [i.e. a man], just *salāmu 'alaykum*', while Charlene felt that talking to men was fine 'as long as it's not in a personal, social way'. Others mentioned that 'flirting', 'idle chit-chat' and personal friendships were unacceptable. Friendships with members of the opposite sex prior to conversion generally had to be given up because the convert felt it was not appropriate to continue having close social relations with them. Charlene found this hard, saying of her friends: 'The ones I was really close to, some of them were boys. That was very difficult to give up, because for ages afterwards we still kind of kept on . . . because the boys were still willing to accommodate even with the whole big thing [gesturing towards her *jilbāb*] . . . But I couldn't do the whole male relationship thing.' Diana found that she really missed male company after she converted: 'As time's gone on I find it's like a relief if I do chat to a guy, it's like, oh finally I can speak to a man properly, having conversations, which isn't good [i.e. Islamically].' Even though she knew it wasn't strictly allowed, she was still talking on the phone to her ex-boyfriend: 'We won't stop talking till I get married, I don't think I really should be talking to him, but it's just nice to hear a man's voice.' One married female interviewee who was normally very cautious in her social contacts with men showed me a letter she had written to a male friend shortly before her conversion, several years ago. In it she had said: 'Because I have grown up in a Western culture (which I am not at ease with) there are still things Western in me that I could not give up – mixing with my male friends, for example.' However, it emerged that she had in fact only stayed in touch with

---

[84] Murad, 'Islam, Irigaray, and the Retrieval of Gender'.
[85] In the case of the other male interviewees, interviews took place in an office (two), or on the phone (two), or in a domestic setting in the presence of the wife (four).

one of her male friends; her contact with this man was infrequent (partly because he lived abroad), and their relationship had become more formal, for example she avoided being alone with him in a non-public space. She was in fact considering breaking off contact with him as she felt that in some ways he was too familiar. He once told her husband that he had 'enjoyed spending time with her'; another time he blew her a kiss when they parted. Another interviewee, Rachel, who was engaged but not yet married, said that she did have male friends with whom she socialized, though she avoided being alone with them in private.

Four of the interviewees said they did not feel comfortable with strict segregation. This included the two men who were happy to be interviewed on their own in a domestic setting, one of whom said: 'I'm absolutely comfortable with male–female interaction ... I'm all for mixed social gatherings, I feel deeply uncomfortable in segregated gatherings.' However, he did also add: 'Strictly speaking, you and I here alone shouldn't be happening,' showing an awareness that his practice was falling short of Islamic norms. Similarly, Lisa's view seemed closer to a mainstream Western paradigm than a traditional Islamic one; she described how she and her husband (from whom she was now separated) had not been able to see the point of going to a party together when they could not have any contact with each other once there. Rachel opposed any kind of strict segregation of the sexes on the grounds that it would inhibit women's active involvement in society: 'I have a convert friend ... she refuses to go to any events that are mixed, which I really really disagree with, because one of the most important things about being Muslim in England is being seen. It's not going to help our position if we're hidden behind closed doors and do nothing.' In two other cases, a slightly more relaxed attitude towards segregation reflected the common practice of the particular Muslim culture from which the convert's spouse came. I found a few examples in published and internet sources of fairly strong opposition to strict segregation on the part of converts, including for example one American woman who feels, like Rachel, that it is disadvantageous to women: 'Why should I sit in the back just because someone thinks men cannot control themselves?' She goes on to say that she will not live her life 'locked up in a cage, or in the back row at a university lecture'.[86] Katherine Bullock feels that 'when carried to an extreme, male/female segregation is a

---

[86] Quoted in Anway, *Daughters of Another Path*, p. 86.

loss that restricts women and inhibits healthy male–female relations by removing opportunities to share insights and perspectives with each other'; however, she also feels that 'extreme mixing . . . leads to a loss in the form of too many dangers for women's security'.[87]

Shaking hands with a non-*maḥram* member of the opposite sex is a matter about which there is some disagreement among Muslim scholars. Yusuf al-Qaradawi deems it permissible, as long as there is no fear of temptation, or any intention of provoking sexual desire or enjoyment.[88] Of the seventeen interviewees who were asked,[89] five said they definitely wouldn't shake hands with a member of the opposite sex, eight said that they tried not to but occasionally found themselves doing so, and four said that they did so in certain circumstances. Most, like Prabha, showed an awareness of the potential for giving offence, and took pains to avoid doing so: 'I really really try not to, and normally if people put their hand forward I try and keep mine at my side for as long as possible, unless they really don't get the hint and their hand is still out and then because I don't want to embarrass them or make them feel humiliated I shake their hand very briefly.' Of the four interviewees who said that they did sometimes shake hands, three did so for professional reasons, because they had a pastoral role and needed to inspire confidence in their clients. This was the case for one woman who worked as a teacher: 'The only time I tend to have to shake hands is when I'm dealing with parents of my kids, and to be honest, I'm teaching their child, they need to be able to feel comfortable with me, that they can trust me, otherwise they're not going to work with me.'[90] Katherine Bullock rationalizes the avoidance of physical contact between unrelated men and women as a way of avoiding misunderstanding: 'There is no need to spend hours wondering whether or not a person intended that touch to be sexual, or dealing with the fallout from a misinterpreted nonsexual touch – there is no touch. It is clean and simple.'[91]

[87] Bullock, *Rethinking Muslim Women and the Veil*, pp. 212–13.
[88] See http://www.islamonline.net/servlet/Satellite?/pagename=IslamOnline-English-Ask_Scholar/FatwaE/FatwaE&cid=1119503546332.
[89] As explained in the introduction, there was some evolution in the content of the questions, so not all questions were asked of all interviewees.
[90] Allievi sees the issue of shaking hands as reflecting a pure–impure dichotomy ('The Shifting Significance of the *Halal/Haram* Frontier', p. 136), but there was no sense of this among my interviewees; for them, it was without exception a matter of maintaining certain boundaries between the sexes.
[91] Bullock, *Rethinking Muslim Women and the Veil*, p. 212.

'Lowering one's gaze' is something that is referred to in a passage of the Qur'an which asks both believing men and believing women to 'lower their gaze and guard their modesty' (24:30–1). Yusuf al-Qaradawi articulates a moderate Islamic scholarly position when he holds that it is not completely forbidden for a man and a woman to look one another in the face, as long as the look is without sexual desire and there is no particular fear of temptation;[92] it is generally agreed also that one should not stare. Most of the interviewees did attempt to apply the principle of 'lowering the gaze' in some way, though usually not in a complete or literal sense. Many were aware of the *ḥadīth* that says that the first glance should not be followed by a second.[93] There was some confusion as to how to apply this teaching, and some difficulty around the fact that different people interpret it differently, as expressed by Fatima: 'I used to just look down completely if I was talking to a Muslim man, but then I found that I did actually need to look to communicate to an extent, so I got into this real internal "Do I look? Do I not look? If I look, will it be interpreted wrongly?" ... I'm only just really learning to be natural.' She found it easier with practising Muslims who understood the issues better, but even with them it was not always straightforward: 'You get the middle Muslims who do give eye contact and then it's "Do I not give eye contact and if I don't give eye contact is that going to be over the top?"' Some said that they tried to adapt to what the other person did, and there was generally quite a lot of concern not to make the person feel uncomfortable, whether by looking too much or not enough. A few, like Eleanor, felt that the need to communicate was paramount: 'If I'm working with a colleague and we're discussing something and he's male, then you can't not look them in the face, because you need to be communicating properly and eye contact is so important in this day and age, at interviews and work, that you would just look very strange, I think, if you didn't look someone in the eye.' Two of the men who were interviewed in their own homes with their wives present engaged in very little eye contact throughout the interview.

Most of the contributors to a discussion on this subject in *Meeting Point* feel that 'lowering one's gaze' is a matter of discretion, and something to be observed according to the spirit rather than the letter; these include one

[92] See http://www.islamonline.net/servlet/Satellite?pagename=IslamOnline-English-Ask_ Scholar/FatwaE/FatwaE&cid=1119503543744.

[93] This *ḥadīth* is included in the collections of al-Tirmidhi, Ahmad ibn Hanbal and Abu Dawud (cited in Bullock, *Rethinking Muslim Women and the Veil*, p. 210).

man who points out that the Prophet was not 'sealed off from women', and who feels that this is 'simply an issue of controlling oneself and exercising a little self-restraint'. Another man expresses impatience with those who advocate strict avoidance of eye contact between unrelated men and women, an approach that he feels can have the unfortunate side-effect of overemphasizing the sexual dimension of life: 'If a man cannot control himself to the extent that every time he sees a woman all he thinks is sexual thoughts then obviously he has a real problem that needs seeing to. I think for the rest of us normal people we should try and lower our gaze when appropriate instead of treating all women like the Medusa.' He feels that 'silliness like turning your back on a woman or looking to the side while talking to her is going to do nothing but make Muslims, especially the men, look like all we do is have sexual thoughts about women'.[94]

There was some flexibility in interpreting Islamic norms according to the context or situation. Very often, different standards were applied when dealing with non-Muslims, not on the 'essentials' (for example the *khalwah* rule was generally upheld), but in areas such as handshaking and eye contact, and general social interaction. Most explained this difference with reference to the fact that non-Muslims simply would not understand, and might therefore interpret the avoidance as rudeness. Rachel for example said that she *did* shake hands and give eye contact with non-Muslim men, but not with Muslim men because 'they know the rules'. Prabha felt that it was okay to have eye contact with non-Muslim men because there was no prospect of her being attracted to them; she explained that, when interacting with a non-Muslim man, 'I just think to myself, I'm never going to look at you that way because you just don't hold any of my values'. In particular, the norms were likely to be relaxed in a work situation, or with non-Muslim family (and in some cases non-practising Muslim in-laws). In the work situation, it was often felt that the professional context provided some boundaries which allowed for a slight relaxation of the rules. Kavindra drew a distinction between home social life and work social life: 'I can't expect to go to a workplace in a country that's not belonging to Muslims and expect my rules to be implemented.' One woman observed 'strict segregation' in her own household, but at work she had a male assistant: 'You have to have some type of banter to keep you going, we have banter and we laugh and we

---

[94] 'Points of View', in *Meeting Point*, 32, June 2004.

joke and things like that.' One man admitted that he was less scrupulous about 'lowering the gaze' when interacting with non-Muslim female colleagues, and was unsure as to whether that made him a 'hypocrite'. Some of those who were prepared to relax the rules with non-Muslims were motivated by the desire to avoid creating an unfavourable image of Islam or Muslims; Eleanor said that if necessary she would shake a non-Muslim man's hand rather than give offence: 'I'm always of the opinion – I don't know whether it's right or not – that you don't want to make yourself look a bit rude, it doesn't do any favours to the Muslim community.' One woman had male cousins. Strictly speaking, she knew she was not supposed to socialize freely with them, as non-*maḥram* males, but she relaxed the rules in view of the fact that they were close family and they grew up together. Kavindra and her husband (the latter's family being non-practising Muslims) felt that they couldn't impose their ways on the members of their respective families: 'You can't apply your strict rules to them and expect the family life to function, so what we do is we try for a middle ground.'

Some women converts speak of a natural bashfulness or modesty they feel in the presence of men, something that they may not have experienced in their pre-conversion days, with many of them saying (as mentioned in chapter 3) that they would now feel naked if they went out without their *ḥijāb*. Linda described the effect that reading the Qur'anic passage that asks men and women to lower their gaze (24:30–1) had on her shortly before her conversion: 'Almost a shyness came over me, it was really strange . . . maybe a seed was planted and it laid dormant for a long time but it was there . . . then I was walking back to work from the library and I almost felt kind of like shy, as men were walking towards me.' Diana described how she and her friend had gone to a mixed Islamic event, and whenever young men went past they had found themselves giggling in a way that they would never have done before. One of Reilly's interviewees, an English convert, talks of the way in which she now curtails her interactions with men, commenting: 'I think it's a mixture of shyness and feeling that it's not right. With women I'm different, I guess. I've always been a shy person but I think it's increased more since I've become a Muslim.'[95] It seems that some of these women acquired this quality of shyness or modesty (*ḥayā'* in the Arabic-Islamic sources) as a result of socialization with other Muslims; or they may have cultivated it

[95] Reilly, *Seeking Sanctuary*, pp. 128–9.

after having read or heard *ḥadīths* that commend the quality, although in Linda's case her experience preceded her conversion.

MARRIAGE

It is rare for a convert to remain single for many years after their conversion; Allievi comments that for women especially, marriage is a 'natural consequence' of conversion.[96] A well-known *ḥadīth* states that marriage is 'half the religion', and this teaching is taken to heart by most converts. Notwithstanding the difficulties that converts sometimes encounter in trying to find a marriage partner, most would agree with the interviewee who commented: 'Islam generally supports people getting married and having kids.' Hermansen observes that for single women converts, it is 'more difficult to find acceptance', and some of Anway's respondents felt that marriage gave them a better standing in the Muslim community.[97] Of my thirty interviewees, twenty-three were married; one was engaged to be married; one was separated; and two were divorced (one of whom was negotiating a possible third marriage, but her first as a Muslim). Of the remaining three, two were in negotiations to marry someone, whilst the other was still relatively young (twenty-one) and living in a rural area where it was not easy to find a marriage partner, although she had made some attempt to do so. The picture was therefore overwhelmingly one of marriage as the norm.

As 'dating' is generally not considered acceptable in Islam, it is common for converts to have some form of arranged marriage, although this differs from arranged marriage as practised in many traditional Muslim cultures in that recourse is had to Muslim friends and acquaintances in the absence of a Muslim family of origin. Other possibilities include meeting someone via the internet, or having limited contact with someone through a work or social setting. Huda al-Khattab describes the Islamic way of arranging marriages as 'diametrically opposed to the western way. Western families, to a large extent, leave their children to sink or swim in the nerve-wracking and confusing world of dates and boyfriend/girlfriend.' She feels that this leads to all sorts of problems, such as one partner wanting more commitment than the other. Ironically perhaps, she likens the Western way to 'Russian

---

[96] Allievi, *Les Convertis à l'Islam*, p. 189.
[97] Hermansen, 'Two-Way Acculturation', p. 198; Anway, *Daughters of Another Path*, p. 7.

roulette', a simile which some Westerners might use to describe arranged marriage. She describes the Islamic way of marriage as involving 'much businesslike talk and negotiation of conditions ... which makes it all seem more like a boardroom deal than the romance of the century', and is aware that many non-Muslims find arranged marriage unromantic: 'People who have over-indulged in Hollywood love stories and Mills & Boon ... may well find it all quite weird, but surely it is better to "lay all one's cards on the table" ... from the outset than to find things out the hard way and have unpleasant surprises later on.' However, she feels that this approach 'does not entirely rule out "romance"'.[98]

Several interviewees had met or married their spouses prior to conversion. Of those who married after conversion, and who described how they met their partners, the overwhelming majority – eleven out of twelve – had had what could be described as an arranged marriage. Of these eleven, five had been introduced to their spouses through Muslim friends or acquaintances, three (all men) had been approached by their future fathers-in-law, two (also men) had had marriages arranged abroad involving negotiations with the families of the prospective spouses, and one woman had met her husband on an Islamic internet site. Although the last might not sound like an 'arranged marriage' in the ordinary sense, contact through the internet site had been followed by a limited number of meetings (they lived on different continents) involving chaperones, after which the two were married.[99] The remaining woman met her husband through work and proposed marriage to him. However, even this case was closer to an arranged marriage than to the prevailing Western pattern, since the work setting was Islamic and there was no free socializing between men and women, and Islamic norms regarding contact before marriage were observed (i.e. not being alone together and having very limited or no physical contact). Of the two who were in negotiations to marry, one had met her potential partner through an internet site. The other had tried internet sites with no luck, and then reverted to what she described as the 'proper Islamic way', through Muslim friends and acquaintances. Most interviewees felt that it was either inadvisable or not permitted to meet without a chaperone even in a public

[98] Al-Khattab, *Bent Rib*, pp. 15–16.
[99] When this woman travelled to her prospective husband's country she took her parents with her, thus fulfilling the requirement that a woman should be accompanied by a non-*mahram* male relative when travelling long distance.

place, as this would be akin to 'dating' and might harm the woman's reputation. Safety was also a concern in cases where contact had been made through the internet. Some, especially women, spoke of being overwhelmed with (often unsuitable) offers, or of receiving offers where the motivation was to acquire a British passport. Several referred to the fact that they had prayed *istikhārah* (a prayer for guidance) when trying to decide whether to marry a particular person.[100]

Several interviewees spoke of the advantages of arranged marriages. Rachel explained:

> From the very first time you meet that person you've got marriage in mind, so you start off with the mindset of, you're using your head before your heart, is this person a suitable partner? Do they have similar interests to me? Will they blend with my family? . . . Do we both have the same aspirations for the future? All those things go through your head when you're meeting a partner, whereas in a non-Muslim situation that doesn't happen, you kind of drift.

She felt that one was more likely to find someone compatible this way than through the usual Western way of dating and living together. Halima, who had been married for two months, also emphasized that romantic love was not necessarily the best starting point: 'The basis is different, you don't necessarily fall head over heels in love with the person. You might, but if you go about it the right way and you trust in Allah, Allah will put love between the two of you, and that happened with us . . . I really didn't expect that we would become close and comfortable with each other so quickly but that's, as we say, Allah's blessing. We didn't have to know each other really well before.' Na'ima Robert, who married her husband after only one meeting, feels, like Huda al-Khattab, that it is possible to have an element of romance in a Muslim marriage, although one of her interviewees remarks that if the husband is not a Westerner, he may need educating in this regard. Robert paints an idyllic picture of the early days of an Islamic marriage as 'full of exploration and discovery, excitement and wonder: you are two individuals getting to know each other, spiritually, mentally and physically.'[101] However, she also maintains that

---

[100]   The prayer, often used when making important decisions, is sometimes followed by opening and reading the Qur'an at random, or by some kind of 'sign', which might simply be a dawning inclination one way or the other on the part of the supplicant.

[101]   Robert, *From my Sisters' Lips*, pp. 171–2 and 165.

Islamic love is different from love in the *jahiliyya*, the 'time of ignorance' before Islam. In essence, Islamic love is based on loving for
Allah's sake, and that means loving what Allah loves about a person:
their *iman* [faith], their submission; their *taqwa* [piety], their Islamic
manners; good character and strong *deen* [religion/way of life] . . .
Loving for Allah's sake does not fluctuate according to your own
whims and desires – it is constant, as long as the other person is also
striving to please Allah.[102]

It seems that the strong contrast between Western and Islamic gender
norms does sometimes give rise to a sense of culture-clash. Matthew Thistle,
an 'Anglo Muslim' (his description) convert living in Saudi Arabia, includes
a description on his blog of a formal meeting between himself and a potential marriage partner, 'the girl in the black chador':

I couldn't help but express to her the weirdness of this situation as a
westerner, how I had many female friends platonic and otherwise . . .
As they say here, of course, true love happens after marriage, but with
my western bohemian, ex-womanising cultural background, it was as
alien as can be, so after a few more minutes with a few embarrassing
silences [I took my leave] . . . How could I really know anything about
her? . . . I felt no attraction, she is a very pious girl so much so that I
couldn't feel 'the woman' behind all the piousness, and that is my own
inevitable cultural conditioning . . . I mean I couldn't see her body or
even her hair! OK nor should I need to, and neither am I meant to, they
are revealed once you are legal but I simply can't see it happening with
such a profoundly different girl-woman-sister.[103]

This convert stays mainly in the register of his original cultural paradigm
but occasionally oscillates between that and the adopted 'Islamic' paradigm,
as when he says 'Okay nor should I need to . . .', and when he adds at the end:
'Then again, I couldn't see me ever becoming a Muslim either, so to God I
turn, for help.' The cultural ambivalence is apparent, as one senses both
alienation and a tentative openness to the possibility that this culture so different from his own might hold something good.

When interviewees were asked about the difference between a Muslim
or Islamic marriage and a non-Muslim marriage, the replies often contained

[102] Ibid., pp. 160–1.
[103] See   http://enthogenesis.blogspot.com/2004/03/i-finally-met-girl-in-black-chador-i.html
(accessed 14/3/06).

some implicit or explicit criticism of the way things are generally done in Western societies. While some acknowledged that non-Muslim marriages could be successful, others tended to generalize and see them in a rather negative light. Sakina, who had been married to a non-Muslim prior to her conversion and who was now married to a Muslim, felt that a Muslim marriage was more likely to be happy than a non-Muslim marriage, 'because non-Muslim marriages, they're always fraught with things like feminist issues and the woman wanting to go out and earn money just because she feels she has to be equal to the husband, or the issue of children being dumped into childcare'. Others also felt that a non-Muslim couple were more likely to experience conflict or friction. Zaynab, who had been in a relationship with the man who was now her husband for several years prior to their conversion and subsequent marriage, felt there was sometimes 'a lot of tit-for-tat' in non-Muslim marriages. Kawthar had been with her husband, a non-practising Muslim, for several years before she converted; he had then 'reverted' and they had married. She described the resulting improvement in their relationship: 'We just have more respect for each other. As a non-Muslim I would have just gone out and it's none of your business because I'm going out and that's it, but as a Muslim that's really disrespectful to leave another one in the dark or worrying about your whereabouts.' Prabha felt that the spiritual aspect was the main distinguishing feature of a Muslim marriage: 'I think a non-Muslim marriage tends to be about keeping each other happy, and a Muslim marriage is about that but the main goal is helping each other to get to Allah, and when you're helping each other get to Allah it doesn't always mean putting up with each other's vices.' This was echoed by Amin: 'A non-Muslim marriage is one of cooperation, whereas a Muslim marriage is one of cooperation for an end, for an obvious end, for the next life, which is a tremendous difference.'

Muslim marriages were generally felt to be more stable and lasting than secular marriages.[104] Prabha commented: 'Here marriage as an institution doesn't have that much weight because of the divorce rate anyway, people actually think, what's the point of getting married just for a piece of paper? ... It doesn't really make a difference now if you're married or not because

---

[104] This is in fact borne out in the British context by research done by the PSI in 1994 showing that divorce was more frequent in the white population than among South Asian, Turkish and Cypriot immigrants. See Ansari, 'The Infidel Within', p. 265.

people can do what they like'; she contrasted this with the Islamic position: 'In a *dīn* [religion, way of life] where any relationship outside of marriage is completely prohibited, obviously marriage is a huge thing.' Rahima felt that an Islamic marriage had a stronger base than a secular marriage: 'It's a commitment that's beyond just love. I think in the West now generally if you fall out of love with someone then the marriage is over. In Islam it's about responsibility and respect, and love is part of that but it's not the only thing.'

The Muslim Marriage Guide by English convert Ruqaiyyah Waris Maqsood is widely read by both converts and born Muslims. It upholds traditional gender roles, with the wife having primary responsibility for the care of the home, and the husband being the provider. These roles include the husband's headship of the household: 'Allah has requested that wives obey their husband and pay them respect in every matter that does not conflict with His will.' Maqsood is careful to stress, however, that the man's headship is dependent upon him fulfilling his duties as a husband, and that 'it does not mean that he is issuing commands at every hour of the day'.[105] Several interviewees spoke of the advantages of having a structure with specific roles for husband and wife, particularly in terms of limiting the potential for conflict in a marriage. One of these was Eleanor:

> In an Islamic marriage there's a clear distinction of your role and you know why you're doing certain things. I mean we may sit at home and moan about the cleaning and the housework but you know that that's your role as a wife and mother, and you'll get the reward for doing that, so although you grumble you feel glad that you've got that role . . . I think that's the beauty of Islam, that the roles of men and women are defined without being derogatory to either sex really. You know what you've got to do and it makes it more harmonious.

Having a set of criteria or rules according to which a household is run was generally felt to be helpful, as was having a shared philosophy of life. Sulayman said of his marriage: 'It's a union based on common outlook, so my wife and I will get up in the morning and pray, we'll discuss various issues, we'll do things because we think it's either Islamic or acceptable in Islam and we won't do things because they're unIslamic. We think that the common outlook, the common practice, will give us the opportunities for getting on with each other, because relationships are very complicated and

---

[105] Maqsood, *The Muslim Marriage Guide*, pp. 77 and 83.

very difficult.' Several interviewees referred to the importance of a Muslim husband and wife having a shared goal. One such was Prabha: 'You support each other in a different kind of way, because you're supporting each other in terms of the *dunyah* [this world], which is what a non-Muslim marriage is, but you're supporting each other also in terms of your *din*, and so you are *inshallah* [if God wills] trying to grow together, gain knowledge together, gain spiritually together.'

Looking at patterns of marriage, childbirth and employment among the sample, it was clear that women preferred to be based in the home when there were children. Of the fourteen women who were currently married, three did not yet have children and these were in paid employment. Of the two with older children (secondary-school age or above), one worked for an Islamic organization and one was a housewife. The remaining nine had younger children (primary-school age or below), and of these one worked part time for an Islamic organization, one was studying, two worked part time from home, and the other five stayed home to care for their children. It was therefore relatively rare for a woman with children below secondary-school age to be going out to work (and none worked full time), with seven out of the nine being based at home. This contrasts with a national figure of about two-thirds of mothers with children of primary-school age or below participating in the labour force.[106]

Most of the interviewees were asked questions along the lines of: 'Do you consider the husband to be the head of the household?' I was aware that this was a loaded question, given that Islam has often been seen or portrayed by non-Muslims as oppressive to women. In view of this, one might have expected interviewees to downplay the husband's authority, yet of the twenty-two respondents who spoke on the subject, all but three or four felt that in some sense the husband was the head of the household, or that he had the final say in cases of disagreement between the spouses (though several mentioned the condition that his opinion should not go against Islamic teachings). Some invoked the 'tie-breaker' argument: that in cases of disagreement it is necessary for one person to have the 'casting vote' in order to ensure harmony and avoid conflict. Most felt that cooperation and

---

[106] The Office for National Statistics found in 2003 that 73% of working-age women whose youngest child was aged five to ten and 55% of women whose youngest child was under five were in the labour force. See http://www.statistics.gov.uk/cci/nugget_print.asp?ID=436 (accessed 21/08/2006).

consultation were the norm, and envisaged that the husband would only exercise his right to prevail on rare occasions. Ali, whose wife was present during the interview, acknowledged that 'every team needs a captain', but went on to say: 'Most decisions that are made in the house are made by my wife, they are not made by me. We're a team, we work as a team, we talk, we cooperate, and we support one another, that's it. There's no handing down laws, I wouldn't be allowed.' Several of the women felt that the man's special position referred to in Qur'anic verses such as 4:34 or 2:228 was not a question of male privilege but one of added responsibility and a duty of protection towards the wife.[107] Charlene used Qur'anic interpretation (referring implicitly to 4:34, which contains the phrase: 'Because of what they [i.e. men] spend of their wealth') to argue that a man's authority derives solely from his role as the breadwinner: 'In the Qur'an it's actually quite clear that he is not actually higher, it's just that Allah has put him higher because he provides, he's the provider, so that's the only reason. I mean, for example if my husband did not provide for me, I would not have to obey him.' In some cases, the question as to whether the husband was considered the head of the household gave rise to considerable amusement, and often to some banter when both husband and wife were present. Sulayman, whose wife has a good command of classical Arabic and is more educated in an Islamic sense than he is, said: 'I keep saying to her she's more intelligent than I am, she just uses intelligence to win the arguments which is absolutely the way to do it.' He did feel that the basic structure of the man having the final say was one that promoted marital harmony, but felt, like Ali quoted above, that the norm was teamwork, open discussion and give-and-take, without the need 'to thump the table'.

Charlene was one of the most wholehearted in her acceptance of a woman's duty of obedience to her husband (albeit conditional upon his being the breadwinner, as mentioned above), but perhaps this should be taken in the light of the fact that she was not yet married. As it happens, she was involved in negotiations to be married, and gave the impression of being a rather spirited and independent woman. She referred to a *ḥadīth* which says that if a women does four things (the five daily prayers; fasting in Ramadan;

---

[107] Q 4:34 refers to men as '*qawwāmūna 'ala al-nisā*'', which may be translated as 'protectors/maintainers of women', and outlines certain disciplinary measures to which the man may resort if necessary; 2:228, on the subject of divorce, refers to the *darajah* or 'degree' that a man has over a woman.

guarding her chastity; and obeying her husband), she can enter Paradise by whatever gate she wants. Although the issue of obedience was something that worried her when she first converted, she said that when she thought about all the things men have to do to gain Paradise, she realized she was lucky: 'I only have to obey him on the things that Allah has said that I should obey him on, and I don't mind doing that because by doing that I'm obeying Allah.' She continued: 'If he says I don't want you to go out, I would actually not go out, not because I really think he's right in telling me not to go out, but because I know that on Judgement Day that would be a good deed for me ... I look at it in terms of the *ākhirah* [afterlife], not the *dunyah* [this life].'

As Franks points out, the issue of 'obedience' is not straightforward and does not lend itself to easy generalizations.[108] It is rarely if ever a question of absolute or unconditional obedience, and space for negotiation is created by, for example, the caveat that the obedience is conditional upon there being no contradiction with Islamic teachings.[109] She also points out that the concept of obedience is difficult to translate from one cultural context to another, having for example connotations of an unthinking and robotic following of authority in the secular context, while in a religious context the obedience is seen as voluntary and in the service of a higher good (for example heavenly reward, marital harmony or societal stability).[110] The 'obedience' that was spoken about by my interviewees was generally a qualified one, and some women in particular showed a certain ambivalence which suggested a degree of latitude in practice, even as they affirmed what they saw as the normative Islamic position. Prahba, when asked whether she saw her husband as the head of the household, replied: 'I'm supposed to, yes. I'm probably not the best person to ask because I'm a rather independent person and I do try but you know, we all struggle with different things, but I mean he does have the final say. I'll ask his permission for things, because I know that he has that right. It doesn't necessarily mean that I always agree and that I necessarily always deal with it in the best way.' Similarly Kavindra, when asked whether she would actually do what her husband said, laughed and said: 'Um ... you know what, I'm not really a good wife. He's certainly head of the household,

---

[108] Franks, *Women and Revivalism in the West*, p. 99.
[109] Ibid., pp. 82 and 100. Interestingly, Franks found that her Christian respondents and interviewees were more likely to see wifely obedience in unconditional terms than the Muslims were.
[110] Ibid., pp. 83–4.

Allah has given him that . . . luckily my husband was born and brought up here and thinks like me and wouldn't insist on everything . . . So in terms of him being the head of the household it's difficult but not that difficult.' One of the male interviewees expressed his frustration that both his current wife and his former wife had gone against his wishes at times: 'In theory what I say goes. I would always try and discuss things and seek consensus, but at the end of the day if a decision has to be made and we're in disagreement, then what I say as the man should be what happens, and it cheeses me off in both my marriages when that wasn't always accepted.'[111]

There is a certain awareness among converts that the idea of 'obedience' might be seen as 'hopelessly old-fashioned, or even demeaning' in the West.[112] When Na'ima Robert was contemplating marriage, she found that the concept of obedience went against the way in which she was brought up, and consequently went through 'much soul-searching' before accepting it, encouraged by a Qur'anic verse that says: 'It may be that you dislike a thing which is good for you and that you like a thing which is bad for you. Allah knows but you do not know' (2:216).[113] While many of the interviewees talked in general terms of the different roles of husband and wife, and of the husband's position as head of the household, most spoke in abstract terms and few gave specific examples. However, there did seem to be a general consensus, even among women who worked, that the husband's role involved being the main provider and protector, and that the woman's role entailed shouldering the bulk of the responsibility for childcare and domestic tasks, or as Huda al-Khattab puts it: 'The husband-manager tends to be in charge of outside activities, whilst the wife tends to be in charge of internal household affairs.'[114] Na'ima Robert describes the rights of the wife in traditional terms as 'being treated well and having all her needs taken care of, being fed, clothed and housed as her husband feeds, clothes and houses himself', while the husband has 'the right to have his needs looked after in his home – the cooking and cleaning and the mending of clothes'.[115] A few of my interviewees gave examples of the kind of decision in which the husband might

---

[111] According to Roald's study, some converts find certain verses of the Qur'an, in particular 4:34, which lays down the husband's right of chastisement, to be 'problematic' (*New Muslims in the Eurpean Context*, pp. 188–9); none of my sample expressed this view, but then they were not directly asked about it.

[112] Al-Khattab, *Bent Rib*, p. 4.

[113] Robert, *From my Sisters' Lips*, p. 169.

[114] Al-Khattab, *Bent Rib*, p. 4.

[115] Robert, *From my Sisters' Lips*, pp. 167–8.

have the last word, and these included whether to send the children to an Islamic or a state school, and whether to settle abroad or stay in Britain. One woman referred to a particular instance in which her husband's wishes had prevailed: 'We had some small Christmas celebration that was going to happen at the school and I kind of felt maybe that my daughter could join in, but he was adamantly no, and he gave me his reasons why it was no, and I thought well fine, he is right, I must go along with it.' For her, the fact that he gave reasons seemed to be very important, as she added: 'If he did feel strongly and he did justify to me why his opinion was such, I don't have a problem.' This account suggests that her husband convinced her through intellectual persuasion, but it may also be that she felt the need to rationalize her acquiescence, either to herself (to ensure ongoing domestic harmony), or to others (to avoid appearing too compliant, a quality which is not valued in Western society).

In practice, my female interviewees did not appear to feel that the husband's authority was overly burdensome, and my overall impression was that any reservations they had about the husband's headship were compensated for by the perceived advantages of being in a Muslim marriage, especially the right of a woman to be financially supported by her husband and to stay at home and care for the children. A few of the women referred to the fact that if they themselves earned money, the husband had no right to it and he still had to support them. Several seemed to enjoy the sense of being protected and cared for. One of these was Hafsa: 'The man is the head of the house and the sister [i.e. the woman] is the foundation of the house ... He's the protector. If we're walking down the road I'd want my husband to be there with me.' One of Anway's respondents is strongly enthusiastic about the gendered division of labour: 'The one right I have that's very important to me is not having to work and getting the chance to be with my daughter! It also is nice to have my husband provide for me at my standards and above without really asking ... I feel the home is for the wife and mother, and I love it.'[116]

My interviewees did not conform to the stereotype of the 'submissive Muslim woman'. In terms of natural assertiveness they seemed to represent a normal cross-section of British womanhood (for example, some gave rather feisty descriptions of the way in which they responded to hostility

---

[116] Anway, *Daughters of Another Path*, p. 89.

they encountered as a result of wearing the *ḥijāb* in public). Diana described herself as 'quite bossy and independent', and gave that as the very reason why she wanted a man to be the head of the household: 'If I could wear the trousers I think I'd probably get bored, I'd get annoyed, and I'd probably lose respect as well for that person.' None of those who spoke on this subject saw the wife's obedience or the husband's authority as unconditional, and this is in accordance with Islamic teachings which make obedience to the husband subject to a higher duty of obedience to God. However, as has been seen above, many people introduced some additional reservations concerning the extent and nature of the husband's authority. This could be attributed partly to apologetic concerns (to counteract a view of Islam as oppressive to women), partly to the influence of a non-Muslim upbringing in which the man's 'headship' was not necessarily the norm, and partly to a natural human desire for a degree of autonomy (in the case of the women).

POLYGYNY

Polygyny is a potentially controversial subject, both amongst Muslims and between Muslims and non-Muslims. While it is universally acknowledged by Muslims that it was practised by the Prophet, and therefore cannot be intrinsically wrong, some prominent modernist or reformist Muslim thinkers, including Muhammad 'Abduh (1849–1905), have tried to show that, based on a variety of arguments, it is no longer appropriate.[117] The practice has been restricted or outlawed in several Muslim countries, especially the more secular ones. Although some people might feel that polygyny is a topic of minor interest and hardly ever occurs, it may be more

---

[117] The most common method employed is to juxtapose the two Qur'anic verses on the subject: 4:3 (which gives permission for polygyny but advises men to keep to one wife if they fear they cannot deal equitably with their wives) and 4:129 (which states that they will not be able to be completely fair between wives no matter how hard they try). I did find one instance of a convert using this argument against polygyny: see Martin, 'What Muslim Women Want'. Opponents of polygyny argue that the latter verse effectively cancels out the permission, while the mainstream view is that the latter verse was revealed in order to reassure the Companions that they could not be expected to have identical feelings towards each of their wives. Others have argued that only a prophet could have the necessary qualities to be able to have a successful plural marriage, or that humans are less virtuous than they used to be and so the undesirable consequences (resulting from jealousy etc.) would outweigh any benefits.

widespread in Britain than is commonly thought (though it is impossible to know the exact numbers involved because those who engage in it rarely broadcast the fact). Shagufta Yaqub, a British Muslim who was commissioned to do a BBC radio documentary on the subject, was surprised by how easy it was to find cases of polygyny in Britain.[118] I had the impression that nearly all of my interviewees had given the matter quite a lot of thought, and, as will be shown below, several had either considered it or practised it themselves.

In an article entitled '"The Polygamy Question": Do we or Don't we in this Day and Age?', second-generation convert Isla Rosser-Owen argues that polygyny is an authentic Islamic practice which has been stigmatized even among Muslims due to a combination of factors: widespread abuse of the practice (with men failing to deal openly and fairly with their wives); and the infatuation of many Muslims with all things Western, and in particular the 'Bollywood factor' (including 'the over-romanticisation of marriage' and 'the quest to find the perfect partner'). She describes prevailing Muslim attitudes in the following terms: 'If a woman is in a polygynous marriage ... she is seen as uneducated, common and at best naïve. She is often sneered at – by other women. It's something that the peasants do, and that no respectable man or woman would have anything to do with.' Her belief that in the UK at least converts are more likely than born Muslims to enter into plural marriages was supported by my own findings. Over half of those who were asked knew, or knew of, at least one convert who was in a plural marriage, and many felt that the practice was increasing. A few of the interviewees had had personal experience of plural marriage: two (one man and one woman) were currently in polygynous marriages, one had been in the past, and two of the women were currently in negotiations to become second or third wives. In addition, one of the men had negotiated for a polygynous marriage with two women, but had ended up marrying them consecutively (having divorced one to be with the other) rather than concurrently. This was due to reservations on the part of the women; he stressed that he himself would have much preferred the option of polygyny. Among the remaining interviewees, one man said that he would like to take a second wife but his wife would not agree, and several interviewees said that they might consider it in

---

[118] One Muslim scholar cited on the programme who was a *muftī* and a member of a *sharī'ah* council said that he had between ten and fifteen cases of polygyny referred to him each month: *Inside the Harem*, Radio 4, 13 October 2004.

the future, depending on circumstances. Only a third of the sample felt that it was definitely not for them, many citing their upbringing and personality as reasons. Some of these admired people who *were* able to enter into such marriages, and one woman hoped that she would be able to bring her daughter up in such a way that she would be capable of being a co-wife. None felt that polygyny was wrong on principle, and only one of the interviewees expressed a sense that it was inappropriate in the British context: 'It takes a certain type of man to be able to marry more than one wife ... also it takes a certain type of woman to be able to fit into that role, which I don't think either the men or the women in the West are particularly geared to doing, because the mindset is so different.' There was very little difference in attitude between the men and the women, except that women were more likely to refer to the possible emotional difficulties of being in a plural marriage.

Such is the level of prejudice and stigma surrounding polygyny (in both Muslim and non-Muslim circles) that of the two interviewees currently practising it, one preferred not to discuss it and the other did not wish to be identified. The latter had been a second wife for just over a year, and told me of her experience: 'Among the [Muslim] community it's really not looked on well and I've had to be very, very careful ... I had one friend who saw me as being a right floozy ... that was the implication.' She felt there was an element of hypocrisy among Muslims who constantly sang the praises of Islam but did not wish to accept what for her is an integral part of it. She added: 'If it was known, a lot of people wouldn't want to speak to me, I mean I would be boycotted ... I've come across quite a few people who have to be very careful about it, and are terribly worried that they're going to be persecuted by the community.'

A few of the women spoke of the potential advantages of plural marriage. The woman quoted above who was a second wife explained that in order to allow the first wife to adjust, she did not insist on her right to spend equal time with her husband. Her description suggests that polygyny and 'romance' are not entirely mutually exclusive: 'I've got more independence, I don't have to cook his dinner every night, I don't have to do a lot of his washing. Maybe we won't get bored with each other because we're not with each other twenty-four hours a day, so we've still got quite a romantic view of each other. He respects my space.' One of the two women who were currently negotiating to be in plural marriages told me that she had given much thought to the matter and explained her reasons for wanting to be in a polygynous relationship. Her account had many resonances with that of the second wife just quoted: 'I couldn't imagine myself cooking every single day and having to deal with a man every single day. I want to be able to do my own stuff, I want to be able to do my projects, I want to be able to do my writing ... and since I'm independent, a man telling me what to do is quite difficult for me, so at least he'll only be telling me what to do part-time.' She was planning to spend weekends with her husband, if the arrangement worked out, and to lay down a condition that she could spend the whole summer abroad, as she wished to do aid work. In a similar vein, Na'ima Robert writes that 'the polygamous system is one that is ideally suited to a certain type of woman: the woman who is busy with her studies or career, whose friends and family play a big part in her life, the woman with children from a previous relationship, the older woman who just doesn't want a man around all the time because she enjoys her own company'. One of her interviewees speaks of her strong, supportive relationship with her co-wife; Robert comments: 'Wives can help each other out, sharing childcare if one has to work or study, cooking for each other if one is sick or has just had a baby, learning and studying the *deen* together.'[119] Clearly there is a perception among some converts that polygyny can be empowering for the wife. In the case of the second wife of one year described above, it may also have given more freedom of movement; she said that she was free to go wherever she wanted, while a few of the wives in monogamous marriages spoke in terms of asking permission to go out.[120]

Several of the interviewees spoke of the potential difficulties attending plural marriage and the heavy degree of responsibility placed on the husband, in particular the requirement to support his wives and treat them equitably and fairly. Some mentioned abuses of the institution that they had heard about or witnessed.[121] These included the man using his second wife as a mistress and his first as a housekeeper, the man not telling his first wife about his second, and the man claiming benefits and forcing his second wife to sign on under false pretences. Amira felt that men entering into such

[119] Robert, *From my Sisters' Lips*, p. 181.
[120] There is a well-known *ḥadīth* which states that a woman should not leave her house without her husband's permission (cited in Roald, *Women in Islam*, pp. 146–7).
[121] See also on this the following books authored by converts: Huda al-Khattab, *Bent Rib*, ch. 4; Philips and Jones, *Polygamy in Islam*.

marriages tended to underestimate their responsibilities, or wished to marry only young virgins, which in her view went against the spirit of polygyny, which was at least in part intended to cater for women who were widowed or divorced, or women who might not otherwise be able to find husbands. She commented that if polygyny was more openly practised and not surrounded by secrecy and furtiveness, it would be easier to regulate and men would find it less easy to get away with abuses. Only one interviewee mentioned the legal complications, saying that although she would consider being in a plural marriage, she wouldn't enter into one in Britain because as a second wife her marriage would not be legally recognized and she would therefore have no rights. Two of the interviewees said that they had been approached by women looking for a co-wife, and one of them commented: 'Often they've got a problem, so they think the solution is for him to have another wife.'

Several female interviewees referred to the fact that in circumstances where women were unmarried, whether due to widowhood, a shortage of men or the difficulty of finding men willing to settle down, polygyny could be a better option than remaining single. Some, including Amira, couched their willingness to be in a plural marriage in terms of their compassion for women who were on their own: 'If I was married, and let's say my neighbour downstairs, she has six children and her husband died, I would ask my husband to marry her so that he could help her with her children. That is the real [i.e. proper] way of getting married to a second wife.' Prabha said that she wished she were the type of person who could be in a polygynous marriage, adding: 'I don't know whether I would be able to share, but if it was a particular situation where there was no other choice, then I would never deny another sister. I would like to think at the time I'd be strong enough.' Eleanor felt it would be difficult to be a co-wife, but commented: 'If the circumstances were a hundred percent right and it was necessary, if for example there was a massive war and loads of Muslim women were left without husbands and needed to be taken care of, as it was at one time in history, I would feel awful if I wasn't willing to accept that.'

As with the other topics in this chapter, rationalizing the Islamic position often entailed a critique of Western society and culture. Some, like David, contrasted Islamic polygyny with the 'serial monogamy' practised in Western societies: 'In the West . . . you marry somebody, later on when she's a bit older you dump her and take on a newer model. I don't think that's fair or kind at all, just because you like the newer model, you should still keep and treat with respect the first one.' Kavindra focused on the social implications of sexual permissiveness: 'If you look at today's society, you can really see that what ails it is the adultery that's going on. You can have a man who's married, but then he's free to have sex with a lady with whom he might have a child – but he's not responsible in any way for his mistress or his off-spring.'[122] She felt that polygyny was 'better than the alternative of having a society like you are now where the kids don't know their fathers, where no one takes responsibility for them. This is unacceptable.' Some, like Ali, drew attention to the double standard whereby multiple partners are tolerated in Western society but not polgyny: 'Before I was a Muslim I was involved in secular polygamy big time . . . secular polygamy is practised far more than Islamic polygamy and people do not understand that.' Abdal-Hakim Murad expresses a similar sentiment, observing that 'the present arrangement in the West where consensual relationships of all kinds are allowed and even militantly defended: homosexual, lesbian, and so on' is regarded as 'an absurdity' by Muslims. He juxtaposes this with the fact that a 'consensual *ménage à trois*' is 'perfectly acceptable in modern Western law as long as the parties to it live "in sin" and do not attempt to marry'.[123]

Isla Rosser-Owen feels that Muslims' defensiveness about polygyny results in confusion and polarized opinions, with some people arguing that it is only allowed in exceptional circumstances, while others promote polygyny as 'the norm', and as preferable to monogamy.[124] Interviewees generally did not engage in apologetics on the subject, but there is a certain amount of this in the literature. For example, English converts Abdal-Hakim Murad and Huda al-Khattab both argue that the lawfulness of polygyny in Islam illustrates the way in which the religion accommodates human nature (*fiṭrah*). As al-Khattab argues: 'Islam . . . takes hold of the natural urges of human beings . . . and limits and channels those energies, setting up safe-guards . . . In the case of polygyny, the natural urge of some men to have more than one partner is controlled.'[125] Murad stresses the 'biological ratio-nale' for polygyny: 'As Dawkins and others have observed, it is in the genetic

---

[122] This is not strictly true in Britain nowadays, as once paternity is established a man can be pursued by a government agency.
[123] Murad, 'Islam, Irigaray, and the Retrieval of Gender'.
[124] Rosser-Owen, ' "The Polygamy Question" '.
[125] Al-Khattab, *Bent Rib*, pp. 42–3.

interest of males to have a maximal number of females; while the reverse is never the case.' He cites Western authors who point out the advantages of polygyny, including catering for bereaved women in a war situation; creating an extended family in which the women can support each other, for example in childcare, in order to help avoid 'the juggling of work and children which is a besetting hazard of modern relationships'; and creating close-knit family networks, which allegedly reduces the incidence of criminal behaviour in the children. He concludes that polygyny can be 'a frankly liberative option for women'. He also cites polygyny as evidence of Islam's superiority over Christianity: 'By his triumphant polygamy, the Blessed Prophet was indicating the end of the Christian war against the body, and rhetorically re-affirmed the sacramental value of sexuality that the Hebrew Prophets had proclaimed.'[126]

CONCLUDING REMARKS

Converts' attitudes towards gender issues are quite distinct from those of mainstream Western or British society. The concept of a wife 'obeying' her husband, for example, is one that has been rejected by many people as outdated and undesirable, with references to it often being omitted from the traditional Christian marriage vows. The way in which converts talk about marriage does, however, have parallels with conservative Christian and Jewish views of marriage, with the emphasis on commitment rather than romantic love, the acknowledgement of the husband's authority or headship, and the spiritual goal.[127] Hajar's comment that a Muslim marriage is in some ways like an 'old-fashioned English marriage' gives rise to the thought that converts are more in harmony with pre-1960s British gender norms than with those of today. Allievi hypothesizes that women seeking to live a traditional lifestyle, one closer to that of the last generation, find in Islam the 'plausibility structure' that enables them to do so.[128]

[126] Murad, 'Islam, Irigaray, and the Retrieval of Gender'.
[127] In fact, a few of the interviewees mentioned that a traditional Jewish or Christian marriage might be similar to a Muslim marriage.
[128] He suggests (citing Yvonne Haddad) that it is easier for women to say: 'It is my religion ... it is the will of God,' than to say: 'It is my choice, I want to be a woman in the "traditional" way': Allievi, 'The Shifting Significance of the *Halal/Haram* Frontier', p. 146.

By and large there is a high degree of correspondence between converts' gender discourse and Islamic (including Islamic feminist) discourse which sees men and women as 'equal but different', and posits the relationship between the sexes as one of complementarity.[129] The concepts of sexuality and female empowerment appear in the *ḥijāb*-related discourse of born Muslims as well as that of converts. In fact, there seems to be a degree of standardization in gender discourse generally, which may be because issues of gender and sexuality are so highly charged: Bourque describes the way in which women converts who attend meetings and study circles learn how to talk about these issues, and in particular how to defend themselves vis-à-vis their families and other non-Muslims.[130] There has been a general tendency in recent years for Muslim scholars and writers to qualify or dilute by various means the concept of the wife's duty of obedience to her husband (following the initiative of Islamic feminist thinkers such as Amina Wadud). One common argument is that the husband's *qiwāmah*[131] consists of his duty to support his wife rather than his having any privileges or authority over her;[132] another is that Qur'an 4:34, which cites the wife's 'recalcitrance' or disobedience (*nushūz*) as cause for chastisement, applies only to adultery.[133] In accordance with this general trend, my interviewees, while upholding the principle of wifely obedience, tended to see it in qualified terms, though without much in the way of detailed reasoning. While they had internalized some aspects of Islamic feminist discourse, their ideas were couched in everyday language and they did not generally produce sustained or sophisticated arguments, or refer to the Qur'anic text. To some extent this is to be expected in the informal, conversational setting of an interview; it also suggests that they did not feel particularly defensive about gender issues, at least in that particular setting.[134] Despite the continuity between

---

[129] On contemporary Islamic gender discourses see, e.g., M. Yamani (ed.), *Feminism and Islam: Legal and Literary Perspectives* (Reading: Garnet, 1996); Roald, *Women in Islam*; M. Cooke, *Women Claim Islam: Creating Islamic Feminism through Literature* (New York: Routledge, 2001).

[130] Bourque, 'How Deborah Became Aisha', p. 243.

[131] The term *qiwāmah* is derived from Qur'an 4:34 which decribes men as '*qawwāmūna 'ala al-nisā*'', which may be translated as 'protectors/maintainers of women'.

[132] This is in fact argued by Fatima Martin in her article 'What Muslim Women Want'.

[133] See Roald, *Women in Islam*, p. 171.

[134] Van Nieuwkerk, however, felt that her interviewees' reaction to her as a non-Muslim Dutch woman may have caused them to be slightly defensive on gender issues ('Gender, Conversion, and Islam', p. 98).

convert and born-Muslim gender discourses, it may be that converts have a slightly enhanced awareness of the way in which mainstream society perceives Islamic teachings on gender, and this enables them to offer a more nuanced apologetic. The Western setting and context means that criticism of Western society is a prominent aspect of this discourse.

The wearing of the *niqāb* by converts (as well as by some Muslims who rediscover their faith) should be distinguished from its traditional, cultural use in places such as Saudi Arabia and the Yemen, where it is reportedly declining.[135] It is more appropriate to see it as an extension of the 'reveiling movement' which gained momentum in the 1990s, representing as it does a strong affirmation of Muslim identity (as discussed in chapter 3) and a distancing from certain aspects of Western culture. It would appear from my sample that converts are well represented in this reclaiming of the *niqāb*, though numbers are too small to draw any firm conclusions.

The contrast between converts and born Muslims becomes more apparent when one observes actual practices, as opposed to discourse. For example, it seems that converts are more likely to be scrupulous about applying Islamic teachings, as they understand them, on gender issues. Linda exemplifies an attitude that I found to be not uncommon; she said that when she converted, polygyny was 'the hardest thing to accept', adding: 'But I do feel that if you accept Islam you should accept all parts of Islam.' Based on this particular sample, converts did not generally opt for the easier, more 'lenient' or modernist interpretation of Islamic law. No one felt that polygyny should be banned, for example (as some Islamic modernists have argued), although a few felt it was more appropriate in special circumstances (such as war), and at least one thought it would not work in the Western context. It was evident that interviewees had put a lot of thought into issues such as lowering the gaze and handshaking, and generally made efforts to apply Islamic teachings (as they understood them) in these areas.[136] Similarly, on the issue of social mixing, converts seem to be quite careful in their observation of Islamic norms as they understand them;[137] by contrast, born Muslims may be part of

---

[135] See, e.g., Roald, *Women in Islam*, p. 212.

[136] Allievi found in his study of European converts that immigrant Muslims were far less likely than converts to abstain from shaking hands with the opposite sex (*Les Convertis à l'Islam*, p. 169).

[137] One should not discount the possibility that favourable attitudes to matters such as polygyny and gender segregation have a positive correlation with living in a society where these

a particular culture which has evolved a more flexible attitude to contact between the sexes (e.g. South East Asian or some African cultures).[138] In the case of two of the interviewees who were among the most easygoing with regard to social mixing, their relatively relaxed approach was based on the particular Muslim culture of their spouse.

Converts' scrupulous interpretation of Islamic norms was often accompanied by a degree of flexibility, particularly when interacting with non-Muslims, and they evinced a willingness to adapt to different situations and contexts and to apply the spirit and not just the letter of the law. Their more lenient attitude to eye contact and handshaking with non-Muslims derived from a concern that Islamic norms should not be misunderstood or construed as hostile. Sometimes this flexibility arose from the need to relate to and interact with non-Muslim family members. Here general principles, such as the importance of not alienating people or giving Islam a bad name, transcended the specific teaching, as long as the teaching did not concern an essential or obligatory matter.

Although women's advocacy groups and agencies which are used to dealing with the problems arising from abuses of polygyny may emphasize the disadvantages of the institution and see it as reflecting gender inequalities in society, it cannot be denied that in some cases women actively choose polygyny to suit their own preferred lifestyle. This is not a wholly new phenomenon; Maryam Jameelah, a prominent American Jewish convert and author of several books, famously moved to Pakistan in the early 1960s to be the second wife of a Muslim scholar (as mentioned in chapter 4), explaining that she wanted the space to pursue her intellectual interests. This phenomenon of women freely choosing polygyny in order to maintain their independence is comparable to the way in which temporary marriage (*mut'ah*) has been used in Iran in recent years by young couples as a way of getting to know each other and finding out whether they are suited for permanent marriage. In both cases an institution that has often been decried (by both Muslims and non-Muslims) as detrimental to women has been reclaimed by some women to fulfil their own purposes.

things are not widely practised, and so the possible resulting abuses are not seen. Arguably in a society with more or less strict gender segregation, for example, there is a risk of women being excluded from decision-making processes.

[138] Islamic law does in some cases accommodate local customs ('*urf*), so long as these do not contravene essential Islamic teachings.

It is perhaps in their attitudes to polygyny that the contrast between converts and born Muslims is most marked. Roald suggests that Muslims who
have lived in Western societies, or who have been exposed to Western influences, tend to have a negative attitude to polygyny. Her reference to
Muhammad Asad's implicit disapproval of it seems to indicate that she
includes converts among these Westernized Muslims, though in the absence
of fieldwork done specifically among converts it may not be appropriate to
set too much store by this. Roald also observes, as does Isla Rosser-Owen, that
polygyny is less favourably viewed in the Muslim world today, not just
because of the idealization of romantic love, but also because it is commonly
portrayed as a social problem.[139] In my own sample, I found a relatively positive attitude to it (even taking into account the possibility that some converts
might be paying lip-service to something perceived as 'Islamic'). Rosser-
Owen's suggestion that the decline of polygyny among Muslims is partly due
to *infatuation* with the West drew my attention to the possibility that if
indeed it is the case that converts have a relatively positive attitude to polygyny, it may be partly because of their sense of *disillusionment* with Western
society. At the same time, white converts in particular may be able to adopt
practices that are seen as questionable by the wider society without having
their Western credentials or 'Britishness' questioned. Another explanatory
factor might be that converts, who are 'still experimenting with how to apply
Islam to their lives', as Rosser-Owen puts it,[140] are more likely than born
Muslims to be open to something they find in the Islamic sources, even if it is
not widely practised, and are unlikely to be affected by any cultural resistance
which may have grown up around that particular phenomenon. Factors that
affect attitudes to polygyny also have a bearing on attitudes to the *ḥijāb*. In
some born-Muslim cultures where the upper classes in particular took on the
attitudes of the colonizers, there is still a residue of anti-*ḥijāb* feeling: the
ḥijāb, like polygyny, may be seen as old-fashioned and unattractive, and as
symbolizing poverty, backwardness, narrow-mindedness and the oppression of women.[141] Such attitudes are hardly found among converts, or for
that matter among Muslims who rediscover their faith.

The suggestion of Franks and Hermansen that women who join religious revivalist movements may thereby gain a sense of empowerment was

---

[139] Roald, *Women in Islam*, chapter 9, 'Polygyny'.
[140] Rosser-Owen, ' "The Polygamy Question" '.
[141] Bullock, *Rethinking Muslim Women and the Veil*, p. 43.

to some extent borne out in my own study; although (as Franks points out) the 'right to stay at home' may seem like a strange right to those women who fought for the right to work outside the home, it does nevertheless provide a solution to the practical problem of the 'double burden' of paid work and domestic duties.[142] In her study of Scandinavian converts, Roald finds that as converts mature, they tend bring their Western cultural background to bear on Islamic teachings, resulting in relatively 'progressive' interpretations of gender issues.[143] I did not find this tendency to be so marked among my own sample; in fact, attitudes to polygyny, *niqāb* and arranged marriages seemed more traditionalist than progressive (and this despite the fact that I took some care to diversify my sample, which included only a few interviewees who could be described as *salafī*).[144] Only two of my interviewees followed a pattern of gender relations that was relatively close to mainstream Western gender norms, such as allowing for the possibility of friendship between unrelated men and women (however, even these two acknowledged the principle that an unrelated man and woman should not be alone together in a non-public place). This is not to say that converts are not influenced by their Western cultural formation, but only that the ways in which this influence is manifested are not always predictable. For example, the insistence of some converts on the compatibility of romance with Islamic marriage norms may be partly due to their Western upbringing; although romance is valued in some Muslim cultures, it is, arguably, a characteristic of secular culture (e.g. the Bollywood and Egyptian film industries) rather than religious culture. The references to romance could also be for apologetic reasons, since Na'ima Robert and Huda al-Khattab, who both mention it, are partly aiming to portray a favourable impression of Islamic marriage norms.

On the whole, on the question of Western influences on Islamic practices I found a rather variegated picture, with a selective synthesis of Islamic and Western attitudes and values. For example, traditional views on gender relations were sometimes combined with an assertively feminist attitude;

---

[142] Franks, *Women and Revivalism in the West*, p. 124.
[143] Roald, 'The Shaping of a Scandinavian "Islam"', p. 59.
[144] Roald's slightly contrasting finding may reflect the fact that female converts in Scandinavia who are married to born Muslims are more likely to be breadwinners, since immigrants there are of relatively recent provenance and so less likely to be established in professions or businesses.

Na'ima Robert in particular sounds almost radically feminist in linking her wearing of *niqāb* to an insistence that men do not have the 'right' to see her face. Similarly, she describes her eventual acceptance of a wife's duty of obedience to her husband and follows this with the spirited remark: 'I also made sure that my husband-to-be knew that I was not about to put up with any nonsense: I wouldn't be ordered around or talked down to.'[145] Gender practices and discourse illustrate the complex relationship between Islamic identity formation and attitudes to Western society; while female covering represents a dramatic departure from prevailing Western norms, the discourse that supports it draws extensively on Western feminist critiques of the commodification of the female body in capitalist societies.

[145] Robert, *From my Sisters' Lips*, p. 169.

Conclusion

M uslim converts draw from their faith certain values, norms and
beliefs that are very different from those of mainstream British
culture. They selectively oppose aspects of British culture, including materialism, consumerism, secularism, the sexualization of society,
hedonism, individualism (to varying degrees) and familial disintegration.
Their opposition is not just intellectual or ideological: it is embodied in
their daily lives. Converts counter the alienating forces of modern secular
society in various ways: by maintaining a strong religious belief, by living a
disciplined and structured life, and by gaining a sense of belonging to a
community (whether local, national or global). They simplify their lives by
voluntarily ruling out certain choices and by selectively rejecting aspects of
Western life (the drinking culture, free mixing of the sexes and prevailing
standards of sexual morality, to name a few). By dressing distinctively (in the
case of the women) they are marking themselves out as 'different' or 'other'
despite the cost in terms of hostility and discrimination from the host culture. As Badran observes, converts voluntarily position themselves as 'outsiders', while immigrant Muslims and their descendants are regarded as
such without having a choice in the matter, mainly due to their physical
characteristics.[1]

To the extent that converts (and also some 'revert' Muslims) consciously
act as cultural critics, and enact that criticism in their own lives by living out
a different pattern, they may be seen as counter-cultural. The term 'counter-
culture' is most often used to refer to the hippy movement which began in

---

[1] Badran, 'Feminism and Conversion', p. 204.

the 1960s.[2] On the face of it, converts are not much like hippies at all (although a number of older converts describe themselves as ex-hippies); British society today is rather different from what it was in the 1960s, so one would not expect a 'counter-culture' to manifest itself in the same way today. In some respects things have come full circle, with some of the practices that hippies advocated such as 'free love' and drug use becoming commonplace activities, and mainstays of British youth culture. On the other hand, some of the aspects of society that the hippy culture stood *against*, in particular its materialism and consumerism (its 'wealth, plenty and gadgets', in Qutb's words), seem to be more prevalent today than in the 1960s. If the Vietnam War was seen by hippies, among others, as an act of imperialism, Muslim converts (and Muslims in general) are talking of a new wave of imperialism, spearheaded by America and Britain, in the present day. Their concern may be heightened by the fact that the main casualties of this neo-imperialism are Muslims, but their arguments are often couched in terms of ethics and social justice.

Those who see individualism as an essential characteristic of counter-culturalism may feel that subscribing to a religion and following its precepts could hardly be described as 'counter-cultural' and that it would be more accurately described as conformist. By and large this corresponds to converts' own self-image – they would certainly see themselves as 'conforming' to Islamic teachings and to God's will. When I asked interviewees if they felt they had a particular purpose in life, the vast majority answered along the lines of: 'To worship God to the best of my ability.' It just so happens that what they are conforming to (even allowing for some diversity in interpretation) is in some respects radically different to mainstream values and practice in twenty-first-century Britain and Western society in general.

This study has observed many ways in which converts bring aspects of their original identity into their Islamic lives. Ansari suggests that in the early phase of Muslim immigration, converting to Islam meant adopting immigrant cultures, as the preservation of ethnic identities was a priority for Muslims at the time.[3] Converts now seem to experience less pressure to conform to these cultures, particularly with the changing attitudes of younger generations of British Muslims. Converts appear to be more confident than

---

[2] See on this Roszak, *The Making of a Counter Culture*.
[3] Ansari, '*The Infidel Within*', pp. 387–8.

they used to be about forging their own cultural patterns and taking what they see as the best from different cultures. This remains true of those who marry born Muslims, as the spouse too is likely to be going through a process of cultural synthesis and adaptation. As observed in chapter 3, many converts acknowledge the continuity of their Islamic faith with the values they were taught as children, and inclusivist attitudes towards British culture on the part of converts are often attributable to their childhood experiences or family background. Western influences are sometimes manifested in unpredictable ways, via a creative combination of Islamic and Western values. This was particularly evident in the fusion of traditional gender norms and female empowerment, as seen for example in the use of polygyny to achieve a more independent lifestyle, described in chapter 5.

Converts are contributing to an indigenous British Islam in various ways. First, they perform the task of cultural mediation. As has been shown in this study, they often have a keen awareness of not only Muslim sensibilities but also prevailing British sensibilities; this makes them potentially very effective as communicators and cultural interpreters in both directions.[4] Their approach to delicate questions such as sexual morality can sometimes be more nuanced and less confrontational, whilst stopping short of challenging central Islamic beliefs. Second, they challenge, on occasion, the boundaries of Islamic thought; it seems that converts can sometimes say things that are difficult for born Muslims to say. Yakoub Islam's championing of the cause of gay and lesbian Muslims, which would be anathema to many Muslims, is a case in point.[5] Scott Siraj al-Haqq Kugle (an American convert) similarly expands the limits of Islamic discourse on homosexuality, but on an academic level. Third, as mentioned in chapters 3 and 4, converts have made a significant contribution to both integrationist and anti-extremist discourse.

There was something of a contrast between convert discourse in the Muslim media and my interview material. This is because, as mentioned in the introduction, most of the convert-authored material was in the more progressive or liberal press, i.e. Q-News and emel. I believe this reflects a

[4] See, e.g., Yahya Birt's insightful article on the Jack Straw/niqāb affair of autumn 2006, 'The Veil and the Limits of English Tolerance'.
[5] As a self-avowed 'progressive Muslim', he suggests the invention of a new shahādah: 'I believe in one God, Allah, and that the rest of my life will be devoted to being less of an idiot than I am now' (Islam, 'White, Weird and Wonderful').

liberal bias in the press rather than a conservative one among the interviewees, though without further research it is difficult to be sure. As mentioned
in chapter 3, it may be appropriate to speak of a tension between a relatively
liberal vocal minority (traditionalists such as Abdal-Hakim Murad and the
perennial philosophers notwithstanding) and a quieter, more conservative
majority. Like Roald, I found that the more highly educated converts were
on the whole more reflective and less conservative in their views. Roald
observed a tendency among converts to become more flexible and lenient in
interpreting Islamic norms as they developed and matured.[6] I found evidence of this in the press and internet material – for example in the evolving
attitudes to music of Yusuf Islam and Rasjid Topham, and the tendency of
some converts to 'return to their roots' after an initial burst of enthusiasm
for all things Islamic. However, my own sample presented a rather mixed
picture. The person with the most liberal views overall had been a Muslim
for only two years; the four interviewees who were *salafi* in orientation were
not particularly recent converts (three of them having been Muslim for over
ten years), and some interviewees had maintained a high level of scrupu-
lousness over many years on matters such as music and handshaking. Two
or three people said that over time they had become stricter or more 'orthodox' in the practice of their Islamic faith. To some extent an increased
leniency *was* apparent in the matter of tolerance of difference among
Muslims. Perhaps the lack of an overall progression towards leniency can be
attributed to the fact the inevitable waning (with time) of the proverbial zeal
of the converted is counteracted by a gradual socialization into the Muslim
community, whereby converts progressively integrate more aspects of
Islamic belief and practice into their lives.

Although converts contest many of the prevalent values of Western
society, they do not reject them all. To some extent they still embody the core
values of liberal democracy: the vast majority positively appreciate living in
a pluralistic society. At the same time, they have a relatively 'strong' Islamic
identity, and are usually diligent in their religious practice. Conservative in
their understanding of Islamic teachings in the area of gender behaviour,
and conscientious in implementing them, they remain flexible in their dealings with non-Muslims. It seems that converts are more likely than born

---

[6] Roald, *New Muslims in the European Context*, pp. 105 and 233. She also observes that some
converts do retain inflexible attitudes.

Muslims to engage in polygynous marriage and to abstain from listening to (instrumental) music, whilst at the same time, paradoxically, they are at the forefront of integrationist discourse. Timothy Bowes for example abjures music while emphasizing the continuity of his Islamic faith with his upbringing (as described in chapter 3).

This creative synthesis between Islamic and Western elements emerged most clearly in the overall picture I gained of each interviewee as an individual. Unfortunately, the limitations of academic writing have made it difficult to do justice to this aspect of the fieldwork in this study. The people I interviewed did not seem to fit very well into the commonly invoked categories of Muslim thought (e.g. traditionalist, modernist, radical Islamist). Instead I found that the views of a given person would often add up to an idiosyncratic mosaic, the separate parts of which would have to be ascribed to different categories. For example, someone's views might be relatively liberal by Islamic standards in one area, and relatively conservative in another. As a result, I was surprised by some of the answers I received to interview questions, in the light of other answers already given by the same person. Perhaps the most striking example of this 'mosaic' effect was provided by one woman who respected the al-Muhajiroun leader Omar Bakri Mohammed and had on occasion consulted him on Islamic issues. This woman was very sceptical about democracy, and believed that the Islamic state or Caliphate offered a better solution. She was also a creative writer of non-religious historical fiction who went to a weekly kick-boxing class and said that she was 'the dominant one' in her marriage.

As mentioned in chapter 4, Muslims and non-Muslims in Britain have shared concerns in many areas, among them British foreign policy, social fragmentation, the decline of moral and behavioural standards, and the supremacy of the market-driven consumer society. For Muslims, Islam provides not only a broad set of values and standards by which to evaluate the society in which they live, but also perhaps a motivation to speak out. An old Chinese proverb advises: 'If you want a definition of water, don't ask a fish'.[7] The possibility cannot be discounted that conversion to Islam enables some people to distance themselves psychologically from the society in which they grew up – in such a way as to see that society more clearly.

---

[7] Quoted in Newbigin, *Foolishness to the Greeks*, p. 21.

Glossary of Arabic and Islamic terms

burqah	an all-enveloping outer garment for women, usually covering the face
da'wah	'call' or 'invitation', i.e. to Islam
dhikr	remembrance of God; devotional act involving the repetition of the names of God, phrases from the Qur'an etc.
fatwā	informal legal ruling
fiqh	Islamic jurisprudence
fiṭrah	human nature; natural goodness; innate disposition
ḥadīth	a report containing a saying or action of Muhammad; a collective term for these reports
ḥalāl	religiously permitted
ḥarām	religiously prohibited
ḥijāb	covering; Islamic dress code for women (which usually involves covering all except the face and hands)
hijrah	'flight' from a place where one is not free to practice one's faith to a place where one is
ijtihād	independent juristic reasoning
imām	religious leader, prayer leader
jihād	struggle for the sake of God (including military engagement)
jilbāb	a woman's gown or dress, which covers her from head to toe (excluding the face)
kāfir (pl. kafirūn/ kuffār)	unbeliever(s)
kufr	unbelief
khalwah	illegitimate seclusion (between a non-*maḥram* male and female)

maḥram	unmarriageable, being in a degree of consanguinity that precludes marriage (e.g. parent, sibling)
niqāb	face veil
salafī	a term used to describe an Islamic tendency which harks back to the earliest Muslim generations; *salafī*s tend to be conservative and puritanical and are often Wahhabi-affiliated
shahādah	declaration of faith, sincere pronouncement of which renders someone a Muslim
tawḥīd	oneness or unity of God
ummah	global Muslim community

Bibliography

Abbas, T. (ed.) *Muslim Britain: Communities under Pressure*. London: Zed Books, 2005.

Abdel Haleem, H. 'Experiences, Needs and Potential of New Muslim Women in Britain', in Jawad and Benn (eds.), *Muslim Women*, 91–106.

Abdullah, A.-L. 'Understanding Conversion: Bridging the Two Selves'. http://www.islamfortoday.com/abdullah06.htm (accessed 04/08/04).

Adnan, A. *New Muslims in Britain*. London: Ta-Ha, 1999.

Ahmed, T.S. 'Reading Between the Lines: Muslims and the Media', in Abbas (ed.), *Muslim Britain*, 109–26.

Alam, F. 'Vision of a New Islam'. *The Observer*, 4 April 2004.

Alam, F. 'Why I Reject the Anarchists Who Claim to Speak for Islam'. *The Observer*, 12 February 2006.

Alam, F. and J. Izagaren. 'From Glamour to Glory'. *Q-News*, no. 343–4, May/June 2002.

Ali, K. *Sexual Ethics and Islam: Feminist Reflections on Qur'an, Hadith and Jurisprudence*. Oxford: Oneworld, 2006.

Allen, C. 'From Race to Religion: The New Face of Discrimination', in Abbas (ed.), *Muslim Britain*, 49–65.

Allievi, S. *Les Convertis à l'Islam: Les Nouveaux Musulmans d'Europe*. Paris: l'Harmattan, 1998.

Allievi, S. 'The Shifting Significance of the *Halal/Haram* Frontier: Narratives on the *Hijab* and Other Issues', in van Nieuwkerk (ed.), *Women Embracing Islam*, 120–49.

AlSayyad, N. 'Muslim Europe or Euro-Islam: On the Discourses of Identity and Culture', in AlSayyad and Castells (eds.), *Muslim Europe*, 9–29.

AlSayyad, N. and M. Castells (eds.) *Muslim Europe or Euro-Islam: Politics, Culture, and Citizenship in the Age of Globalization*. Oxford: Lexington Books, 2002.

Amina. 'Amina's Story'. http://www.islamfortoday.com/amina.htm (accessed 04/08/04).

Ansari, H. *'The Infidel Within': Muslims in Britain since 1800*. London: Hurst & Co., 2004.

Anwar, M. 'Issues, Policy and Practice', in Abbas (ed.), *Muslim Britain*, 31–46.

Anway, C. *Daughters of Another Path: Experiences of American Women Choosing Islam*. Lee's Summit, MO: Yawna Publications, 2002 [1995].

Anway, C. 'American Women Choosing Islam', in Haddad and Esposito (eds.), *Muslims on the Americanization Path*, 145–60.

Badran, M. 'Feminism and Conversion: Comparing British, Dutch and South African Life Stories', in van Nieuwkerk (ed.), *Women Embracing Islam*, 192–232.

Bagguley, P. and Y. Hussain. 'Flying the Flag for England? Citizenship, Religion and Cultural Identity among British Pakistani Muslims', in Abbas (ed.), *Muslim Britain*, 208–21.

Barker, E. *New Religious Movements: A Practical Introduction*. London: HMSO Publications, 1989.

Barker, I. and R. Currie. 'Do Converts Always Make the Most Committed Christians?'. *Journal for the Scientific Study of Religion* 3, 1985, 305–13.

Bearman, P., T. Bianquis, C.E. Bosworth, E. van Donzel and W.P. Heinrichs. 'Liwāṭ'. *Encyclopaedia of Islam*. Brill Online, http://www.brillonline.nl/public/.

Beit-Hallahmi, B. *Prolegomena to the Psychological Study of Religion*. London: Associated University Press, 1989.

Bennassar, B. and L. Bennassar. *Les Chrétiens d'Allah*. Paris: Perrin, 1989.

Berger, P. *Invitation to Sociology*. London: Penguin, 1991.

Berger, P. and T. Luckmann. *The Social Construction of Reality: A Treatise in the Sociology of Knowledge*. New York: Doubleday, 1966.

Berrington, L. 'The Spread of a World Creed'. *The Times*, 9 November 1993.

Berrington, L. 'Islam Sheds its Image as Purely Eastern Religion'. *The Times*, 10 November 1993.

Birt, Y. 'Building New Medinas in These Sceptred Isles'. *Q-News*, no. 343–4, May/June 2002 (available at http://www.yahyabirt.com).

Birt, Y. 'Lies, Damn Lies, Statistics and Conversion!'. *Q-News*, no. 350, October 2002 (available at http://www.yahyabirt.com).

Birt, Y. 'Lobbying and Marching: British Muslims and the State', in Abbas (ed.), *Muslim Britain*, 92–106.

Birt, Y. 'Between Nation and Umma: Muslim Loyalty in a Globalizing World', orig. pub. http://www.yahyabirt.com; *Islam21* 40, January 2006, 6–11).

Birt, Y. 'Islamic Citizenship in Britain after 7/7', in Malik (ed.), *The State we are in*, 3–13.

Birt, Y. 'We Muslim Converts are not Traitors in your Midst'. *The Spectator*, 19 August 2006.

Birt, Y. 'The Veil and the Limits of English Tolerance'. http://www.yahyabirt.com (posted 11 October 2006; accessed 10/01/07).

Bourque, N. 'Being British and Muslim: Dual Identity amongst New and Young Muslims', in Jones (ed.), *University Lectures*, 1–18.

Bourque, N. 'How Deborah Became Aisha: The Conversion Process and the Creation of Female Muslim Identity', in van Nieuwkerk (ed.), *Women Embracing Islam*, 233–49.

Bowes, T. 'At This Point in my Life'. *The Neurocentric: The Journey of a Self-Centred Soul*, 8 May 2005, http://neurocentric.blogspot.com/2006/05/at-this-time-in-my-life.html (accessed 10/05/06).

Bowes, T. 'The Legacy of my Christian Upbringing'. *The Neurocentric*, 7 March 2006, http://neurocentric.blogspot.com/2006/03/legacy-of-my-christian-upbringing.html (accessed 16/03/06).

Brown, C. *The Death of Christian Britain: Understanding Secularisation 1800–2000*. London: Routledge, 2001.

Bruce, S. *Religion in Modern Britain*. Oxford: Oxford University Press, 1995.

Bulliet, R. *Conversion to Islam in the Medieval Period: An Essay in Quantitative History*. Cambridge, MA: Harvard University Press, 1979.

Bullock, K. *Rethinking Muslim Women and the Veil: Challenging Historical and Modern Stereotypes*. Herndon, VA: International Institute of Islamic Thought, 2002.

Bullock, K. 'The Hijab Experience of Canadian Muslim Women'. http://www.islamfortoday.com/hijabcanada.htm (accessed 12/10/05).

Bullock, K. 'Twelve Hours Old'. http://www.islamfortoday.com/12hours.htm (accessed 27/10/05).

Chaudhry, S. 'Getting Spiritual in Syria'. *emel*, issue 8, November/December 2004.

Compton, N. 'The New Face of Islam'. *Evening Standard*, 15 March 2002.

Davies, G. *Religion in Britain since 1945: Believing without Belonging*. Oxford: Blackwell, 1994.

Dawood, K.B. 'Face to Faith'. *emel*, issue 5, May/June 2004.

Dean, Y. 'A Day in the Life'. *Meeting Point*, no. 36, October 2005.

Deen, S. 'What Women Want'. *emel*, issue 4, March/April 2004.

Dibbell, J. 'In Gold we Trust'. *Wired News*, issue 10:01, January 2002. http://www.wired.com/wired/archive/10.01/egold_pr.html (accessed 21/12/06).

Dutton, Y. 'Conversion to Islam: The Qur'anic Paradigm', in Lamb and Bryant (eds.), *Religious Conversion*, 151–65.

Eaton, C. le G. *Islam and the Destiny of Man*. Cambridge: Islamic Texts Society, 1994.

Eaton, H. le G. 'The Radical Middle Way'. *Q-News*, no. 365, February 2006.

Eickelman, D. and J. Piscatori. *Muslim Politics*. 2nd edn., Princeton: Princeton University Press, 2004.

Emerick, Y. 'You and your Family'. *Meeting Point*, no. 22, March 2001.

Evans, G. 'In Search of Tolerance', in Park et al. (eds.), *British Social Attitudes*, 213–30.

Ford, P. 'Why European Women are Turning to Islam'. *The Christian Science Monitor*, 27 December 2005.

Fowler, J.W. *Stages of Faith: The Psychology of Human Development and the Quest for Meaning*. London: Harper & Row, 1981.

Franks, M. 'Crossing the Borders of Whiteness? White Muslim Women who Wear the *Hijab* in Britain Today'. *Ethnic and Racial Studies* 23, 2000, 917–29.

Franks, M. *Women and Revivalism in the West: Choosing 'Fundamentalism' in a Liberal Democracy*. Basingstoke: Palgrave, 2001.

Fulat, S. 'Recognise our Role in Society'. *The Guardian*, 21 January 2006.

Garcia-Arenal, M. 'Jewish Converts to Islam in the Muslim West'. *Israel Oriental Studies* 17, 1997, 227–48.

Garcia-Arenal, M. 'Les Conversions d'Européens à l'Islam dans l'histoire: esquisse générale'. *Social Compass* 46, 1999, 273–81.

Geaves, R. 'Who Defines Moderate Islam "Post"-September 11?' in Geaves et al. (eds.), *Islam and the West*, 62–74.

Geaves, R. 'Negotiating British Citizenship and Muslim Identity', in Abbas (ed.), *Muslim Britain*, 66–77.

Geaves, R., T. Gabriel, Y.Y. Haddad and J.I. Smith (eds.). *Islam and the West Post 9/11*. Aldershot: Ashgate, 2004.

Gent, S. 'It was as if the Scales had been Lifted from my Eyes'. http://thetruereligion. org/modules/xfsection/article.php?articleid=180 (accessed 11/08/04).

Gerholm, T. 'Three European Intellectuals as Converts to Islam: Cultural Mediators or Social Critics?', in Gerholm and Lithman (eds.), *The New Islamic Presence*, 263–77.

Gerholm, T. and Y. Lithman (eds.) *The New Islamic Presence in Western Europe*. London: Mansell, 1988.

Giddens, A. *Sociology*. 5th edn., Cambridge: Polity Press, 2006.

Gillespie, V.B. *The Dynamics of Religious Conversion*. Alabama: Religious Education Press, 1991.

Gilliat-Ray, S. 'Multiculturalism and Identity: Their Relationship for British Muslims'. *Journal of Muslim Minority Affairs* 18, 1998, 347–54.

Gilliat-Ray, S. 'Rediscovering Islam: A Muslim Journey of Faith', in Lamb and Bryant (eds.), *Religious Conversion*, 315–32.

Glasser, B. and A. Strauss. *The Discovery of Grounded Theory: Strategies for Qualitative Research*. New York: Aldine Publishing Co., 1967.

Gordon, B. 'That Muslim Woman Could be Happier Than you . . .'. *Daily Telegraph*, 25 April 2005.

Green, A. 'Why I Embraced Islam'. Interview, *Islamic Voice* 11–11, 130, November 1997. Also http://www.themodernreligion.com/convert/convert_anthonygreen. htm (accessed 04/08/04).

Greil, A.L. and D. Rudy. 'What Have we Learned from Process Models of Conversion? An Examination of Ten Case Studies'. *Sociological Focus* 4, 1984, 305–23.

Griffith, P. and M. Leonard (eds.) *Reclaiming Britishness: Living Together after 11 September and the Rise of the Right*. London: Foreign Policy Centre, 2002.

Haddad, Y.Y. (ed.) *The Muslims of America*. New York: Oxford University Press, 1991.

Haddad, Y.Y. 'The Quest for Peace in Submission: Reflections on the Journey of American Women Converts to Islam', in van Nieuwkerk (ed.), *Women Embracing Islam*, 19–47.

Haddad, Y.Y. and J.L. Esposito (eds.) *Muslims on the Americanization Path*. Oxford: Oxford University Press, 2002.

Hafeez, S. 'Mecca2Medina'. *emel*, issue 8, November/December 2004.

Hall, S. 'The Question of Cultural Identity', in Hall et al. (eds.), *Modernity*, 273–316.

Hall, S., D. Held and T. McGrew (eds.). *Modernity and its Futures*. Cambridge: Polity Press, 1992.

Hauser, C. 'From a Bathing Suit to a Hijab'. http://thetruereligion.org/modules/xfsection/article.php?articleid=181 (accessed 11/08/04).

Henzell-Thomas, J. 'Passing Between the Clashing Rocks: The Heroic Quest for a Transcendent Identity'. Paper presented at the AMSS 32nd Annual Conference, Indiana Unversity, 26–28 September 2003. http://www.amss.net/Abstract_32nd Conference/JeremyHenzell-Thomas19.htm (accessed 04/02/05).

Henzell-Thomas, J. 'Taking Responsibility for Others'. http://theamericanmuslim. org/tam.php/features/print/taking_responsibility_for_others/ (accessed 18/01/07); orig. pub. in *emel*, issue 27, December 2006.

Hermansen, M. 'Two-Way Acculturation: Muslim Women in America Between Individual Choice (Liminality) and Community Affiliation (Communitas)', in Haddad (ed.), *The Muslims of America*, 188–201.

Hermansen, M. 'Roads to Mecca: Conversion Narratives of European and Euro-American Muslims'. *Muslim World* 89, 1999, 56–89.

Hermansen, M. 'Keeping the Faith: Convert Muslim Mothers and the Transmission of Female Muslim Identity in the West', in van Nieuwkerk (ed.), *Women Embracing Islam*, 250–75.

Hesse, B. (ed.) *Un/Settled Multiculturalisms: Diasporas, Entanglements, 'Transruptions'*. London: Zed Books, 2000.

Hewitt, I. 'Alien Nation, or Alienation?'. *Q-News*, no. 334, August 2001.

Hewitt, I. 'Schools of Good Faith'. *Q-News*, no. 339–40, January/February 2002.

Hussain, D. 'British Muslim Identity', in Seddon et al. (eds.), *British Muslims Between Assimilation and Segregation*, 83–118.

Hussain, D. 'The Impact of 9/11 on British Muslim Identity', in Geaves et al. (eds.), *Islam and the West*, 115–29.

Hussain, D. 'Muslim Political Participation in Britain and the "Europeanisation" of *FIQH*'. *Die Welt des Islams* 44, 2004, 376–401.

Islam, Yakoub. 'Dissident Sexualities: Muslim and Gay in the UK'. http://www.muslimwakeup.com/sex/archives/2004/12/002546print.php (accessed 09/03/06).

Islam, Yakoub. 'Gender Jihad'. http://www.bayyinat.org.uk/gender.htm (accessed 09/03/06).

Islam, Yakoub. 'White, Weird and Wonderful'. http://www.muslimwakeup.com/ main/archives/2004/12/002238print.php (accessed 02/10/06).

Islam, Yusuf. 'Music: A Question of Faith or Da'wah?'. http://www.mountainoflight. co.uk/talks.html (accessed 10/12/06).

Jacobson, J. *Islam in Transition: Religion and Identity among British Pakistani Youth.* London: Routledge, 1998.

Jawad, H. and T. Benn (eds.) *Muslim Women in the United Kingdom and Beyond.* Leiden: Brill, 2003.

Jenkins, S. 'The Journey of a Lifetime'. http://www.themodernreligion.com/ convert/convert-jenkins.html (accessed 04/04/04).

Jones, A. (ed.) *University Lectures in Islamic Studies 2.* London: Altajir World of Islam Trust, 1997.

Joseph, S. 'More Than Just a Scarf'. Editorial, *emel*, issue 4, March/April 2004.

Joseph, S. 'The Future of our History'. Editorial, *emel*, issue 5, May/June 2004.

Joseph, S. 'Surmountable Obstacles'. Editorial, *emel*, issue 7, September/October 2004.

Joseph, S. 'Count Yourself In'. Editorial, *emel*, issue 10, March/April 2005.

Joseph, S. 'A Career Path for Tomorrow'. Editorial, *emel*, issue 20, May 2006.

Khattab, H. al-. *Bent Rib: A Journey through Women's Issues in Islam.* London: Ta-Ha, 1997.

Kissoon, A. 'A Different Childhood: A Ten Year Journey to Islam'.http://www. islamonline.net/english/journey/2005/03/jour01.shtml (accessed 09/ 06/05).

Knott, K. and S. Khokher. 'Religious and Ethnic Identity among Young Muslim Women in Bradford'. *New Community* 19, 1993, 593–610.

Köse, A. *Conversion to Islam: A Study of Native British Converts.* London: Kegan Paul International, 1996.

Köse, A. and K. Loewenthal. 'Conversion Motifs among British Converts to Islam'. *International Journal for the Psychology of Religion* 10, 2000, 101–10.

Kugle, S. Siraj al-Haqq. 'Sexuality, Diversity, and Ethics in the Agenda of Progressive Muslims', in Safi (ed.), *Progressive Muslims*, 190–234.

Lamb, C. and M. Bryant (eds.). *Religious Conversion: Contemporary Practices and Controversies.* London: Cassell, 1999.

Levtzion, N. (ed.). *Conversion to Islam.* New York and London: Holmes & Meier, 1979.

Lewis, P. *Islamic Britain: Religion, Politics and Identity among British Muslims*. 2nd edn., London: Tauris, 2002.

Lings, M. *The Eleventh Hour: The Spiritual Crisis of the Modern World in the Light of Tradition and Prophecy*. Cambridge: Archetype, 2002 [1987].

Lofland, J. and N. Skonovd. 'Conversion Motifs'. *Journal for the Scientific Study of Religion* 4, 1981, 373–85.

Lofland, J. and R. Stark. 'Becoming a World-Saver: A Theory of Conversion to a Deviant Perspective'. *American Sociological Review* 30, 1965, 862–75.

Lyall, S. 'Hungry for Fresh Recruits, Cult-Like Islamic Groups Know Just When to Pounce'. *New York Times*, 17 August 2006.

Malik, A.A. (ed.) *The State we are in: Identity, Terror and the Law of Jihad*. Bristol, Amal Press, 2006.

Mandaville, P. 'Reimagining the *Ummah*? Information Technology and the Changing Boundaries of Political Islam', in Mohammadi (ed.), *Islam Encountering Globalisation*, 61–90.

Mannion, D.A. 'Dawud's Story: My Conversion to Islam'. http://www.na65.com/mwhs/New%20Project.asp (accessed 18/03/05).

Maqsood, R.W. *The Muslim Marriage Guide*. New Delhi: Goodword Books, 2006 [1998].

Martin, F. 'What Muslim Women Want'. http://www.qalamonline.com/2006/05/what_muslim_women_want_by_fati.html (accessed 22/08/06).

Masterton, A. 'Think about This'. http://islamic-college.ac.uk/newsletter2/jan04page4.htm (accessed 08/11/05).

McCall, M.Z. 'Window on my World'. *Meeting Point*, no. 20, June 2000.

McCloud, B. *African American Islam*. New York and London: Routledge, 1995.

McRoy, A. *From Rushdie to 7/7: The Radicalisation of Islam in Britain*. London: Social Affairs Unit, 2006.

Modood, T. 'The Place of Muslims in British Secular Multiculturalism', in AlSayyad and Castells (eds.), *Muslim Europe*, 113–30.

Modood, T. *Multicultural Politics: Racism, Ethnicity and Muslims in Britain*. Edinburgh: Edinburgh University Press, 2005.

Mohammadi, A. (ed.). *Islam Encountering Globalisation*. Richmond, Surrey: RoutledgeCurzon, 2002.

Moll, Y. ' "Beyond Beards, Scarves and Halal Meat": Mediated Constructions of British Muslim Identity'. *Journal of Religion and Popular Culture* 15, Spring 2007, http://www.usask.ca/relst/jrpc/.

Moore, D.A.-H. 'Against Mediocrity: Poetry and the Point of Inspiration'. *Q-News*, no. 365, February 2006.

Murad, A.-H. See also T. Winter.

Murad, A.-H. 'British and Muslim?' http://www.islamfortoday.com/murad05.htm (accessed 04/08/04), 1997.

Murad, A.-H. 'Islam, Irigaray, and the Retrieval of Gender'. http://www.masud.co.uk/ISLAM/ahm/gender.htm (accessed 16/03/06), 1999.

Murad, A.-H. 'Seeing with Both Eyes'. http://www.masud.co.uk/ISLAM/ahm/cardiff.htm (accessed 16/03/06), 2000.

Murad, A.-H. 'Recapturing Islam from the Terrorists'. http://www.islamfortoday.com/murad02.htm (accessed 04/08/04), 2001.

Murad, A.-H. 'Faith in the Future: Islam after the Enlightenment'. http://www.masud.co.uk/ISLAM/ahm/postEnlight.htm (accessed 16/03/06), 2002.

Murad, A.-H. 'Tradition or Extradition?' http://www.themodernreligion.com/world/extradition.html (accessed 01/11/05), 2003. Also in A.A. Malik (ed.), *The Empire and the Crescent: Global Implications for a New American Century*. Bristol: Amal Press, 2003, 142–55.

Murad, A.-H. 'Bin Laden's Violence is a Heresy against Islam'. http://www.islamfortoday.com/murad04.htm (accessed 04/08/04).

Murad, A.-H. 'Bombing without Moonlight'. http://www.masud.co.uk/ISLAM/ahm/moonlight.htm (accessed 29/12/06), 2004.

Murad, A.-H. 'Muslim Songs of the British Isles'. *Meeting Point*, no. 36, October 2005.

Murad, A.-H. 'Diana and Dionysus'. http://www.masud.co.uk/ISLAM/ahm/di.htm (accessed 16/03/06).

Murad, A.-H. 'The Fall of the Family (Part I)'. http://www.islamfortoday.com/murad06.htm (accessed 23/02/06).

Murad, A.-H. 'The Fall of the Family (Part II)'. http://www.islamfortoday.com/murad08.htm (accessed 23/02/06).

Murad, A.-H. 'The Poverty of Fanaticism'. http://www.islamfortoday.com/murad02.htm (accessed 04/08/04).

Murray, S. 'The Will Not to Know: Islamic Accommodations of Male Homosexuality', in Murray and Roscoe (eds.), *Islamic Homosexualities*, 14–54.

Murray, S. and W. Roscoe (eds.) *Islamic Homosexualities: Culture, History and Literature*. New York: New York University Press, 1997.

Muslim World League. *Islam: Our Choice.* Mecca: Mecca Printing and Information Est., n.d.

Napier, E. 'Articles of Faith'. *The Guardian*, 24 February 2004.

Newbigin, L. *Foolishness to the Greeks.* Grand Rapids, MI: Eerdmans, 1986.

Nielsen, J. *Muslims in Western Europe.* 3rd edn., Edinburgh: Edinburgh University Press, 2004.

Nock, A. *Conversion: The Old and the New in Religion from Alexander the Great to Augustine of Hippo.* Oxford: Oxford University Press, 1933.

Omar, K. 'Reflecting on the Ways of our Ancestors'. *Meeting Point*, no. 3, Autumn 1994.

O'Sullivan, J. 'If you Hate the West, Emigrate to a Muslim Country'. *The Guardian*, 8 October 2001.

Park, A., J. Curtice, K. Thomson, L. Jarvis and C. Bromley (eds.) *British Social Attitudes: The 19th Report.* London: Sage Publications, 2002.

Parrucci, D. 'Religious Conversion'. *Sociological Analysis* 29, 1968, 144–54.

Paterson, A. 'My Journey to Islam'. http://www.islamicity.com/Mosque/MyJourney/ AbdulWahid_Paterson.htm (accessed 04/08/06).

Paterson, J. 'Would you Swap Fun, Fashion and Freedom . . . for This?'. *Real Magazine*, 11–24 February 2003.

Peach, C. 'Britain's Muslim Population', in Abbas (ed.), *Muslim Britain*, 18–30.

Percy, M. (ed.). *Previous Convictions: Conversion in the Present Day.* London: SPCK, 2000.

Petre, J. 'My Dad Buys me Books about Islam'. *Daily Telegraph*, 30 December 2001.

Philips, A.A.B. and J. Jones. *Polygamy in Islam.* Riyadh: Tawheed Publications, 1990.

Poston, L. *Islamic Da'wah in the West: Muslim Missionary Activity and the Dynamics of Conversion to Islam.* New York: Oxford University Press, 1992.

Qaradawi, Y. al-. 'Singing and Music'. http://www.radwan.cwc.net/music.html (accessed 18/03/05).

Qwidi, M. al-. 'Understanding the Stages of Conversion to Islam: The Voices of British Converts'. Ph.D. thesis, University of Leeds, 2002.

Rahman, S. 'The Talented Mr Gai Eaton'. *emel*, issue 1, September/October 2004.

Rahman, S. 'Framing Life'. *emel*, issue 21, June 2006.

Ramadan, T. *To be a European Muslim.* Leicester: Islamic Foundation, 1999.

Ramadan, T. *Western Muslims and the Future of Islam*. Oxford: Oxford University Press, 2004.

Rambo, L. *Understanding Religious Conversion*. New Haven: Yale University Press, 1993.

Rashid, M. al-. 'Thinking about the Good Things to Come'. *emel*, issue 9, January/February 2005.

Reilly, H. *Seeking Sanctuary: Journeys to Sudan*. London: Eye Books, 2005.

Rippin, A. *Muslims: Their Religious Beliefs and Practices*. London: Routledge, 2005.

Roald, A.S. *Women in Islam: The Western Experience*. London: Routledge, 2001.

Roald, A.S. *New Muslims in the European Context: The Experience of Scandinavian Converts*. Leiden: Brill, 2004.

Roald, A.S. 'The Shaping of a Scandinavian "Islam": Converts and Gender Equal Opportunity', in van Nieuwkerk (ed.), *Women Embracing Islam*, 48–70.

Robert, N. *From my Sisters' Lips: A Unique Celebration of Muslim Womanhood*. London: Bantam Press, 2005.

Rocher, L. and F. Cherqaoui. *D'Une foi l'autre: Les Conversions à l'Islam en occident*. Paris: Éditions du Seuil, 1986.

Rosser-Owen, I. 'British Muslim? A Venting of Steam'. *Q-News*, no. 343–4, May/June 2002.

Rosser-Owen, I. 'A Top Brother'. *emel*, issue 9, January/February 2005.

Rosser-Owen, I. 'In Search of a Muslim Literati'. *Q-News*, no. 365, February 2006.

Rosser-Owen, I. ' "The Polygamy Question": Do we or Don't we in This Day and Age?'. http://www.zawaj.com/articles/ThePolygamyQuestionArticle1.pdf (accessed 14/03/06).

Roszak, T. *The Making of a Counter Culture*. Berkeley and Los Angeles: University of California Press, 1968.

Runnymede Trust. *Islamophobia: A Challenge for us All*. London: Runnymede Trust, 1997.

Runnymede Trust. *Islamophobia: Issues, Challenges and Action*. London: Runnymede Trust, 2004.

Safi, O. (ed.) *Progressive Muslims: On Justice, Gender and Pluralism*. Oxford: Oneworld, 2003.

Said, S. 'Face to Faith'. *emel*, issue 4, March/April 2004.

Sardar, Z. 'The Excluded Minority: British Muslim Identity after 11 September', in Griffith and Leonard (eds.), *Reclaiming Britishness*, 51–5.

Saunders, H. 'Why I Took the Hijab'. *The Guardian*, 20 June 2002.

Sayyid, S. 'Beyond Westphalia: Nations and Diasporas – the Case of the Muslim *Umma*', in Hesse (ed.), *Un/Settled Multiculturalisms*, 33–50.

Schmidt, G. 'Islamic Identity Formation among Young Muslims: The Case of Denmark, Sweden and the United States'. *Journal of Muslim Minority Affairs* 24, 2004, 31–45.

Scott, H. 'Right This Way'. *Q-News*, no. 352, December 2003.

Scott, H. 'Islamophobia: The Language and Politics of Dependence'. *Q-News*, no. 360, February 2005.

Seddon, M.S. 'Locating the Perpetuation of "Otherness": Negating British Islam'. *Encounters* 8, 2002, 139–61.

Seddon, M.S. ' "Some Thoughts on the Formation of British Muslim Identity" – A Response to T.J. Winter'. *Encounters* 8, 2002, 185–91.

Seddon, M.S. 'British Muslims or Muslims in Britain?'. *Q-News*, no. 354, March 2004.

Seddon, M.S. 'The X Factor'. *Q-News*, no. 364, November 2005.

Seddon, M.S. 'A Day in the Life of . . . Mohammad Siddique Seddon'. http://www.newmuslimsproject.net/NLissue17/dayIn.html (accessed 18/03/05).

Seddon, M.S., D. Hussain and N. Malik (eds.). *British Muslims between Assimilation and Segregation: Historical, Legal and Social Realities*. Leicester: Islamic Foundation, 2004.

Seddon, M.S., D. Hussain and N. Malik (eds.). *British Muslims: Loyalty and Belonging*. Leicester: Islamic Foundation, 2004.

Shadid, W. and S. van Koningsveld. 'Loyalty to a Non-Muslim Government: An Analysis of Islamic Normative Discussions and of the Views of some Contemporary Islamicists', in Shadid and van Koningsveld (eds.), *Political Participation*, 86–114.

Shadid, W. and S. van Koningsveld (eds.) *Political Participation and Identities of Muslims in Non-Muslim States*. Kampen: Kok Pharos, 1996.

Sheriff, S. 'The Muslim News Survey Reveals Majority of British Muslims are against Bombing of Afghanistan and are Comfortable with Being British but not British Foreign Policy'. *Muslim News*, no. 152, 21 December 2001.

Stanford, P. 'Preaching from the Converted'. *Independent on Sunday*, 16 May 2004.

Starbuck, E. *The Psychology of Religion: An Empirical Study of the Growth of Religious Consciousness*. London: Walter Scott Publishing, 1914.

Stockton, A. 'Halal Middle Englanders?'. *Q-News*, no. 323, September 2000.

Sufi, A.-Q. as-. *Jihad: A Groundplan*. Norwich: Diwan Press, 1978.

Sufi, A.-Q. as- [ad-Darqawi]. *Letter to an African Muslim*. Norwich: Diwan Press, 1981.

Sultan, M. 'Choosing Islam: A Study of Swedish Converts'. *Social Compass* 46, 1999, 325–35.

Taylor, B. 'Recollection and Membership: Converts' Talk and the Ratiocination of Commonality'. *Sociology: Journal of the British Sociological Association* 12, 1978, 316–24.

Thomson, A. *Dajjal: The AntiChrist*. London: Ta-Ha, 1986 (rev. edn. 1997).

Thomson, A. 'Martyr or Murderer? The Muslims' Rules of Engagement'. *Q-News*, no. 356, May 2004.

Toma, B. al-. 'Your Mother, your Mother, your Mother . . . '. Editorial, *Meeting Point*, no. 21, December 2000.

Toma, B. al-. 'Enjoin Good . . . '. Editorial, *Meeting Point*, no. 26, June 2002.

Tufail, O. and H. al-Zoubeir. 'Anas Sillwood'. Interview, http://deenport.com/subsections/interviews/printerfriendly.php?interviewid=29 (accessed 30/03/06).

Ullman, C. *The Transformed Self: The Psychology of Religious Conversion*. New York: Plenum Press, 1989.

Van Nieuwkerk, K. (ed.). *Women Embracing Islam: Gender and Conversion in the West*. Austin: University of Texas Press, 2006.

Van Nieuwkerk, K. Introduction entitled 'Gender and Conversion to Islam in the West', in van Nieuwkerk (ed.), *Women Embracing Islam*, 1–16.

Van Nieuwkerk, K. 'Gender, Conversion, and Islam: A Comparison of Online and Offline Conversion Narratives', in van Nieuwkerk (ed.), *Women Embracing Islam*, 95–119.

Wadud, A. *Qur'an and Woman: Rereading the Sacred Text from a Woman's Perspective*. New York: Oxford University Press, 1999.

Walker, M. 'The Seeds of my own Re-evaluations'. http://thetruereligion.org/modules/xfsection/article.php?articleid=187 (accessed 04/08/04).

Weller, P., A. Feldman and K. Purdam. *Religious Discrimination in England and Wales*. London: Home Office, 2001.

Winter, T. See also A.-H. Murad.

Winter, T. 'Conversion as Nostalgia: Some Experiences of Islam', in Percy (ed.), *Previous Convictions*, 93–111.

Winter, T. 'Some Thoughts on the Formation of British Muslim Identity'. *Encounters* 8, 2002, 3–26.

Winter, T. 'Muslim Loyalty and Belonging: Some Reflections on the Psychosocial Background', in Seddon et al. (eds.), *British Muslims: Loyalty and Belonging*, 3–22.

Wohlrab-Sahr, M. 'Conversion to Islam: Between Syncretism and Symbolic Battle'. *Social Compass* 46, 1999, 351–62.

Wohlrab-Sahr, M. 'Symbolizing Distance: Conversion to Islam in Germany and the United States', in van Nieuwkerk (ed.), *Women Embracing Islam*, 71–92.

Young, M. 'Frustrations of a Muslim Convert'. http://www.islamfortoday.com/ frustrations.htm (accessed 04/08/04).

Young, M. 'The Islamic Rules of Warfare'. http://www.islamfortoday.com/war.htm (accessed 04/08/04).

Young, M. 'Much Ado about Nothing'. http://www.islamfortoday.com/ bbcarenaniqaab.htm (accessed 11/05/05).

Young, M. 'Why are you Here?'. http://www.islamfortoday.com/why.htm (accessed 11/05/05).

Young, M. 'Yes to Hijab, No to Niqaab'. http://www.islamfortoday.com/ niqaab.htm (accessed 11/05/05).

Yusuf, H. 'Islam has a Progressive Tradition Too'. *The Guardian*, 19 June 2002.

Yusuf, H. 'A Spiritual Giant in an Age of Dwarfed Terrestrial Aspirations'. *Q-News*, no. 363, June 2005.

Yusuf, H. 'Just Enough Religion to Hate'. *Q-News*, no. 364, November 2005.

Zebiri, K. *Muslims and Christians Face to Face*. Oxford: Oneworld, 1997.

Zebiri, K. 'Muslim Anti-Secularist Discourse in the Context of Muslim–Christian Relations'. *Islam and Christian–Muslim Relations* 9, 1998, 47–64.

Index

Index of Qur'anic Citations